DESKTOP PUBLISHING BASICS

Suzanne Weixel

THOMSON

COURSE TECHNOLOGY ™

Australia • Canada • Mexico • Singapore • Spain • United Kingdom • United States

THOMSON
━━━━━━━━★━━━━━━━ ™
COURSE TECHNOLOGY

Desktop Publishing BASICS
By Suzanne Weixel

Senior Vice President
Chris Elkhill

Managing Editor
Chris Katsaropoulos

Senior Product Manager
Dave Lafferty

Product Manager
Robert Gaggin

Product Marketing Manager
Kim Ryttel

Associate Product Manager
Jodi Dreissig

Development Editor
Custom Editorial Productions Inc.

Production Editor
Anne Chimenti, Custom Editorial
Productions Inc.

Compositor
GEX Publishing Services

Get Back to the Basics...
With these *exciting new products*

This new book from our *BASICS* series provides a step-by-step introduction to the most popular multimedia applications and concepts. Other books include:

Web Design BASICS by Barksdale and Stubbs
15+ hours of instruction for beginning through intermediate features

0-619-05969-8	Textbook, Perfect Bound Cover
0-619-05966-4	Instructor Resource Kit

Internet BASICS by Barksdale, Rutter, & Teeter
35+ hours of instruction for beginning through intermediate features

0-619-05905-2	Textbook, Soft Spiral Bound Cover
0-619-05906-0	Instructor Resource Kit

Microsoft Office v.X Macintosh BASICS by Melton and Walls
75+ hours of instruction for beginning through intermediate features

0-619-05563-4	Textbook, Hard Spiral Bound Cover
0-619-05566-9	Instructor Resource Kit
0-619-05566-7	Review Pack (Data CD)
0-619-05568-5	Activities Workbook

Computer Projects BASICS by Korb
80+ hours of instruction for beginning through intermediate features

0-619-05987-7	Textbook, Perfect Bound Cover
0-619-05988-5	Instructor Resource Kit

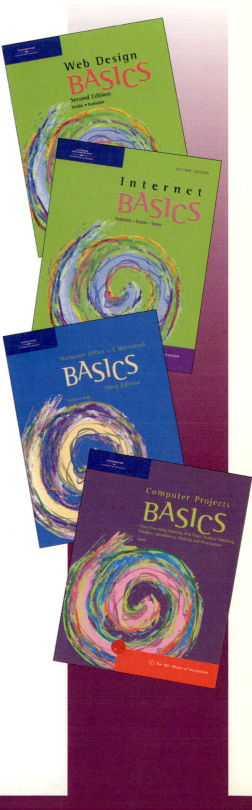

How to Use This Book

What makes a good computer instructional text? Sound pedagogy and the most current, complete materials. Not only will you find an inviting layout, but also many features to enhance learning.

Objectives— Objectives are listed at the beginning of each lesson, along with a suggested time for completion of the lesson. This allows you to look ahead to what you will be learning and to pace your work.

Step-by-Step Exercises—Preceded by a short topic discussion, these exercises are the "hands-on practice" part of the lesson. Simply follow the steps, either using a data file or creating a file from scratch. Each lesson is a series of these step-by-step exercises.

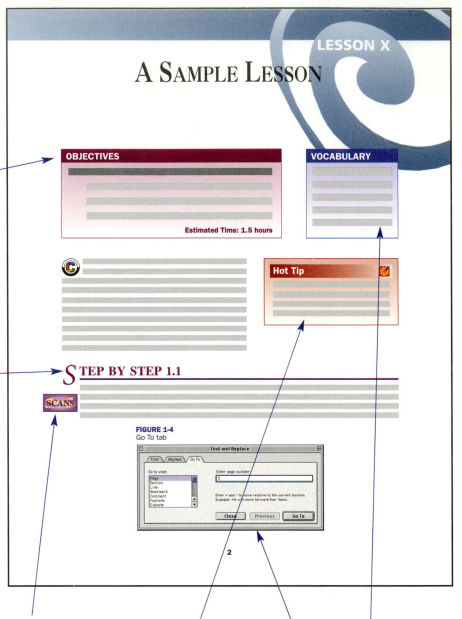

LESSON X

A SAMPLE LESSON

OBJECTIVES

Estimated Time: 1.5 hours

VOCABULARY

Hot Tip

STEP BY STEP 1.1

SCANS

FIGURE 1-4
Go To tab

Find and Replace

Find / Replace / Go To

Go to what:
Page
Section
Line
Bookmark
Comment
Footnote
Endnote

Enter page number

Enter + and – to move relative to the current location.
Example: +4 will move forward four items.

Close   Previous   Go To

2

SCANS—(Secretary's Commission on Achieving Necessary Skills)—The U.S. Department of Labor has identified the school-to-careers competencies.

Marginal Boxes— These boxes provide additional information, such as Hot Tips, fun facts (Did You Know?), Computer Concepts, Internet Web sites, Extra Challenges activities, and Teamwork ideas.

Vocabulary—Terms identified in boldface throughout the lesson and summarized at the end.

Enhanced Screen Shots—Screen shots now come to life on each page with color and depth.

How to Use This Book

Summary—At the end of each lesson, you will find a summary to prepare you to complete the end-of-lesson activities.

Vocabulary/Review Questions—Review material at the end of each lesson and each unit enables you to prepare for assessment of the content presented.

Lesson Projects—End-of-lesson hands-on application of what has been learned in the lesson allows you to actually apply the techniques covered.

Critical Thinking Activities—Each lesson gives you an opportunity to apply creative analysis and use various resources to solve problems.

End-of-Unit Projects—End-of-unit hands-on application of concepts learned in the unit provides opportunity for a comprehensive review.

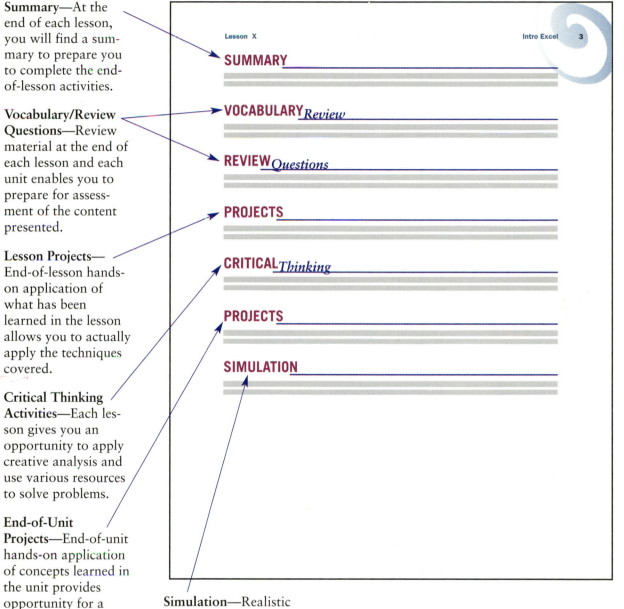

Lesson X   Intro Excel   3

SUMMARY

VOCABULARY *Review*

REVIEW *Questions*

PROJECTS

CRITICAL *Thinking*

PROJECTS

SIMULATION

Simulation—Realistic simulation jobs are provided at the end of each unit, reinforcing the material covered in the unit.

PREFACE

Despite talk of a "paperless" office, printed documents are still very much a part of business today. Organizations have discovered that with the right people, a PC, and a printer, they can generate high-quality publications ranging from pamphlets and posters to booklets and brochures. Distributing information has never been so fast or convenient.

Desktop Publishing BASICS takes a generic, non-software–specific approach to learning the most popular desktop publishing tools. This text covers the following applications: Microsoft Publisher 2002 and Adobe PageMaker 7. You may also find it useful for working with other programs.

By completing the lessons and activities in this book, you'll learn to use desktop publishing to create professional documents such as postcard mailers, flyers, brochures, and newsletters. *Desktop Publishing BASICS* is divided into six lessons. You will learn a concept and then apply it through hands-on, step-by-step activities. The book will take you through each step in a logical, easy-to-follow manner.

In *Lesson 1: Working with Documents*, you are introduced to the fundamentals of planning and creating a document using a template or design. You'll learn how to create a mock-up and select a publication type. You'll learn how to manage publication files, key text, replace sample graphics, and check the spelling. Finally, you'll preview and print your publication.

In *Lesson 2: Formatting Text*, you'll get into the nitty-gritty of organizing and formatting text in a publication. You'll learn how to control the page layout, how to create new text boxes, and how to select and apply font formatting. You'll experiment with different alignments, indents, and tabs, as well as spacing characters, lines, and paragraphs.

In *Lesson 3: Formatting Pages*, you'll learn how to use guides and master pages to ensure consistency within a publication. You'll also learn how to insert page numbers, add and delete pages, and create a publication template. Finally, you'll learn about color schemes and font schemes and how to use styles to format text

In *Lesson 4: Working with Objects*, you'll learn about different types of objects and how you can use them to enhance your publications. You'll learn how to create new drawings and how to import graphics from an external source, such as a scanner, digital camera, or the World Wide Web. You'll learn to format objects with colors and lines and how to integrate objects with text.

In *Lesson 5: Enhancing Documents*, you'll learn how to work with color when creating printed documents. You'll learn how to enhance objects and text with special effects such as dropped shadows, dropped capitals, and horizontal rules. You'll also learn how to create a watermark and how to use design objects.

In *Lesson 6: Publishing a Document*, you'll learn how to select a method of publication: desktop printer, copy shop, or commercial printer. You'll learn how to prepare a document for any type of publication, including performing prepress checks, setting properties, and printing separations. Finally, you'll learn how to prepare and deliver publication files to a commercial printer.

For those who need a refresher on Windows, Appendix A covers Windows basics such as working with folders, launching a program, and installing hardware and software.

Acknowledgments

The author would like to express her appreciation to her family as well as to the many individuals who have contributed to the completion of this book. Putting this book together has been a pleasant experience due largely to the good work of the people whose names appear here.

- Robert Gaggin, Product Manager, Course Technology
- Dave Lafferty, Senior Product Manager, Course Technology
- Jodi Dreissig, Associate Product Manager, Course Technology
- Chris Katsaropoulos, Managing Editor, Course Technology
- Betsy Newberry and Anne Chimenti of Custom Editorial Productions Inc., with writing and editing contributions from Cat Skintik
- Reviewer Donna Occhifinto
- GEX Publishing Services

About the Author

Suzanne Weixel is a self-employed writer and editor specializing in the technology industry. Her experience with computers began in 1974 when she learned to play football on the Dartmouth Time-Sharing terminal her brother installed in a spare bedroom. She graduated from Dartmouth College in 1981 with a degree in art history and currently lives in Marlborough, MA, with her husband, Rick, their sons Nathaniel and Evan, and their dog, a Samoyed named Cirrus.

Suzanne has written or contributed to numerous books including, but not limited to, *Learning Microsoft Office XP*, *Learning Microsoft Word 2002*, *Learning Flash 5*, *Learning Microsoft Office 2000 Advanced Skills: An Integrated Approach*, and *Office 2000 For Teachers*, all published by DDC Publishing, and *Personal Computing Essentials*, published by Pearson Education.

GUIDE FOR USING THIS BOOK

Please read this Guide before starting work. The time you spend now will save you much more time later and will make your learning faster, easier, and more pleasant.

Conventions

The different type styles used in this book have special meanings. They will save you time because you will soon automatically recognize from the type style the nature of the text you are reading and what you will do.

ITEM	TYPE STYLE	EXAMPLE
Text you will key	**Bold**	Key **Don't litter** rapidly.
Individual keys you will press	**Bold**	Press **Enter** to insert a blank line.
Web addresses that you might visit	*Italics*	More information about this book is available at *www.course.com*.
Web addresses that you should key	**Bold**	Start your browser and go to **www.course.com**.
Glossary terms in book	***Bold and italics***	The ***menu bar*** contains menu titles.
Words on screen	*Italics*	Click before the word *pencil*.
Menus and commands	**Bold**	Choose **Open** from the **File** menu.
Options/features with long names	*Italics*	Select **Normal** from the *Style for following paragraph* text box.

Review Pack and Instructor Resources CD-ROMs

The *Review Pack* CD-ROM contains all the data files needed to complete the exercises in the text. Data files in both Microsoft Publisher 2002 and Adobe PageMaker 7.0 formats are provided.

The *Instructor Resources* CD-ROM contains a wealth of instructional material you can use to prepare for teaching this course. The CD-ROM stores the following information:

- Data and solution files. Data and solution files in both Microsoft Publisher 2002 and Adobe PageMaker 7.0 formats are provided.

- ExamView® tests for each lesson. ExamView is a powerful testing software package that allows instructors to create and administer printed, computer (LAN-based), and Internet exams. ExamView includes hundreds of questions that correspond to the topics covered in this text, enabling learners to generate detailed study guides that include page references for further review. The computer-based and Internet testing components allow learners to take exams at their computers, and also save the instructor time by grading each exam automatically.

- Electronic *Instructor Manual* that includes lecture notes for each lesson, lesson plans, Quick Quizzes, and troubleshooting tips.

- Answers to the lesson and unit review questions, and suggested/sample solutions for Step-by-Step exercises, end-of-lesson activities, and Unit Review projects.

- Copies of the figures that appear in the text, which can be used to prepare transparencies.

- Suggested schedules for teaching the lessons in this course.

- Additional instructional information about individual learning strategies, portfolios, and career planning, and a sample Internet contract.

- PowerPoint presentations that illustrate objectives for each lesson in the text.

SCANS

The Secretary's Commission on Achieving Necessary Skills (SCANS) from the U.S. Department of Labor was asked to examine the demands of the workplace and whether new learners are capable of meeting those demands. Specifically, the Commission was directed to advise the Secretary on the level of skills required to enter employment.

SCANS workplace competencies and foundation skills have been integrated into *Desktop Publishing BASICS*. The workplace competencies are identified as 1) ability to use resources, 2) inter-personal skills, 3) ability to work with information, 4) understanding of systems, and 5) knowledge and understanding of technology. The foundation skills are identified as 1) basic communication skills, 2) thinking skills, and 3) personal qualities.

Exercises in which learners must use a number of these SCANS competencies and foundation skills are marked in the text with the SCANS icon.

System Requirements

Concepts in this book are illustrated using screen captures from Microsoft Publisher 2002. However, the concepts and exercises in this book are designed to be compatible with different software programs, including, but not limited to, Microsoft Publisher 2002 and Adobe PageMaker 7.

Computer systems that support these programs include PCs running Microsoft Windows. In order to complete some of the Step-by-Step activities and projects in this book, you should have access to the Internet via a modem or a direct connection.

TABLE OF CONTENTS

DESKTOP PUBLISHING UNIT

DESKTOP PUBLISHING

Unit

Estimated Time for Unit: 10.5 hours

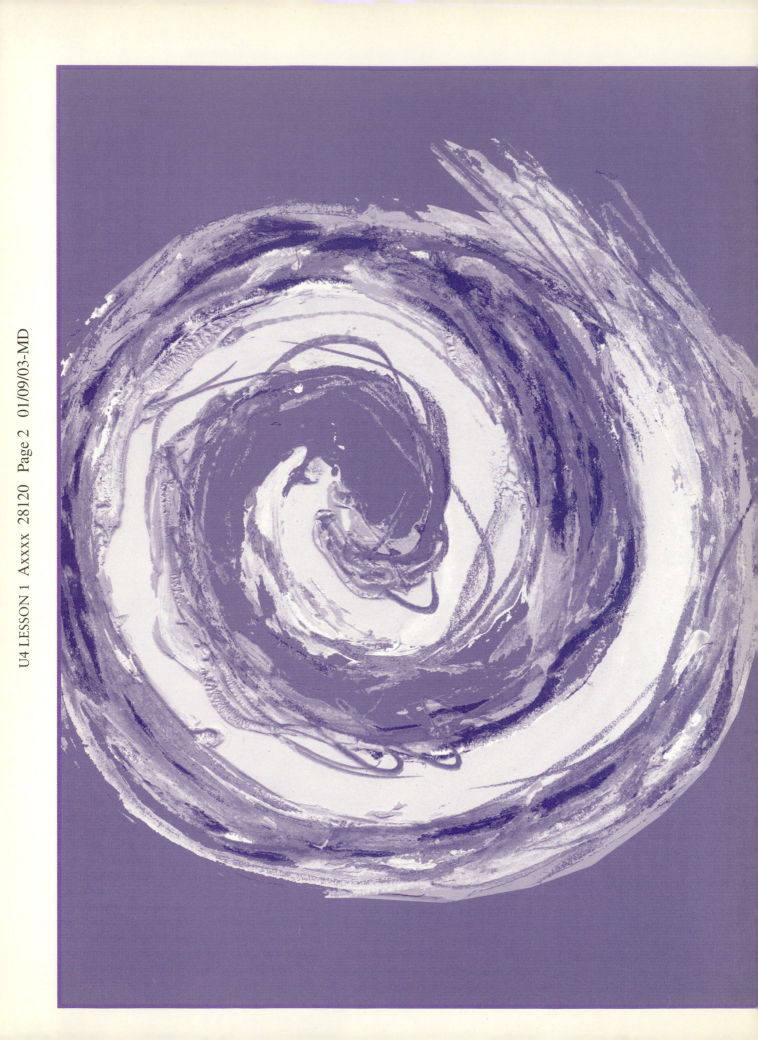

WORKING WITH DOCUMENTS

OBJECTIVES

Upon completion of this lesson, you should be able to:

- Plan a publication.
- Create a new file.
- Save, close, and reopen a document.
- Change the document view.
- Add and edit text.
- Save changes to a file.
- Insert a picture.
- Check spelling.
- Preview and print a document.

Estimated Time: 1.5 hours

VOCABULARY

Active

Clip art

Default

Frame

Graphics

Hardware devices

Mock-up

Orientation

Page size

Publication type

Scratch area

Shapes

Sheet size

Template

Text box

Toggles

View

Wrap

Zoom

Desktop publishing is used to design and produce printed documents such as business cards, brochures, booklets, nametags, product packaging, posters, banners, calendars, invitations, and newsletters. Although all desktop publishing programs have features you can use to arrange and format text and graphics, the programs differ in their level of sophistication. For example, programs designed for professional use, such as Microsoft Publisher or Adobe PageMaker, include features used to prepare a document for commercial printing, while home-use programs, such as Microsoft Greetings or Microsoft Works, assume you will print your documents on a desktop printer. Some word processing programs also offer low-level desktop publishing features for simple documents such as letters, memos, and reports. In this book, you will learn how to use a full-featured desktop publishing program to design, create, and publish professional-level documents.

No matter which program you use, there are six basic steps to producing a desktop publishing document:

1. Plan the document.
2. Select a design.

3. Insert text.

4. Insert graphics.

5. Prepare the document for publication.

6. Print the document.

In this lesson, you will learn to use these steps to create a document quickly and easily. Later lessons cover these steps in greater detail.

Plan a Publication

The first phase of desktop publishing is to plan the basic format for your document. You must make decisions about the physical aspects of the document, such as the page size, the paper stock, color scheme, single-sided or double-sided printing, *binding* options, and the number of copies.

As you think about these issues, you should keep your budget in mind. The amount of money you have available significantly affects the type of document you can produce. For example, color printing costs more than black and white, and paper stocks range widely in price.

You should also consider the program you are using. Make sure it supports all the features you want to include, and that it is *compatible* with other programs and ***hardware devices*** you may need to use. A compatible program can exchange data easily with another program or device. A device is a piece of equipment attached to your computer, such as a scanner. For example, can you use your desktop publishing program to create graphics, or will you need to import graphics from another source, such as a graphics program, a scanner, or a digital camera? Can you easily enter as much text as you need, or will you need to copy the text from a word processing program?

You also need to make decisions about the content of the document: Who will be reading it? What is its goal? There are many different reasons for creating a publication. Marketing publications, such as direct mail postcards, are designed to sell a product, while informational publications, such as corporate newsletters, are designed to educate and inform. Invitations, playbills, and product packaging have very different purposes, and therefore require different approaches. The content of a brochure to be distributed at a conference for neurosurgeons will certainly differ from the content of a flyer that is part of a mass mailing to the customers of a retail store.

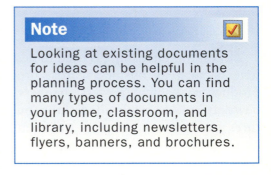

Note

Looking at existing documents for ideas can be helpful in the planning process. You can find many types of documents in your home, classroom, and library, including newsletters, flyers, banners, and brochures.

To ensure the success of your publication, you should create a ***mock-up*** or prototype. A mock-up is a rough draft or sample of the publication that represents the finished product, without including fine details. Creating a mock-up lets you experiment with ***page size, sheet size***, and ***orientation*** as well as positioning text and graphics. It is important to note that in desktop publishing, page size and sheet size are not the same thing. Page size is the dimensions of the finished document page, while sheet size—which is sometimes called *paper size*—is the size of the paper on which the document is printed. Orientation is the position of the paper in relation to the printed content. *Portrait orientation*—sometimes called *tall*—prints the content across the short side of the page, while *landscape orientation*—sometimes called *wide*—prints the content along the long side of the page.

Although you may be able to use your desktop publishing program to preview sample documents, the most effective method for creating a mock-up is to actually take a piece of paper the same size and shape that you envision for the finished product, and then mark it with the location of text and graphics. For example, you can create a mock-up of a tri-fold brochure by folding a standard 8.5-inch by 11-inch sheet of paper into thirds. Or you can create a mock-up of a postcard mailer by using a ruler to draw a rectangle the size of the postcard on a sheet of paper, and then using a pencil to indicate the placement of an address label, text, and graphics.

S TEP-BY-STEP 1.1

1. Hold a blank sheet of 8.5-inch by 11-inch paper with the 8.5-inch sides at the top and bottom. This is portrait orientation. You are going to make a mock-up of a postcard mailer. The page size of the mailer is approximately 8.5 inches wide by 5.5 inches high, which is about half the sheet size. The postcard has two pages—the front and the back.

2. Fold the top edge of the sheet down to meet the bottom edge, and then unfold the page. If you plan to print on 8.5-inch by 11-inch paper, you can fit two postcards on a page. However, you need to create a mock-up of only one. In this case, use the top half of the sheet.

3. Using a ruler, draw 0.5-inch margins on all sides of the rectangle, and then mark the locations where you would position a headline, informational text, and a picture. Refer to Figure 1-1.

FIGURE 1-1
Mock-up of a postcard mailer

Return Address
Line 2
Line 3
Line 4

Stamp

Mailing Addess Line 1
Line 2
Line 3
Line 4

Page 2

Headline

Information text
More text
More text
More text

Picture
Can
Go Here

Page 1

Business Name
Address information
Contact information

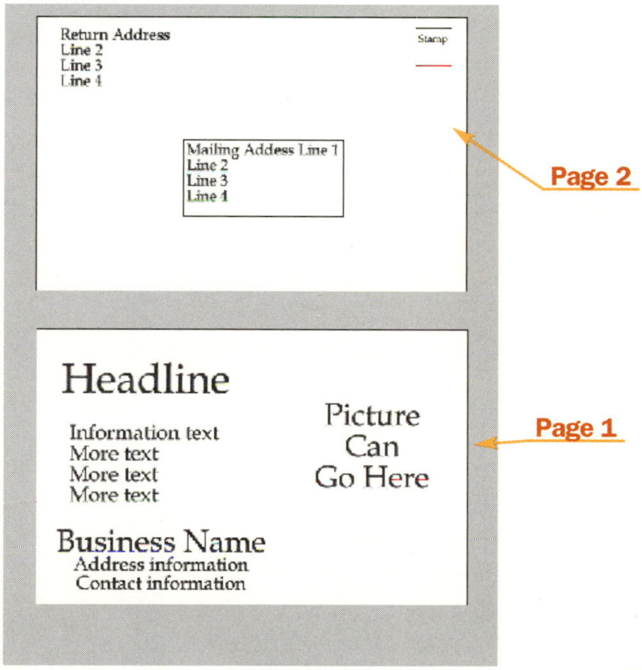

4. Draw the same margins on the back, and then mark the locations of the mailing address, return address, and stamp.

5. Keep this sheet of paper as a reference for creating a postcard mailer in the rest of this lesson.

Create a New File

To create a new desktop publishing file, use the New command on the File menu, or click the New button on the main or standard toolbar. There are many variations or options for creating a new publication, depending on the program you are using. Some programs automatically create a blank file using the *default* settings for options, such as page size and orientation, but most programs display a dialog box where you can select the *publication type*—such as a newsletter or a calendar—and then select the publication design, or *template,* or where you can customize the settings. The default settings are the standard options already selected in the program. A template is a file used as a model for creating other files. It usually contains page layout and text formatting settings as well as objects such as sample text and graphics.

Using a template is the fastest and easiest way to create a professional-looking document, because it already has a coordinated font scheme, color scheme, and layout. All you have to do is replace the sample text and graphics. You can select options to customize the individual settings at any time.

An alternative to creating a publication from a template is to create a blank document and build it from scratch. You will learn how to create a publication this way in a later lesson.

Depending on your program, the available publications are listed in a New dialog box, a Templates dialog box, or New Publication task pane, similar to the one in Figure 1-2. When you select a publication type, most programs list the designs or templates available for that type. In some programs, actual thumbnail-sized previews appear in the dialog box or in a window called a Design Gallery. Click the design or template you want to use to create the new document, and then, if necessary, click a button such as Open or Create Publication.

FIGURE 1-2
Publication types listed in a task pane

New files usually have a generic name such as Publication or Untitled and are numbered consecutively. So, the first file you create is Publication1; the second is Publication2; and so on. You customize the name when you save the file. Most programs let you have more than one file open at a time, although only one can be *active*. The active file is the one in which you are currently working.

Some desktop publishing programs use contact information such as names and phone numbers to automatically enter data in a new publication. You may have supplied some of this information when you installed the program. If the contact information has not already been filled in, the program prompts you to enter it when you create a new document. Simply select a category for the information set, such as home or business, and key the desired information. This contact information will be used in most future publications created with a template or design.

STEP-BY-STEP 1.2

1. Launch your desktop publishing program. The New dialog box, Templates dialog box, or New Publication task pane displays. If the program is already open, or the dialog box is not open, click **File** on the menu bar, and then click **New**. If you are using Adobe PageMaker 7and the Templates dialog box is not open, click **Window**, click **Plug-in Palettes**, and then click **Show Template Palette**.

Note ✅

In some programs, publication types are sorted into categories to help you quickly locate an appropriate design. Click the publication type to expand the list to display categories, and then click a category to scroll quickly to the designs for that category.

Did You Know?

You can edit the contact information at any time. Click Edit on the menu bar and then click the command to open the information set. Select the set you want to use, make the changes, and then click the Update button.

STEP-BY-STEP 1.2 Continued

2. Select a postcard mailer publication type. A postcard mailer is usually a simple, two-page document similar to the mock-up you created in the previous exercise. One page is set up for entering text and graphics and the other page is set up for entering address information and postage. Once you select a publication type, the available designs are displayed on the screen, as shown in Figure 1-3.

> **Note**
>
> If you cannot find postcards in the list of publications, your program probably uses a different name, such as mailers, or lists them as a category under cards. Also, don't worry if your screen looks different from the one in the illustration. You may be using a program that lists the publications and designs in a different format, such as in a dialog box or without previews.

FIGURE 1-3
Sample designs for postcard mailers

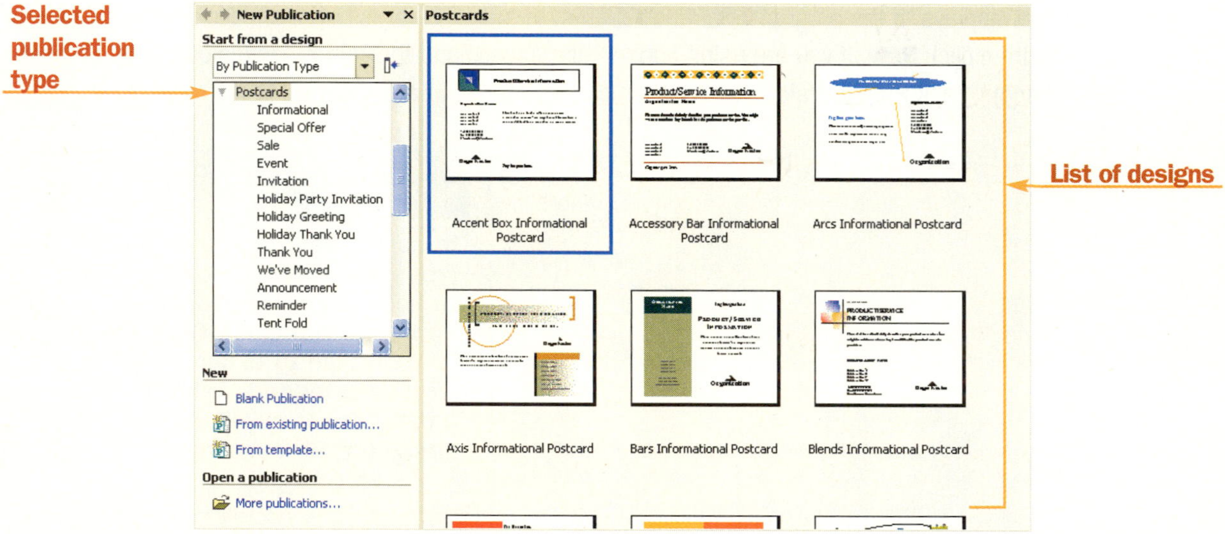

Selected publication type

List of designs

3. Scroll through the list of designs to see what is available, and then click a simple design such as the Level Informational design in Microsoft Publisher or the 2000640.pmt template in Adobe PageMaker 7. If necessary, click the **Open** or **Create Publication** button to create the document.

4. If prompted, cancel the dialog box that asks you to enter contact information. Your program creates and displays the publication on screen with default sample information. Depending on your program and the publication type, options for changing the layout and content may be displayed as well.

> **Note**
>
> If your program displays a dialog box listing font substitutions necessary for the template you selected, you may choose another font or accept the default substitution. You will learn more about fonts in the next lesson.

STEP-BY-STEP 1.2 Continued

5. If available, select the option to change the size of the document from quarter page (4.25 inches × 5.5 inches) to half page (5.5 inches × 8.5 inches). The document should look similar to Figure 1-4.

FIGURE 1-4
Sample page of postcard mailer document

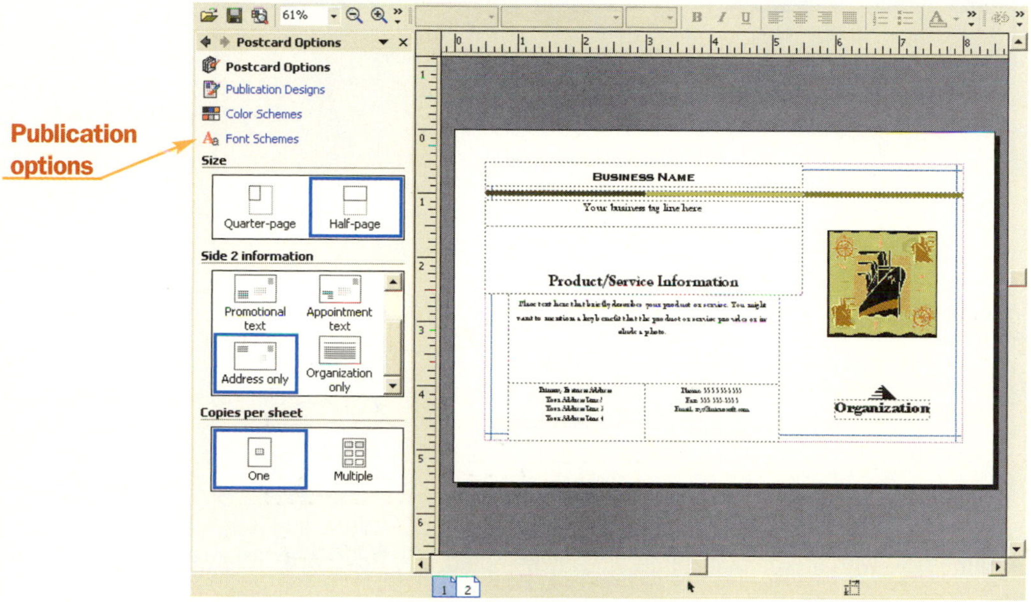

6. Leave the publication open to use in the next exercise.

Save, Close, and Reopen a Document

The first time you save a publication, use the Save As command on the File menu to give it a name and select a storage location. As with all new files, you should use filenames that help to identify the file contents, and, of course, you must follow standard filename rules. That means you cannot use the following characters: /, \, >, <, *, ?, ", !, :, ; , .

By default, most programs save a new publication file in the My Documents folder on your local hard disk, or in the same folder where you most recently saved a file. However, you can select a different location. You can save a file on a local hard disk, on a network drive, or on removable media, such as a 3½-inch disk or a CD-R.

STEP-BY-STEP 1.3

1. Click **File** on the menu bar, and then click **Save As**. The Save As dialog box opens, as shown in Figure 1-5.

FIGURE 1-5
Save As dialog box

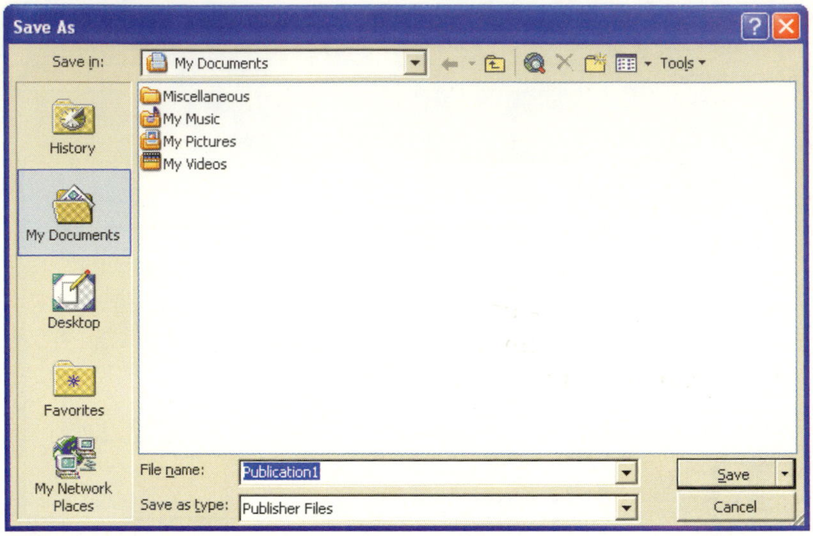

2. In the **File name** box, with the default name already selected, key **Postcard**. This will be the name of the new file.

3. From the **Save in** list, select the location where you want to store the file.

4. Click the **Save** button in the dialog box. The file is saved with the new name in the selected storage location.

5. Leave the **Postcard** file open to use in the next exercise.

Once you have saved a file for the first time, you can use the Save As command to save the file with a new name or in a new location. The original file will remain unchanged.

Close a File

When you have finished using a publication file, you should close it. You can close a file by using the Close command on the File menu. Some programs remain open after you close a file so you can continue using it, while others close unless there are other publication files still open.

If you have not saved the file before selecting the close command, the program displays a dialog box asking if you want to save. Click the Yes button to save the changes and close the file. Click the No button to close the file without saving the changes. Click the Cancel button to close the dialog box and continue working in the file. If you close the file without saving, all changes that you made since the last time you saved will be lost.

STEP-BY-STEP 1.4

1. Click **File** on the menu bar, and then click **Close**. The **Postcard** file closes.

2. Leave your desktop publishing program open to use in the next exercise.

Open an Existing File

To work again with a file you have already closed, you must open it in your desktop publishing program. You can use the Open button on the main or standard toolbar or the Open command from the File menu to display the Open dialog box. By default, the Open dialog box displays the files in the My Documents folder. Or the dialog box may display the location from which you last opened a file. You can use the Open dialog box to locate and select the file you want to open.

> **Note** ☑️
>
> You can close the program and all open files at the same time if you are finished using the program. Use the Exit command on the File menu. If you haven't saved an open file, the program will prompt you to save before closing.

STEP-BY-STEP 1.5

1. Click **File** on the menu bar, and then click **Open**. The Open or Open Publication dialog box appears, as shown in Figure 1-6. Don't worry if your Open dialog box does not look exactly the same as the one in the figure.

FIGURE 1-6
Open Publication dialog box

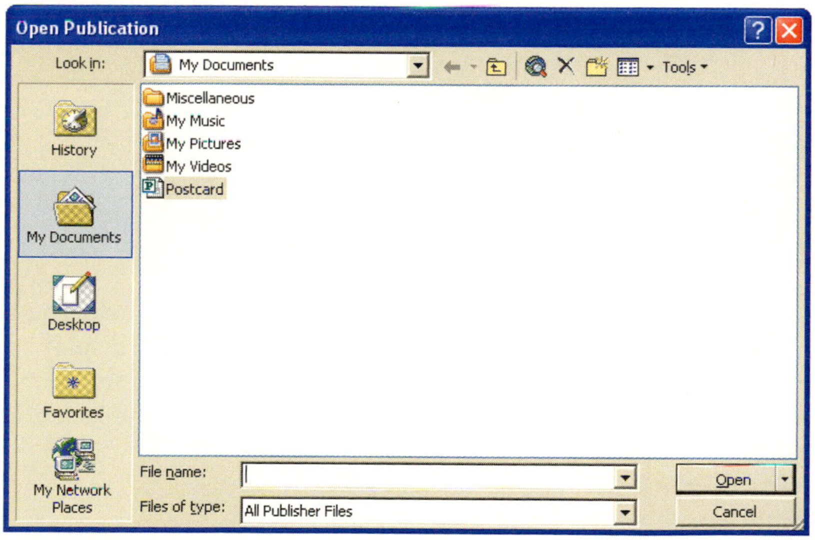

2. If the Postcard file is not listed in the dialog box, click the **Look in** list drop-down arrow and then select the location where the file is stored.

3. In the list of files, click **Postcard**.

4. Click the **Open** button in the dialog box. The file opens in the program window.

5. Leave the **Postcard** file open to use in the next exercise.

Change the Document View

When a publication file is open, it may appear in a program window similar to Figure 1-7. The appearance of the screen depends on the program you are using as well as on default options set for your computer, so don't worry if your screen doesn't look exactly the same as the one in the illustration. However, most desktop publishing programs have a number of standard screen elements in common, such as a document window, menu bar, toolbars, scroll bars, rulers, and panels or task panes where you can select options.

Did You Know?

Some programs also have a command for opening recently used files. The most recently used files may be listed at the bottom of the File menu, so you can just click the File menu and then click the name of the file you want to open. Or, recently used files may be listed on a submenu. Click the File menu, click a command such as Open Recent or Recent Publications to display the submenu, and then click the name of the file you want to open.

FIGURE 1-7
Typical desktop publishing window

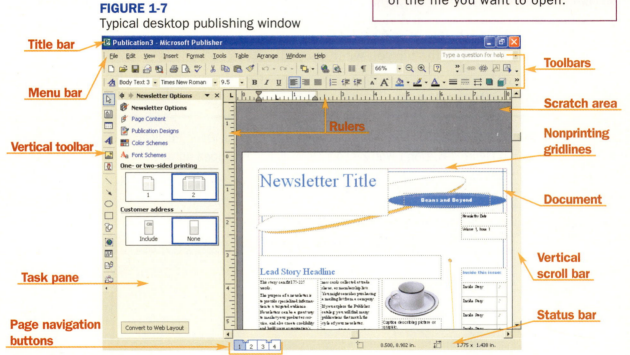

Title bar · Menu bar · Vertical toolbar · Task pane · Page navigation buttons · Rulers · Toolbars · Scratch area · Nonprinting gridlines · Document · Vertical scroll bar · Status bar

In addition, your program probably has nonprinting gridlines that help you align objects on a page; page navigation buttons, which are icons you can click to shift the display to show a different page; and a *scratch area*, which is a portion of the screen where you can temporarily store text and graphics. Even if the element names are not the same in all programs, the functions are similar.

View Options

While you are working in your desktop publishing program, you may want to change the *view* to get a different look at your publication. The view is the way your file is displayed onscreen. Most programs let you display your file in different view modes such as normal or standard, whole page or two-page spread, or preview. You can also choose to show or hide specific elements such as the rulers, the task pane, the guides, and the toolbars.

Most of the commands you use to change the view are located on the View menu. Other commands may be on a different menu, such as the Arrange menu or the Window menu, or available as buttons on a toolbar. Notice that many commands controlling the way a program is displayed are *toggles*, which means they are either on or off. Each time you select the command, it switches from on to off, or off to on. When a command is on, it usually has a check mark beside it on the menu.

STEP-BY-STEP 1.6

1. In the **Postcard** file, click **View** on the menu bar, and then click a command such as **Rulers**. If the rulers were not displayed before, this command toggles them on. If they were displayed, the command toggles them off.

2. Choose the command that shows or hides the toolbars. For example, in Microsoft Publisher click **View** on the menu bar, click **Toolbars**, and then click **Formatting** on the submenu. This toggles the Formatting toolbar on or off. Or, in Adobe PageMaker click **Window** on the menu bar, and then click **Hide Tools**.

3. Repeat steps 1 and 2 until the rulers and the Formatting toolbar are displayed. In other words, toggle the rulers and toolbar on.

4. Use the page navigation feature in your program to display page 2 of the postcard. For example, click the page 2 icon on the Status bar. Page 2 in the Postcard document is the reverse side of the mailer, as shown in Figure 1-8. Use the same feature to display page 1 again. In some programs, you can press the Page Up or Page Down key to change pages.

FIGURE 1-8
Page 2 of the postcard mailer

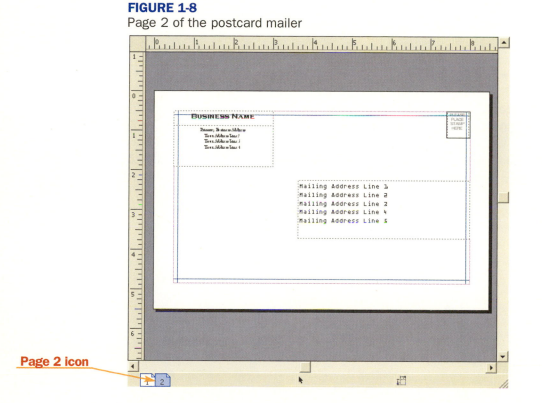

Page 2 icon

5. If your program has a task pane or panel displayed, select the command to close it. For example, click **View** on the menu bar, and then click **Task Pane**.

STEP-BY-STEP 1.6 Continued

6. Practice toggling other elements on and off to change the view, including options that may be on different menus. For example, show and hide special characters or boundaries and guides.

7. Leave the **Postcard** file open to use in the next exercise.

> ### Did You Know?
> Most panels and task panes have close buttons in the upper-right corner. Click the button to close the task pane. They may also have drop-down arrows you can click to display option menus.

Change the Zoom

When you need to get a closer look at a publication, *zoom* in. Zooming increases or decreases the magnification of the file on your screen by a percentage of its original size. For example, zoom in to 200% to display the file at twice its actual size, or zoom out to 50% to display it at half its actual size. Zooming in gives you a closer look and makes it easier to see and work with a particular area, while zooming out makes the publication look smaller and lets you get an overall look at the composition.

You can use the Zoom or Zoom To command on the View menu to select a magnification percentage from a list. You may be able to use a Zoom box on a standard toolbar to key a specific percentage. You can also simply click the Zoom In tool to zoom in or the Zoom Out tool to zoom out.

> ### Did You Know?
> In some programs, you can click the drop-down arrow next to the Zoom box on the toolbar to display a list of magnifications like the one available on the Zoom submenu.

STEP-BY-STEP 1.7

1. In the **Postcard** file, use the **Zoom** or **Zoom To** command on the **View** menu to change the magnification to **200%**. The magnification increases so you get a closer look at the publication.

2. Click the **Zoom Out** tool on the toolbar, or click **View** on the menu bar, click **Zoom**, and then click **150%**. The magnification decreases.

STEP-BY-STEP 1.7 Continued

3. Adjust the zoom to 75%. For example, click the **Zoom Out** button repeatedly until the magnification is 75%, or click the **Zoom** box on the Standard toolbar, key **75**, and press **Enter**. The magnification is adjusted to 75% of the document's actual size. It should look similar to Figure 1-9.

FIGURE 1-9
File displayed at 75% of its actual size

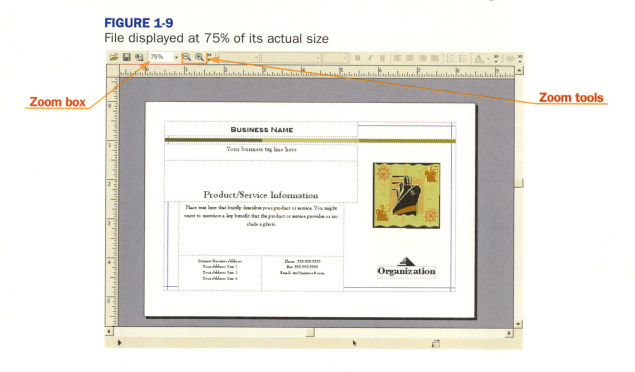

Zoom box

Zoom tools

4. Leave the **Postcard** file open to use in the next exercise.

Add and Edit Text

Text in a desktop publishing file is inserted in a ***text box*** or ***frame***. A text box or frame is an object you can easily move and resize, which makes it easy to position and format the text in the publication. (Some programs have an additional feature called a text block, which is also used for holding text.) When you create a publication file based on a design or template, your program automatically inserts text boxes to hold the contact information and sample text. You replace the sample text to customize the publication. You can also enter new text and edit existing text at any time, as well as insert new text boxes. You learn more about working with text in Lesson 2.

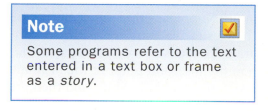

Note ✔️

Some programs refer to the text entered in a text box or frame as a *story*.

Enter Text

In some programs, such as Microsoft Publisher, you simply click the mouse pointer in the text box to position the insertion point so you can enter and edit text. In other programs, such as Adobe PageMaker, you first select the Text tool in the toolbox, and then click in the text box. When the insertion point is inside the text box, a border and sizing handles may appear, as shown in Figure 1-10. In some programs, a rotation handle displays as well. To select the text box, click its border with the mouse pointer, or click the selection tool in the toolbox and then click the border.

FIGURE 1-10
Select text box

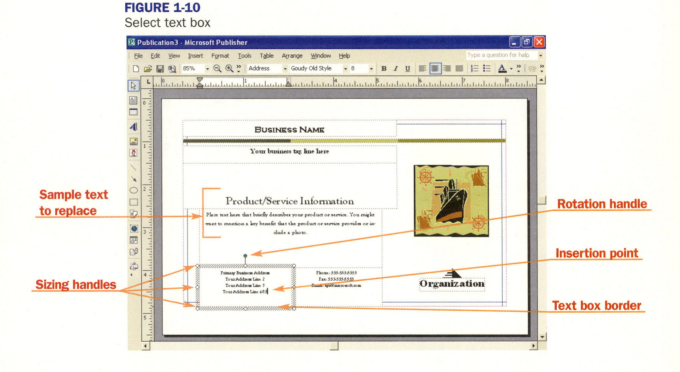

In most desktop publishing programs, you use the same standard text entry, editing, and selection commands that you use in other programs to move the insertion point within a text box or frame and to make changes to the text. For example, to select text, simply drag the mouse across it, or, with the keyboard, position the insertion point at the beginning of the selected text; press and hold Shift; and then press arrow keys to define the selection. To insert new text, simply position the insertion point and begin keying. Table 1-1 describes some of the common keystrokes used to work with text.

TABLE 1-1
Common text-editing keystrokes

PRESS THIS KEY	TO DO THIS
↑	To move insertion point up one line.
↓	To move insertion point down one line.
←	To move insertion point one character to the left.
→	To move insertion point one character to the right.
← BACKSPACE	To delete the character to the left of the insertion point.
DELETE	To delete the character to the right of the insertion point.
↵ ENTER	To start a new paragraph.

As you type in a text box, the text is automatically formatted according to the settings determined by the publication type and design. For example, the text may automatically be centered within the text box, or aligned to the right or left. Usually, the text is automatically sized to fit within the text box. Also, you do not have to press Enter to start a new line, because the text *wraps* within the text box. When text wraps, it automatically starts a new line when the current line is full. If automatic hyphenation is on, words that are split from one line to the next are automatically hyphenated. Although you can change the formatting, in most cases, the default design formatting is appropriate for the publication type and design you have selected.

S TEP-BY-STEP 1.8

1. In the **Postcard** file, replace sample information with specific company information as follows. (You may have to switch pages to enter all the information, and some information may be entered more than once.)

   a. Locate sample text for the company name (such as *Business Name* or *Organization*) and zoom in, if necessary, to get a better view. Then, key **Beans and Beyond**.

   b. Locate sample text for the company address and key the following street address:
   622 Elm Street
   Sudbury, MA 01776

   c. Locate sample text for other contact information and key the following replacement text:
   Phone: 555-555-5555
   Fax: 555-555-5555
   Email: vmcgill@mail.com

   d. If you see sample text for a company tag line or slogan, key **Fine Coffee and Tasty Treats from Around the World**.

> **Note** ☑
>
> Some programs use sample text designed to help you decide where to enter replacement text, while other programs may use gibberish or foreign language text as placeholders.

STEP-BY-STEP 1.8 Continued

2. Locate the sample headline (such as *Product/Service Information*) in the publication and select the sample text. (If necessary, switch to page 2.)

3. Key **Jazz in the Mornings**. The new text replaces the selected text.

4. Click the sample text in the text box below the headline, or wherever there is a text box for entering information, and key the following text. Remember, you do not have to press Enter to begin a new line.

> **Extra for Experts**
>
> You may need to adjust the width and/or height of the text box that holds the address information if items of information run over to two lines. Use a pointer tool to select the text box and drag side handles to widen the box.

Beans and Beyond is pleased to announce a series of Sunday morning jazz concerts beginning the first Sunday in September and continuing through the end of the year. Each week will feature a different ensemble or solo artist, specially selected to complement your weekend. Join us for a relaxing blend of music, beverages, and pastry delights. 9:30 a.m. until 2:00 p.m.

5. Locate the sample mailing address for the postcard and replace it with your name and address.

6. Replace any other sample text in the document. For example, click the sample text *Organization* and replace it with the text **Beans and Beyond**. Notice that the text is automatically resized to fit within the text box. Delete any text boxes you do not need, such as a text box giving information about the template used to create the publication. Now, go back and edit some existing text.

> **Note**
>
> To delete a text box, click the text box border, and then press Delete.

7. Click the text *Jazz in the Mornings* with the pointer or text tool. The insertion point appears where you clicked.

STEP-BY-STEP 1.8 Continued

8. Select the text *in the* and replace it with the text **on Sunday**. The document should look similar to the one in Figure 1-11.

FIGURE 1-11
Postcard with replacement text

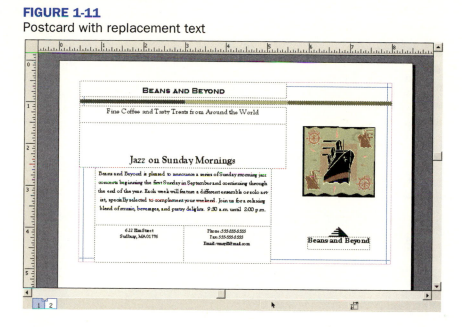

9. Leave the **Postcard** file open to use in the next exercise.

Use Undo and Redo

If you are unhappy with the results of a command or selection in your desktop publishing program, you can use the Undo command to reverse it. Undo lets you reverse the most recent action, or, in some programs, a series of actions. You can use the Redo command to reverse the results of an Undo action. Undo and Redo are available as commands on the Edit menu and may also be available as buttons on a toolbar. The first time you use the command, the most recent action is reversed. Repeat the command to reverse the action prior to that, and so on.

> **Note**
>
> Some programs let you automatically undo or redo a series of commands. Click the drop-down arrow on the Undo toolbar button to display a list of commands that can be reversed. When you click an item in the list, it and all items above it are undone. You can use the same steps on the Redo button to redo a series of actions.

STEP-BY-STEP 1.9

1. In the **Postcard** file, select the **Undo** command from the **Edit** menu, or click the **Undo** button on the toolbar. Your program undoes the most recent action, which is the replacement of the text *in the* with the text *on Sunday*.

2. Select the **Redo** command from the **Edit** menu, or click the **Redo** button on the toolbar. The previous action is reversed.

3. Leave the **Postcard** file open to use in the next exercise.

Save Changes to a File

Y ou can quickly save changes to a file by clicking the Save button on the toolbar, or by using the Save command on the File menu. Saving changes ensures that you don't lose your work if there's a problem with your computer or the software. In some programs, depending on the edits you have made, a dialog box may ask if you want to save changes to your contact information. Click Yes to save the changes to the contact information, or click No to save the file, but leave the contact information unchanged.

Important

Save your files frequently! In the event of a mechanical problem or a power failure, all data you have entered or edited since the last time you saved will be lost. Saving is the only way to ensure that your work is safe.

S TEP-BY-STEP 1.10

1. Click **File** on the menu bar, and then click **Save**. If a dialog box asks if you want to save the changes to your contact information, click **No**. The changes are saved.

2. Leave the **Postcard** file open to use in the next exercise.

Insert a Picture

W hen you create a publication file based on a design or template, your program may automatically insert sample *graphics*, sized and positioned to enhance the document. Graphics are picture files that are generally inserted as objects directly in your desktop publishing files, although in some programs you must insert them into frames. Depending on the publication type and design, the sample graphics may be *shapes* or *clip art* pictures. Shapes are exactly that— lines, ovals, rectangles, and polygons inserted and formatted to enhance the appearance of the document. Clip art pictures are images already saved in a graphics file format. (You learn more about working with graphics and other objects in Lesson 4.)

While you probably want to keep the shapes that are part of the publication design, you may just as likely want to replace the sample clip art in your document with something that represents the content of the publication. To replace the clip art, you open a dialog box in which you locate and select the graphics file you want to insert instead.

In some programs, you first select the object you want to replace, then click Insert on the menu bar, click Picture, and then click From File to open the Insert Picture dialog box. Once you locate and select the file you want, click the Insert button to insert it in the publication. In other programs, you must first delete the sample graphic, then use the Place command on the File menu to open the Place dialog box. Once you locate and select the file, click the Open button, then drag the insertion pointer to define the size and location where you want the picture placed in the publication. For example, drag where the previous clip art image was positioned.

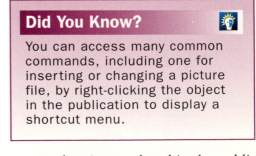

Did You Know?

You can access many common commands, including one for inserting or changing a picture file, by right-clicking the object in the publication to display a shortcut menu.

S TEP-BY-STEP 1.11

1. In the **Postcard** file, select the picture you want to replace. (If you are using Adobe PageMaker, you should delete the sample LOGO graphics objects first.)

2. Select the command to open the dialog box where you can locate and select the picture file you want to insert.

3. Locate and select **DP Step 1-11** from the data files.

4. Click the **Insert** or **Open** button in the dialog box. If necessary, click **Yes** to accept information about the picture file size and then click and drag the insertion pointer to insert the picture where the original object(s) had been and size it at about 1.25 inches square. The replacement graphic should look similar to Figure 1-12.

FIGURE 1-12
Replacement picture in the Postcard file

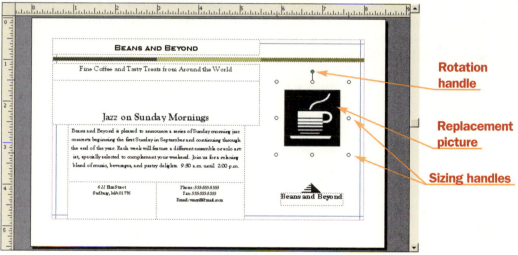

5. Save changes and leave the **Postcard** file open to use in the next exercise.

Check Spelling

At a minimum, most desktop publishing documents include some text, such as a caption on a poster, and often they include a lot of text, such as an eight-page newsletter. Spelling errors can take all the credibility out of a publication, so it is very important to check the spelling in a publication before you print it or send it to be published.

All desktop publishing programs include a spelling checker feature that you can use to locate and correct spelling errors. The spelling checker compares the words in the document to a built-in dictionary. If the spelling checker cannot find the word, it highlights the word. You can correct the spelling, ignore the word, or add the word to the dictionary so that it will not be marked as incorrect in the future.

Some programs also offer a feature that checks spelling as you type and automatically flags words that may be incorrect with a visual mark on the screen, such as a wavy colored underline. You can ignore the flag and continue typing, correct the spelling, or add the word to the dictionary.

Of course, even the best spelling checker won't catch all spelling errors. For example, if you key the word *threw* when you mean to key *through*, the spelling checker does not identify the mistake. The only way to be certain your text is correct is to proofread it carefully.

Extra for Experts

If your program automatically inserts text stored in your contact information into a publication file, it will not mark the text as misspelled, even if it includes a proper name or an unusually spelled word. The program recognizes that these words may not be in its dictionary.

To start a spelling checker in your desktop publishing program, click in the text box you want to check, then click the Spelling button on the toolbar, or select the check spelling command. Your program may open the text box's text in a *story editor* window, which is a separate window used for editing text. When the spelling checker identifies a word that is not in the dictionary, it displays a dialog box similar to the one in Figure 1-13. Select the correct spelling in the list and then click the Change or Replace button, or click one of the other command buttons, such as Ignore or Add to Dictionary. There may also be an option to extend the spell check to all text boxes (or stories) in the document.

FIGURE 1-13
Check Spelling dialog box

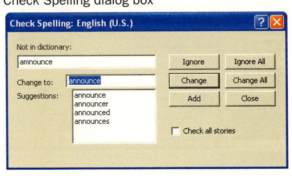

If your program has an automatic spelling checker, you may already have noticed flagged words. The program checks the spelling as you key new text and marks words that are not in the dictionary. To correct the spelling, you can delete the error and rekey the text, or you can right-click the word and select an option from the shortcut menu that displays. Usually, you can choose the same options that are available in the spelling dialog box, including selecting the correct spelling, ignoring the error, or adding the word to the dictionary.

Note

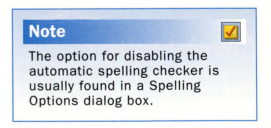

The option for disabling the automatic spelling checker is usually found in a Spelling Options dialog box.

S TEP-BY-STEP 1.12

1. In the **Postcard** file, click in the headline text *Jazz on Sunday Mornings* and change the *a* in *Jazz* to an **e**, then change the *d* in *Sunday* to a **b**. Click the text box border to select the text box. If your program has an automatic spelling checker, it probably flagged the incorrectly spelled words *Jezz* and *Sunbay*.

2. If your program displays a wavy underline beneath the word *Jezz*, right-click on the word. A shortcut menu displays, similar to the one in Figure 1-14.

FIGURE 1-14
Spelling shortcut menu

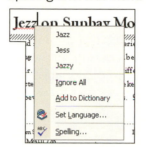

3. Click the correctly spelled word *Jazz* on the shortcut menu. Your program corrects the spelling. Now use the spelling checker to locate other errors in the publication.

4. Click the **Spelling** button on the toolbar, or select the command to start the spelling checker. You may need to click the **Start** button in the spelling dialog box if the text opens in a story editor window.

5. If you have not already corrected the word *Jezz*, your program will highlight it. Click the **Change** or **Replace** button to replace the incorrect word.

6. The spelling checker highlights the word *Sunbay*. Click the **Change** or **Replace** button, or key the correct spelling.

7. Select the option to check all text boxes or stories in the publication. You may need to ignore the proper names used in the address. When the check is complete, close all open dialog boxes and/or the story editor window(s).

8. Save changes to the **Postcard** file and leave it open to use in the next exercise.

Historically Speaking

Before computers took over so many publishing tasks, authors and editors checked text on long sheets of proofs called *galleys*. They marked the text using standard *proofreaders' marks* that printers and typesetters understood to specify changes in the text. Although computers have automated a good part of document production, some jobs are still best done the old-fashioned way, and that includes proofreading. For best-quality results, final proofs should still be printed, read, and marked by hand. Reading a document for errors is a vital part of creating a first-class publication.

Figure 1-15 illustrates just a few of the standard proofreaders' marks used to indicate errors and changes. One mark is made in the margin beside the text, and one mark is made in the text itself. An editor or production specialist reading the marked copy knows immediately how to correct the document. You can find a complete list of proofreaders' marks in most standard dictionaries or on the Internet.

FIGURE 1-15
Common proofreaders' marks

INSTRUCTION	MARK IN MARGIN	MARK IN TEXT
Delete		the happy dog
Insert	happy	the dog
Let it stand	stet	the happy dog
Make capital	cap	the dog
Make lowercase	lc	the Dog
Set in italics	ital	the dog
Set in boldface	bf	the dog
Transpose	tr	dog the
Close up space		d og
Insert a space	#	thedog
Start a paragraph	¶	"where is the dog?" "Over there."
Move left	⊏	the dog
Move right	⊐	the dog
Align	‖	the dog / the dog / the dog

Preview and Print a Document

The goal of creating a desktop publishing document is to see it in print. Even if you intend to have the actual publication prepared by a commercial printer, you can use your program to preview the publication onscreen the way it will look when it is printed and to quickly print a sample copy.

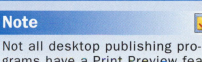

To preview a document before printing, you can simply change the zoom setting or use a Print Preview button or menu command if available. Programs with Print Preview usually display the entire first page, as shown in Figure 1-16. The Print Preview may also have a toolbar with buttons you can use to change pages, display multiple pages at the same time, change the zoom, change some printer settings, and print the document.

> **Note** ✓
>
> Not all desktop publishing programs have a Print Preview feature. This may be because in regular view, the publication is displayed the way it will print.

FIGURE 1-16
Postcard in Print Preview

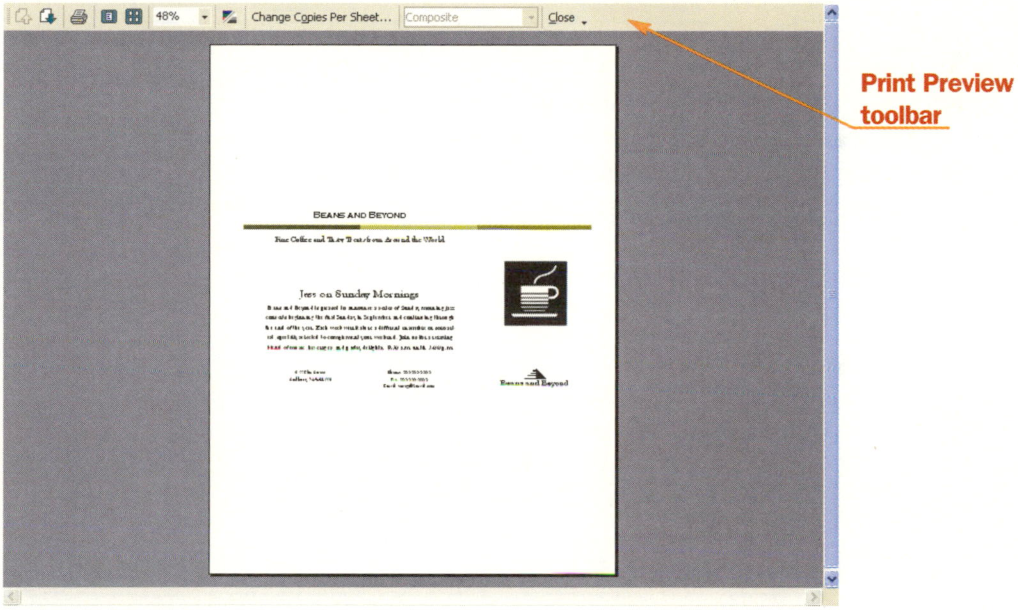

Print Preview toolbar

To quickly print a single copy using the default print settings, you can usually simply click the Print button on the toolbar. If you want to change any print settings, you must select the Print command from the File menu to open the Print dialog box. The Print dialog box, shown in Figure 1-17, lists options such as the number of copies to print, whether to use two-sided printing, and even which printer to use. The options depend on the specific printer and program you are using. In Lesson 6, you learn how to prepare a publication for printing on your desktop or network computer and for commercial printing.

FIGURE 1-17
Print dialog box

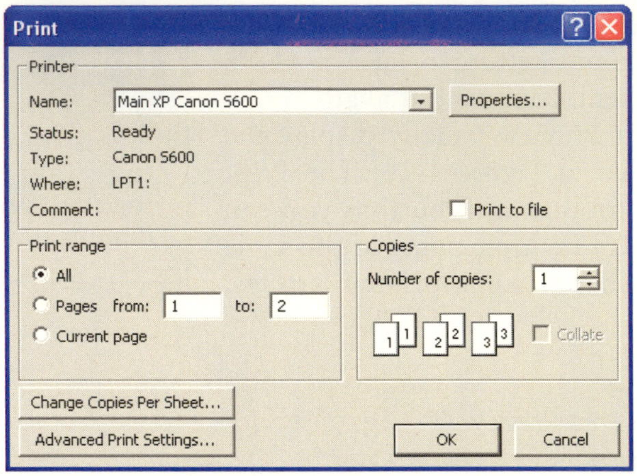

By default, most programs are set up to print a single page of a document on a single sheet of paper. If you want to see how a two-sided publication will look, you must use two-sided printing. Most desktop printers cannot print on two sides at the same time, so you print one side and then reinsert the paper into the printer and print the other side. Some printers will instruct you on how to position the paper in the paper feed to be sure the document prints correctly, or you can consult the printer manual. In some cases, you may have to experiment by feeding a sheet through and marking the top, bottom, back, and front.

If your printer supports two-sided printing, you may select that option before completing the following steps. Otherwise, follow the steps to manually print the publication on two sides. In addition, make sure your printer is correctly connected to your computer or network, that it is on, and that there is paper in the paper feeder.

STEP-BY-STEP 1.13

1. In the **Postcard** file, click the **Print Preview** button on the toolbar if available, or change the zoom to see the whole page.

2. Display page 2 by either clicking **Page Down** on the Print Preview toolbar or by pressing **Page Down** on your keyboard. Page 2, the reverse side of the mailer, is displayed.

3. Change back to page 1 and then close the Print Preview window if you have one open.

4. Click **File** on the menu bar, and then click **Print**. The Print dialog box opens.

5. Choose to print only page 1 by keying **1** in a page range box, or key **1** in both the *from* and the *to* boxes.

STEP-BY-STEP 1.13 Continued

6. Click the **OK** or **Print** button. The page prints. Return the page to the printer feeder, being sure to insert it correctly so that the second page prints on the blank side, top to bottom.

7. Click **File** on the menu bar, and then click **Print**. Choose to print only page 2 of the publication.

8. Click the **OK** or **Print** button. The page prints. You can crop the blank areas off the paper and compare the printed document to the mock-up you created at the beginning of this exercise.

9. Save changes and close the **Postcard** file. Close your desktop publishing program.

SUMMARY

In this lesson, you learned:

■ It is a good idea to plan a publication before you create it using your desktop publishing program.

■ Desktop publishing programs are used to produce printed documents.

■ You can create a blank publication file or use built-in templates and designs to create a document that already includes formatting, text, and graphics.

■ When you save a file, you give it a name and select a storage location.

■ You can change the way a file is displayed onscreen and toggle screen elements off and on.

■ In a desktop publishing file, text is inserted in a text box or frame.

■ You can insert different types of pictures into a desktop publishing file.

■ Desktop publishing programs come with spelling checkers that can help you locate and correct spelling errors.

■ You can preview and print a publication at any time.

VOCABULARY *Review*

Define the following terms:		
Active	Orientation	Template
Clip art	Page size	Text box
Default	Publication type	Toggles
Frame	Scratch area	View
Graphics	Shapes	Wrap
Hardware devices	Sheet size	Zoom
Mock-up		

REVIEW *Questions*

TRUE / FALSE

Circle T if the statement is true or F if the statement is false.

T   F   **1.** Zooming in increases the size of the publication displayed on your screen.

T   F   **2.** A template is another word for newsletter.

T   F   **3.** Some word processing programs offer desktop publishing features that can be used to create simple publications.

T   F   **4.** To include text in a desktop publishing document, you must import it from a word processing file.

T   F   **5.** Most desktop printers can print on two sides of a sheet of paper at the same time.

T   F   **6.** Automatic spelling checkers flag misspelled words as soon as you type them.

T   F   **7.** Once you insert a picture in a publication, you cannot replace it.

T   F   **8.** When you create a publication using a template or design, your program may automatically insert graphics and sample text in the document.

T   F   **9.** When you type in a text box, the text is automatically formatted according to the current settings.

T   F   **10.** Many programs display nonprinting gridlines onscreen in a publication to help you align objects on a page.

WRITTEN QUESTIONS

Write a brief answer to the following questions.

1. What are some things to consider when you plan a publication?

2. What are some reasons for using a publication design or template instead of creating a blank publication?

3. List at least five types of publications you can create with a desktop publishing program.

4. Why would you want to change the zoom while working with a publication?

5. Why should you check the spelling in a publication?

FILL IN THE BLANK

Complete the following sentences by writing the correct word or words in the blanks provided.

1. To quickly print a single copy of a publication using the default print settings, click the _____ button on the toolbar.

2. Graphics are _____ files that are usually inserted as objects directly into a desktop publishing file.

3. Use the _____ command to reverse the results of the Undo command.

4. You do not have to press Enter to start a new line if the text is set to _____ in the text box.

5. Another term for text box is _____.

6. When a command is _____ on, it usually has a check mark beside it on the menu.

7. Some programs automatically customize publications by inserting contact _____.

8. While planning a publication, you can create a(n) _____ to represent what the finished product will look like.

9. The first time you save a publication, you use the _____ dialog box to enter a filename and select a storage location.

10. Some programs have a(n) _____, which is a portion of the screen where you can temporarily store text and graphics.

PROJECTS

PROJECT 1-1

1. Launch your desktop publishing program and choose to create a flyer.

2. Select a simple design or template appropriate for advertising an event.

3. Save the file as **Speaker**.

4. Close the task pane if there is one, and then zoom in to 75%.

5. Replace the sample text with the following information:

Event title: Guest Speaker

Date: Date: April 22

Time: Time: 12:00 p.m.

Location: Location: Building 8, Cafeteria B

Contact: Contact person: 555-7777, ext. 3456

Description: Dr. Keith Lancaster, a specialist in retirement planning, will be giving a lecture about investing for the future, targeted toward those nearing retirement age. At the end of the talk, Dr. Lancaster will answer questions from the audience.

> **Note** ☑
>
> If you are using a template from a program such as Adobe PageMaker, you may need to adjust fonts, font sizes, and text boxes to fit information, and you may also have to decide how to arrange the information given above. Ask your instructor for help if necessary.

6. Replace the sample picture with **DP Project 1-1** from the data files. Adjust the size of the graphic frame if necessary.

7. Check the spelling in the file. Remove any unnecessary text boxes, frames, or graphics.

8. Preview the file, and then print a single copy.

9. Save changes and close the **Speaker** file, but leave your desktop publishing program open to use in Project 1-2.

PROJECT 1-2

1. In your desktop publishing program, choose to create a business card.

2. Select a design or template, such as the Punctuation template in Microsoft Publisher or the 1000768.pmt template in Adobe PageMaker 7.

3. Save the file as **KeithL**.

4. Close the task pane if there is one, and then zoom in to 150%.

5. Replace the sample text with the following information. (You may need to adjust fonts, font sizes, and text box sizes in some programs.)

Company name: Lancaster and Associates

Name: Keith Lancaster

Title: Retirement Specialist

Address: 5454 Main Street
Suite 7B
San Jose, CA 95110

Phone: 408-555-5555

Fax: 408-555-5666

Email: klanc@mail.com

Logo, organization, or other text: Retirement Planning

6. Check the spelling in the publication. If your template includes more than one business card on the page, you need modify only the first sample. Delete any text boxes or graphics you don't need.

7. Preview the publication, and then print one copy.

8. Save changes, close the **KeithL** file, and close your desktop publishing program.

WEB PROJECT

Use the Internet to look up and compare the features of at least two desktop publishing programs. You might try searching for desktop publishing, or looking up the Web sites of software companies you know sell desktop publishing programs, such as Microsoft and Adobe. Try to find a program designed for professional use and one designed for home use. Look for information that you can use to decide whether to buy the program. For example, most sites have feature lists that you can save or print, as well as pricing information. Compare the information you find and see if you can pick a program you would like to own.

TEAMWORK PROJECT

As a group, plan the development and production of a publication. Start by deciding the type of publication you want to produce as well as the target audience and the message you want the publication to convey. Agree on how you want the finished product to look, how it will be printed, and how it will be distributed. If possible, research the costs of producing the publication, including paper costs, printing costs, and delivery costs. You can call or write to a commercial printer to ask for a price list. Your school may even have a resource you can ask about paper and copying costs. Enter the pricing information into a spreadsheet, or write it on paper. See if you can save money by changing some of the project specifications. For example, could you print fewer copies, use fewer pages, or distribute the publication by hand instead of mail? Once you have settled on a budget and a publication plan, try making a mock-up that you can share with the class.

CRITICAL *Thinking*

ACTIVITY 1-1

Use your desktop publishing program to create an invitation to a party at your school or home. Start by planning how you want the invitation to look. For example, do you want it to be a single, unfolded sheet of paper, or do you want it to be folded card? Look at the designs or templates available in your program for ideas; then, create a mock-up. Create the document by selecting the publication type and design. Replace the sample text and graphics with customized text and graphics. Before you print the invitation, be sure to check the spelling.

WORKING WITH TEXT

LESSON 2

OBJECTIVES

Upon completion of this lesson, you should be able to:

- Create a blank document.
- Work with text boxes.
- Work with fonts.
- Align text.
- Set indents and tabs and create lists.
- Adjust spacing.
- Copy, move, and import text.
- Control text flow.

Estimated Time: 2 hours

VOCABULARY

Clipboard

Color scheme

Font

Font effects

Font size

Font style

Horizontal alignment

Indents

Insertion point

Kerning

Leading

Margins

Points

Sans serif font

Serif font

Tabs

Tracking

Vertical alignment

White space

Text is an important component of most desktop publishing documents. Sometimes, the text makes up the bulk of the publication, such as in a newsletter that includes lengthy articles. Other times, the text is used to highlight or complement other content, for example, in a sales flyer that may use short bullet lists or a travel brochure that may have photo captions. All desktop publishing programs include tools that help you enhance the appearance of your publications and ensure that the text is easy to read. Most of the tools are similar to those found in word processing programs that allow you to apply boldface or indent a paragraph. Other tools are designed specifically for fine-tuning documents for publication, such as adjusting spacing between lines, characters, and paragraphs. In this lesson, you learn how to create a blank document, insert and delete text boxes, format text, and control text flow.

Create a Blank Document

In Lesson 1, you learned to create a publication using your program's built-in designs or templates. If none of the templates or designs is suitable for your publication, you can create a new blank document and start from scratch. Once you create a blank document, you insert text and graphics and apply formatting to design your publication.

Although some desktop publishing programs start with a new blank document open on the screen, most start displaying a dialog box or task pane listing designs or templates. Click the option for creating a blank document or publication to display a default blank document. Alternatively, click the New button on the toolbar. Some programs first display a Document Setup dialog box in which you can select settings to control the appearance of the new document or just click OK to create a document with the default settings. In most programs, the default blank document is a full 8.5-inch by 11-inch page with 1-inch *margins* marked by margin guides on all sides. Margins are the area between the edge of the page and the objects in the publication. Some programs may have different default margins.

STEP-BY-STEP 2.1

1. Launch your desktop publishing program. If necessary, close the template dialog box or window.

2. If necessary, click the option to create a blank full-page document, or click the **New** button on the toolbar. If your program displays a Document Setup dialog box, key **1** in each of the margin boxes and then click the **OK** button. Your program creates and displays a document similar to the one shown in Figure 2-1.

FIGURE 2-1
Blank full-page document

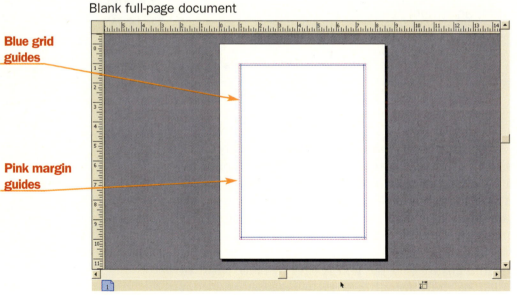

Blue grid guides

Pink margin guides

3. Save the file as **Meeting** and leave it open to use in the next exercise.

Work with Text Boxes

As you have already learned, text in a desktop publishing document is inserted in a text box, which is sometimes called a *frame* or *text frame*. When you create a document based on a template or design, your program automatically inserts and formats text boxes. You can manually insert text boxes at any time, and you can delete text boxes you no longer need. Once a text box is inserted in a document, you can easily change its size and/or position on the page.

> **Note** ☑
> Some programs let you create two types of text boxes—text blocks and text frames. For the exercises in this lesson, you should use text frames.

Insert and Delete Text Boxes

To insert a text box, use a tool or command such as Text Box, or use a frame tool. Click the appropriate tool and then click and drag the mouse pointer to define the size and position of the object on the page. As you drag, guidelines appear on both the horizontal and vertical ruler. Use these lines to help you gauge the text box dimensions. When you release the mouse button, the new text box is inserted in the document, and it is selected. The appearance of a selected text box varies depending on the program you are using. Most display sizing handles and a nonprinting border, like other selected objects. Some display a thin black printing border called a *stroke* and *windowshade handles* on the top and bottom. You learn how to add, modify, and remove strokes in Lesson 4.

Usually, the new text box has an ***insertion point*** flashing in it, but in some programs, you have to click a text tool and then click in the new frame to place the insertion point. The insertion point is a flashing vertical bar that indicates where keyed text will be inserted. New text is generally inserted to the left of the insertion point. You use standard text entry and editing techniques to key text in a desktop publishing program. To delete a text box, click its border to select it, and then press Delete, or choose Delete or Clear from the Edit menu.

> **Note** ☑
> You should always use proper typography and keyboarding when keying text in a publication.

S TEP-BY-STEP 2.2

1. In the **Meeting** file, adjust the zoom to at least 75% so you have a good look at the top part of the document.

2. Click the tool that allows you to insert a text box or rectangular frame, and then position the mouse pointer at the top margin halfway across the page, at about 4.25 inches on the horizontal ruler.

> **Extra for Experts**
> In some programs, you can drag the rulers closer to the work area so you can measure the objects in your publication.

STEP-BY-STEP 2.2 Continued

3. Press and hold the mouse button and drag diagonally down and to the right to draw a box about 1 inch high and 3 inches wide. Use the rulers for help sizing the object. Release the mouse button to insert the object in the file. It should look similar to Figure 2-2. Don't worry if your text box or frame has a stroke, or line, around it.

> **Note** ☑
>
> If you want to remove the stroke, select None from the Stroke list in the Fill and Stroke dialog box.

FIGURE 2-2
Blank text box

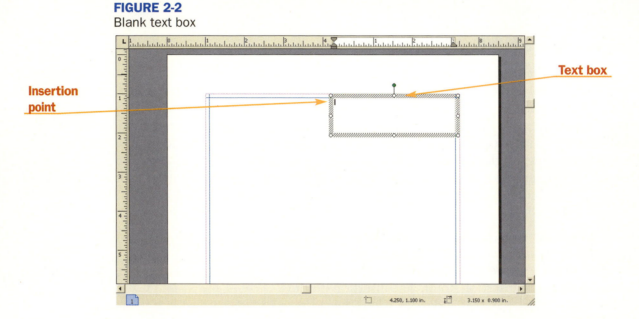

4. If necessary, click in the text box with the text tool to position the insertion point, and then key the text **Leadership Association Meeting**. The text displays in the default formatting. You learn how to change the formatting later in this lesson.

5. Click the text box or frame tool again, and then position the mouse pointer in the lower left corner of the document.

6. Press and hold the mouse button and drag diagonally up and to the right to draw a box about 2 inches high and 6 inches wide. Again, use the rulers to help size the object. Release the mouse button to insert the object in the file.

7. Key the text **Join us on Friday**. Now, try deleting a text box.

8. Use the pointer or selection tool to click the border of the text box you drew in step 6 to select it, and then press **Delete**. The text box is removed from the file.

9. Save changes and leave the **Meeting** file open to use in the next exercise.

Resize, Position Text Boxes

When you select a text box, sizing handles display around its border. Drag a sizing handle to quickly resize the text box. When the mouse pointer is positioned over a sizing handle, it may change to a double-headed arrow and include the word *Resize*. Drag a top or bottom handle to change the text box height. Drag a side handle to change the width, or drag a corner handle to change both the height and width at the same time.

To position a text box, simply place the mouse pointer over the object's border and then drag the object to a new location. When the mouse pointer is over the border, it may change to a four-headed arrow and include the word *Move*.

> **Note**
>
> Most programs display the *X* and *Y coordinates* of a text box or frame, as well as the width and height of the object, in the status bar or in a control palette. You can use these coordinates and measurements to position or size a text box precisely.

STEP-BY-STEP 2.3

1. In the **Meeting** file, select the text box.

2. Position the mouse pointer over the object's border (the Move pointer may appear), and then press and hold the mouse button and drag the object to the upper-left corner of the document, where the top and left margins meet. Release the mouse button to move the object.

3. Position the mouse pointer over the sizing handle in the lower-right corner of the text box.

4. Press and hold the mouse button and drag across to the right margin and down to the 3-inch mark on the ruler, as shown in Figure 2-3. As you drag, the mouse pointer may change to a cross-hair, and a dashed line may define the text box size. Release the mouse button to resize the object.

FIGURE 2-3
Resize a text box

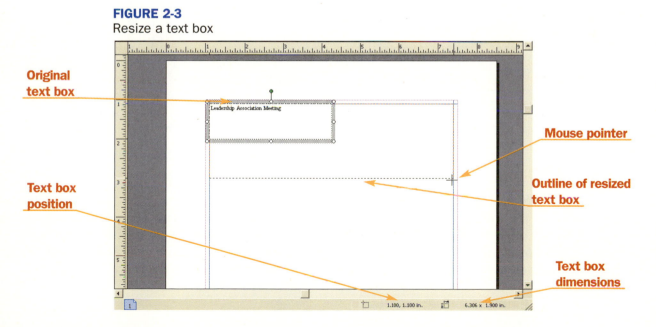

5. Save changes and leave the **Meeting** file open to use in the next exercise.

Work with Fonts

Change the look of text in a publication using font formatting. A *font* is the typeface or design of a set of characters, including letters, numbers, and symbols. Although the main goal in selecting a font is to make text easy to read, appropriate use of fonts can also make an impact in your publications and help define the tone and message you want to convey. Fonts can be elaborate or simple, decorative or plain. It is worth spending some time to select just the right font or combination of fonts to complement your publication.

In addition to selecting a font, you can set font size, font style, font effects, and font color. You can apply font formatting to selected text, or you can select the options before you key new text. Many font formatting options can be set using toolbar buttons, palette options, or menus. In addition, most programs have a Font or Character Specifications dialog box similar to the one shown in Figure 2-4, in which you can select any of the font formatting options. To open the Font dialog box in most programs, click Format on the menu bar and then click Font. To open the Character Specifications dialog box in PageMaker, click Type on the menu bar and then click Character.

FIGURE 2-4
Font dialog box

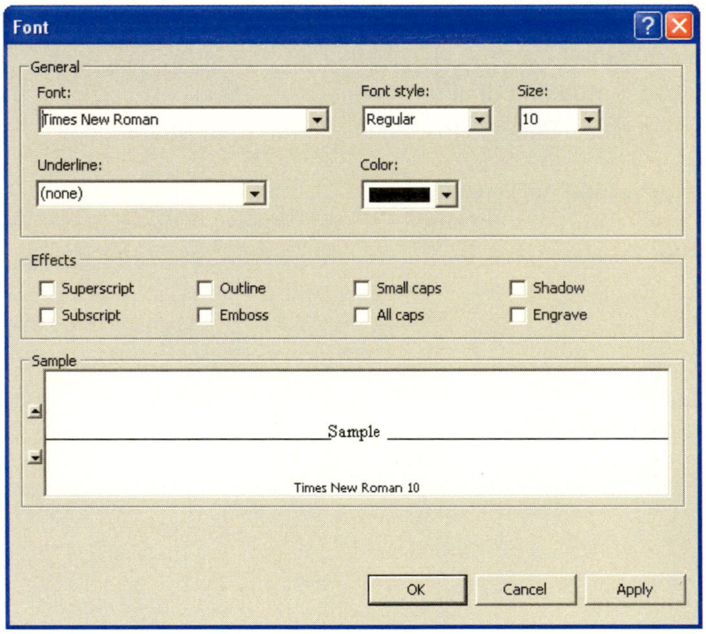

Select a Font and Font Size

There are two basic types of fonts: serif fonts and sans serif fonts. *Serif fonts* have short lines and curlicues at the ends of the lines that make up each character. Serif fonts are generally easy to read and so are often used for lengthy paragraphs, reports, or letters. Some common serif fonts include Times New Roman, Garamond, and Century. *Sans serif fonts* have straight lines without serifs and are often used for headlines and titles. Some common sans serif fonts are Arial, Impact, and Tahoma. Other types of fonts include script fonts, which imitate handwriting decorative, or fantasy fonts, and symbol fonts, which include sets of symbols you can insert as characters into text. Figure 2-5 shows examples of different fonts.

FIGURE 2-5
Sample fonts

Serif Fonts	Script Fonts
Times New Roman	*Brush Script MT*
Sylfaen	*Edwardian Script ITC*
Georgia	*Freestyle Script*
Sans Serif Fonts	Decorative or Fantasy Fonts
Arial	Chiller
Comic Sans MS	CASTELLAR
Gill Sans MT	Curlz MT
	Jokerman
	Ravie

Your program probably has a default font and font size for text inserted in a blank document. For example, in Microsoft Publisher, the default font is 10-point Times New Roman. To choose a font, locate your program's font list on a menu, toolbar, or in a dialog or task pane. In most cases, the fonts are listed in alphabetical order, and you can sometimes see a preview of a font when you select it in the list. Most desktop publishing programs come with a long list of built-in fonts, and you may have other fonts available on your computer as well. You can buy and install font sets you need, or locate free fonts on the Internet.

> ### Extra for Experts
>
> Some programs let you scale the width of selected text by a percentage of its original size. For example, scale text to 200% to stretch it to twice its original width. Scale text to 50% to shrink it to half its original width.

Too many fonts can make a publication difficult to read. In general, you should try to use no more than three fonts on a page, and you should avoid mixing similar fonts on the same page. For example, use a serif font for body text and a sans serif font for headlines. You can add a third font for captions or subheadings, or better yet, change the size and/or style of one of the other fonts you are already using.

Font size is the height of an uppercase letter in the font set, measured in ***points***. There are 72 points in an inch. Select a new font size by locating your program's font size list on a toolbar, menu, or palette, or in the Font dialog box. You can choose one of the sizes on the list or key a size in the font size box. Many programs have Increase Font Size and Decrease Font Size toolbar buttons that you can use to quickly change the font in 1-point increments.

Some programs also offer a copy fitting option, which you use to automatically adjust the size of text to fit within a text box. Copy fitting, which may be called AutoFit Text, is usually a toggle that is turned on or off using a menu command or a dialog box. When copy fitting is on, text you key in a text box automatically resizes to fit within the text box borders. When copy fitting is off, text is sized according to the current font size selection.

> **Note** ☑
>
> If you open a file that uses a font that is not installed on your computer, your program may automatically substitute a similar font, or it may display a dialog box asking if it is OK to substitute a font. You learn more about font substitution in Lesson 6.

STEP-BY-STEP 2.4

1. In the **Meeting** file, select all of the text in the text box.

2. Click the **Font** box drop-down arrow on the toolbar or Control palette, and then click **Arial** on the list of fonts. You may have to scroll to the top of the list to locate the correct font.

3. Click the **Font Size** box on the toolbar or palette and key **36**, or click **36** on the Font Size list. The text should now be formatted in 36-point Arial, as shown in Figure 2-6.

FIGURE 2-6
Modified font and font size

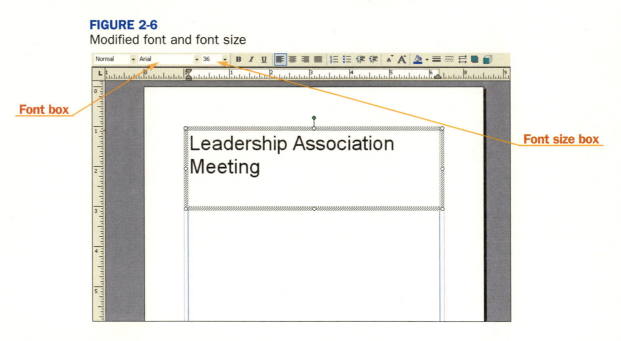

4. Save changes and leave the **Meeting** file open to use in the next exercise.

Apply Font Styles, Font Effects, and Font Color

Font style is used to call attention to specific text without changing the font itself. The style is the slant and *weight*—or thickness—of characters in a font set, such as bold and italic. Some programs also offer underlining as a font style. Bold is usually used to highlight text and make it stand out, while italic is usually used for subtle emphasis. Click a toolbar button to apply a style, or select it in the Font dialog box.

B
I
U

Font effects are attributes applied to characters such as superscript, subscript, shadows, or small caps. Font effects are sometimes used for decorative purposes, but are sometimes necessary for correct typography. For example, to key the chemical formula for water correctly you need to use a subscript 2: H_2O. Font effects are usually available in the Font dialog box or on a palette. You can often combine effects to achieve different results.

Font color is simply the color used for text. By default, font color is usually black. To change the font color, click the Font Color button on the toolbar or in the Font or Character Specifications dialog box to display a palette of available colors, then click the color you want to use. Some programs display only colors that are part of the current *color scheme*, which is a set of coordinated colors. There may be an option for displaying or creating additional colors, or a color chart from which you can select any color you want. You learn more about working with color in Lesson 5.

STEP-BY-STEP 2.5

1. In the **Meeting** file, select all of the text in the text box and click the **Bold** button on a toolbar or Control palette. The text is formatted in bold style.

2. Open the dialog box in which you can change character formats. For example, click **Format** on the menu bar and click **Font** to open the dialog box.

3. Select the **Small caps** effect.

4. Change the font color to blue.

5. Click the **OK** button in the dialog box to apply the font formatting to the selected text. It should look similar to Figure 2-7. In PageMaker, you may have to set hyphenation to manual in order to keep the word *Meeting* from hyphenating. Click **Type** on the menu bar, click **Hyphenation**, click the **Manual Only** option, and then click the **OK** button.

FIGURE 2-7
Modified font style, effect, and color

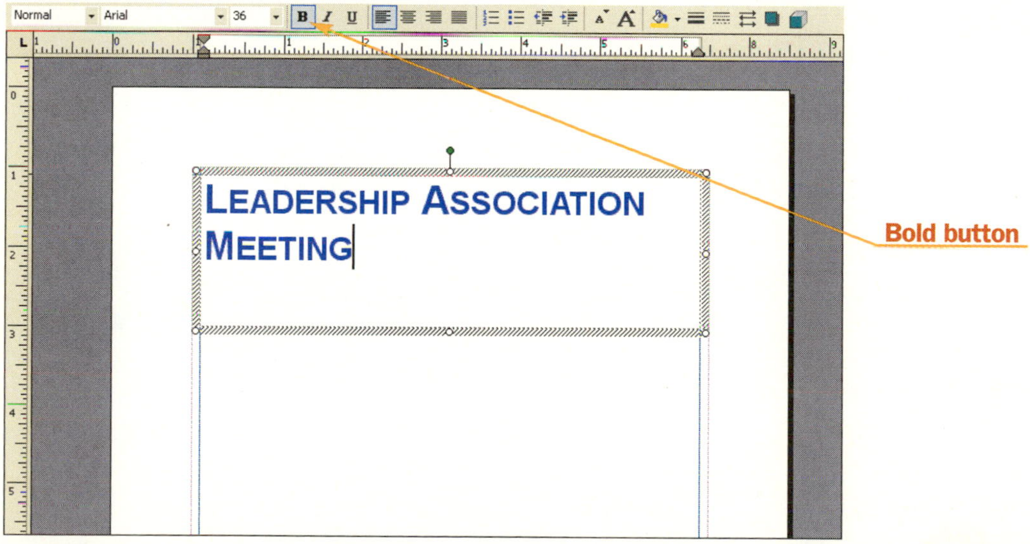

Bold button

LEADERSHIP ASSOCIATION MEETING

STEP-BY-STEP 2.5 Continued

6. Save changes and leave the **Meeting** file open to use in the next exercise.

Align Text

In desktop publishing programs, you can set text alignment to position paragraphs in relation to the borders of a text box. You can set the *horizontal alignment* of text to adjust the position of paragraphs in relation to the left and right margins of the text box. You can set the *vertical alignment* to adjust the position of all text in a text box in relation to the top and bottom margins of the text box. Figure 2-8 shows examples of different alignments.

FIGURE 2-8
Sample text alignments

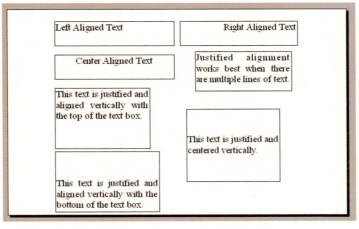

Set Horizontal Alignment

Most programs offer four horizontal alignment options: left align, which positions a paragraph so that text is even with the left margin; right align, which positions a paragraph so that text is even with the right margin; center align, which positions a paragraph so text is centered between the margins; and justify, which spaces the text so that both the left and right margins are even. Some programs may also have a *force justify* option that justifies all lines in a paragraph, even short lines at the end of the paragraph.

To set horizontal alignment, position the insertion point within a paragraph or select multiple paragraphs and then click an alignment button on the toolbar or control palette's paragraph settings. You can also select an alignment before you key new text. You may also select alignment options from a menu. Horizontal alignment is carried forward to the next paragraph when you press Enter. However, each paragraph of text can have a different horizontal alignment.

STEP-BY-STEP 2.6

1. In the **Meeting** file, make sure the insertion point is positioned in the text, and then click the **right align** button on the toolbar or Control palette. You may have to click the **Paragraph** button on the Control pallette to display the alignment buttons. The text in the text box aligns with the right margin.

2. Click the **justify** button. The text is justified between the left and right text box margins. (If the word *Meeting* spaces itself out across the frame, you used the Force Justify button, not the Justify button.)

3. Click the **center** button. The text is centered between the left and right margins.

4. Save changes and leave the **Meeting** file open to use in the next exercise.

Set Vertical Alignment

Most programs offer three vertical alignments: top, which positions the text to start immediately below the top border; bottom, which positions the text to end immediately above the bottom border; and center, which positions the text between the top and bottom borders. In most programs, you set vertical alignment in a dialog box such as Format Text Box or Frame Options. You can set only one vertical alignment for a text box, no matter how much text it contains.

> **Note** ✅
>
> Do not confuse vertical alignment, which spaces text within a text box, with vertical text direction, an effect in which text characters are positioned vertically instead of horizontally. To achieve a vertical text effect, you usually have to create a graphics object using a different program or a utility such as WordArt. Using WordArt is covered in Lesson 5.

STEP-BY-STEP 2.7

1. In the **Meeting** file, open the dialog box in which you can set vertical alignment. For example, click Format on the menu bar and then click Text box. If necessary, click the Text Box tab. In some programs, such as PageMaker, click Element on the menu bar, click Frame, and then click Frame Options.

2. Select the option to center the text vertically. For example, click the **Vertical alignment** drop-down arrow and click **Middle**.

STEP-BY-STEP 2.7 Continued

3. Click the **OK** button in the dialog box. The text should look similar to Figure 2-9.

FIGURE 2-9
Text is centered vertically and horizontally

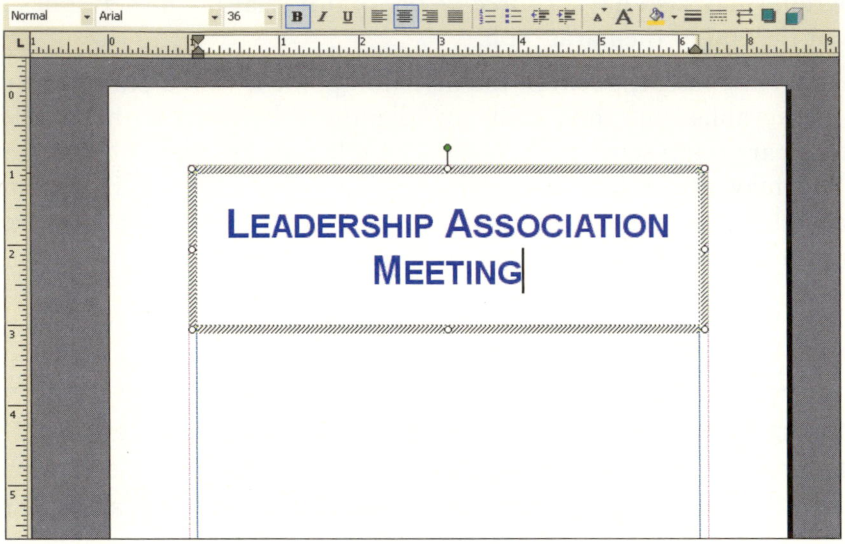

4. Print one copy of the **Meeting** file.

5. Save changes and close the **Meeting** file. Leave your desktop publishing program open to use in the next exercise.

Set Indents and Tabs and Create Lists

You can set indents and tabs within a text box in much the same way you do in a standard word processing document. *Indents* are used to set temporary margins for a paragraph or series of paragraphs. *Tabs* are used to adjust the horizontal position of text across a single line. To set indents and tabs for a single paragraph, simply position the insertion point in the paragraph and then select the options you want to apply. To format multiple paragraphs, select the paragraphs before selecting the options. You can also select the options before you key new text. Indents and tabs are carried forward to new paragraphs when you press Enter.

Lists are an effective way to present information so that readers can quickly identify and digest the important points you are trying to make. In addition, lists are useful for breaking up the layout of a page to make it more interesting and appealing. Use numbered lists when the order of items matters and use bulleted lists when the order does not matter. For example, number directions to a building and bullet facts about a product or service.

Most programs offer many different methods to apply indents, tabs, and lists. Usually, you can set precise values or select options in a dialog box or control palette, but it is often faster and easier to simply drag the indent or tab markers on the horizontal ruler or on the Indents/Tabs ruler.

Set Indents

Most programs offer five types of indents, as shown in Figure 2-10. A first-line indent indents the first line of a paragraph from the left margin. A left indent indents all lines in a paragraph from the left margin. A right indent indents all lines from the right margin. A double or quotation indent indents all lines from both the left and right margins. A hanging indent indents all lines except the first line from the left margin.

FIGURE 2-10
Sample indent styles

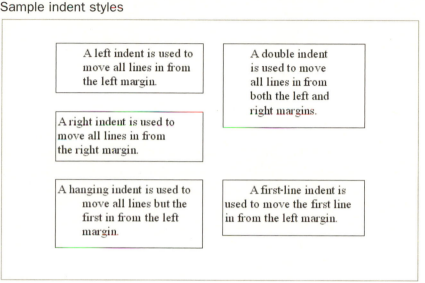

> A left indent is used to move all lines in from the left margin.

> A double indent is used to move all lines in from both the left and right margins.

> A right indent is used to move all lines in from the right margin.

> A hanging indent is used to move all lines but the first in from the left margin.

> A first-line indent is used to move the first line in from the left margin.

Indents may be set by dragging indent markers on a ruler, by specifying values in a Control palette, or by using a dialog box. Some programs have Increase Indent and Decrease Indent toolbar buttons that you can use to quickly adjust a left indent in 0.5-inch increments. To open the Indents and Lists dialog box, click Format on the menu bar and then click Indents and Lists. To open the control palette, click Window, Show Control Palette. (You may have to click the Paragraph formatting button to make the indents options available.) To display the Indents/Tabs ruler, click Type on the menu bar and then click Indents/Tabs. Your instructor may want you to use a particular method to complete the following exercise. If not, select the method you want to use.

S TEP-BY-STEP 2.8

1. In your desktop publishing program, open **DP Step 2-8** from the data files. This publication is similar to the Meeting file you worked with earlier in this lesson, but it includes additional text.

2. Save the file as **Meeting2**.

3. Increase the zoom to at least 75%, and then select the text of the quotation, including the quotation marks, but not the speaker's name or title.

4. Apply a double or quotation indent by indenting the text 0.5 inches from both the left and right margins. You can do this by dragging the indent markers on the horizontal or Indents/Tabs ruler, or by setting values in the Indents and Lists dialog box or Control palette.

STEP-BY-STEP 2.8 Continued

5. Select the speaker's name and title and indent the lines 3 inches from the left margin. When you deselect the text, the text box should look similar to the one in Figure 2-11.

FIGURE 2-11
Indents applied to text

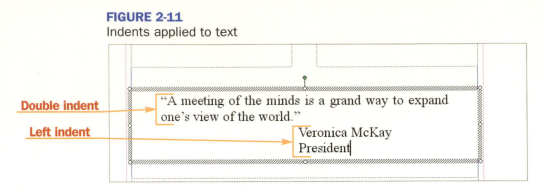

6. Save changes and leave the **Meeting2** file open to use in the next exercise.

Set Tabs

A tab is a stopping point at a specific point along the horizontal ruler. Each time you press the Tab key, the insertion point advances to the next tab stop. There are four types of tab stops in most programs. Left sets text to start flush with the tab stop. Right sets text to end flush with the tab stop. Center centers text on either side of the tab stop. Decimal aligns decimal points or periods flush with the tab stop. Most programs have default left tab stops set every 0.5 inch. In most programs, you can also set *tab leaders*, which are characters repeated on the line preceding the tab stop. Common tab leader characters include dots, lines, dashes, and bullets.

Set tabs by selecting the type of tab stop in the tab stop box near the ruler and then clicking on the horizontal ruler or the Indents/Tabs ruler to position the tab, or by using the Tabs dialog box.

You can usually change one type of tab to another by double-clicking the tab to display a dialog box where you can select the new tab type. Move a tab if necessary by simply dragging it on the ruler. To delete a tab, drag it off the ruler or use a dialog box to delete it.

S TEP-BY-STEP 2.9

1. In the **Meeting2** file, position the insertion point to the right of the colon after the word *Date:* in the last text box on the page.

2. Set a left tab stop at 1.25 inches on the horizontal ruler or on your program's Indents/Tabs ruler. You can set the tab stop by clicking on the ruler or, in some programs, by using the Tabs dialog box.

3. Press **Tab**, key **Saturday, March 22**, and then press **Enter**. (You may need to close the Indents/Tabs ruler before you can begin working with the text.)

4. Key **Time:**, press **Tab**, and key **10:00 a.m.**

STEP-BY-STEP 2.9 Continued

5. Press **Enter**, key **Location:**, press **Tab**, and key **Midtown Hotel**. The text box should look similar to the one in Figure 2-12.

FIGURE 2-12
Align text using tabs

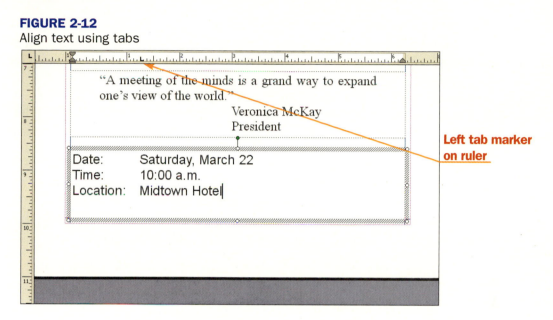

6. Save changes and leave the **Meeting2** file open to use in the next exercise.

Create Lists

To create a list, you simply apply a list format or style to the current paragraph or to selected paragraphs. Most lists are formatted automatically using a hanging indent, but in some programs, such as Adobe PageMaker, you must adjust the indents manually on the Indents/Tabs ruler. Usually, the formatting is carried forward when you press Enter. You can also select the list format before you key new text.

Most programs include a set of built-in bullet styles that you can quickly apply to lists. Click the Bullets button on the toolbar to apply the default bullet style or the most recently used bullet style to the current paragraph, or select the bullet size and other options in a dialog box. In some programs, you must specify how many paragraphs you want formatted as part of the list.

Likewise, most programs include built-in number formats. Click the Numbering button on the toolbar to quickly apply the default number style or the most recently used number style to the current paragraph. Options for customizing the *separator character* and indent are usually found in a dialog box.

S TEP-BY-STEP 2.10

1. In the **Meeting2** file, select the five paragraphs (6 lines) of text under the heading *Morning Agenda.* Do not select the heading.

2. Click a button such as **Bullets** or **Bullets & Numbering** to apply bullet formatting. In some programs, you may have to select the formatting manually. If so, select a large square bullet style and specify to format 6 paragraphs as part of the list. You may also have to manually set a hanging indent of 0.25 inches.

3. In the text box to the right of the one where you created the bulleted list, select the last three lines of text in the text box: *Pick up an application, Fill out an application,* and *Submit an application.*

4. Click a button such as **Numbering** or **Bullets & Numbering** to apply number formatting. In some programs, you may have to format the number style manually. If so, select a period as the separator and specify to apply the formatting to 4 paragraphs as part of the list. When you deselect the text, it should look similar to Figure 2-13. Don't worry if the formats of the numbers and bullets are not the same as in the illustration. Your program may have different defaults.

FIGURE 2-13
Text formatted as lists

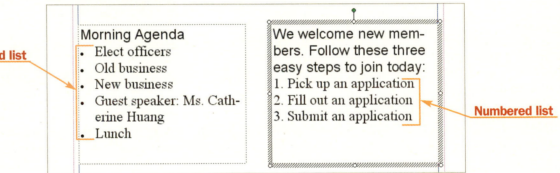

5. Save changes and leave the **Meeting2** file open to use in the next exercise.

Adjust Spacing

When you create a desktop publishing document, you should consider the amount of **white space** in and around text boxes as well as the text box content. White space is the area on a page that has no text or graphics. Spacing between characters, spacing between lines in a paragraph, and spacing between paragraphs can dramatically affect ease of reading a document, as well as the document's appearance. In most programs, there are many ways to ensure the correct amount of space is placed in and around your text. To adjust the space between all characters in a text box, you set the

Extra for Experts

In some programs you can insert three types of *relative spaces* in place of regular spaces—em spaces (double the width of a regular space), en spaces (half the width of an em space), and thin spaces (one quarter the width of an em space). Unlike regular spaces, relative spaces change width in relation to point size and font only, even when text is justified.

tracking. To adjust the space between two specific characters, you set the *kerning*. You can set the line spacing or *leading* to change the amount of space between lines of text, and you can specify the amount of space to leave before and/or after each paragraph. Finally, you can set the top, bottom, left, and right margins for a text box to control the amount of white space between the text and the text box borders.

Set Character Spacing

The amount of space allotted for the width of each character is determined by the font set. You can increase or decrease the spacing between all characters in a selection by setting the tracking. Kerning is used when you can see uneven spacing between a pair of characters within a word. Uneven spacing causes the reader's eye to hesitate, making it harder to read the text. Good kerning spaces characters so that the reader views each word as a single unit.

Tracking and kerning are usually set in a dialog box, or you may be able to select options or key values on a control palette. To open the dialog box, click Format on the menu bar and then click Character Spacing. To open the Control palette, click Window on the menu bar and then click Show Control Palette. (You may have to click the Type button to make the character formatting options available.) Tracking is usually set as a percentage of the original spacing. However, some programs let you select relative spacing, such as tight, which decreases spacing, or loose, which increases spacing. In most programs, you increase or decrease the kerning between a selected pair of characters by a specific number of points. In some programs, you select to expand or condense the spacing between the selected pair and then enter the distance in points. Some programs have automatic kerning options you can set to automatically increase the space between wide characters when the text is larger than a specified size.

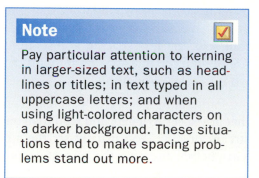

Note

Pay particular attention to kerning in larger-sized text, such as headlines or titles; in text typed in all uppercase letters; and when using light-colored characters on a darker background. These situations tend to make spacing problems stand out more.

S TEP-BY-STEP 2.11

1. In the **Meeting2** file, select the heading text *We welcome new members. Follow these three easy steps to join today.*

2. Open the Character Spacing dialog box or the Control palette and change the tracking to tight or to 88% of the original tracking. This decreases the amount of spacing between all characters. As a result, some character pairs may appear to run together. Next, adjust the kerning to increase the space between pairs of characters.

3. Select the *o* and the *d* in the word *today*, and expand the kerning until the characters no longer run together.

4. Repeat step 3 to expand the kerning between the *t* and the *h* in the word *these* and in the word *three*, and between the *r* and the *s* in the word *members*.

5. Save changes and leave the **Meeting2** file open to use in the next exercise.

Set Line and Paragraph Spacing

Line spacing, or leading (pronounced to rhyme with *wedding*), is important because if there is too much or too little space between lines, the reader's eye has trouble following from one line to the next. In general, you want the space between lines to be greater than the space between words, but some situations, such as short lines of text, call for tighter leading.

In most programs, you can set the leading in a Line Spacing dialog box or using the Leading menu accessed from the Type menu. To open the Line Spacing dialog box, click Format on the menu bar and then click Line Spacing. You can usually use either lines or points as the unit of measure. If you use lines and then change the font size, the line spacing adjusts automatically. If you use points, the line spacing remains constant, no matter what font size you apply.

Paragraph spacing helps break content into chunks that are easier to locate and read than one long continuous stream of text. You usually set the amount of space to leave before and after the current paragraph in points.

You should set paragraph and line spacing instead of pressing Enter to insert extra lines. Setting spacing options gives you greater control over the appearance of your publication and makes editing and rearranging text much easier. Both paragraph spacing and line spacing can be applied to the current paragraph, to selected paragraphs, or to new paragraphs before you key the text. The formatting is carried forward to the next paragraph when you press Enter. Line and paragraph spacing options are usually available in a dialog box or in a control palette.

Note

If you set space lines too close together, *ascenders*, which are the parts of characters that extend above the rest of the text, may run into the text in the line above, and *descenders*, which are the parts of characters that extend below the baseline, may run into the text in the line below.

Note

Display special characters to show nonprinting paragraph marks at the end of each paragraph in your document. To display special characters, click the Special Characters button on the toolbar, or select the appropriate command from the View menu.

Note

Instead of trying to fit many paragraphs into one text box, you can break the text up into multiple text boxes. Using multiple text boxes gives you more flexibility in terms of position, size, alignment, and other options.

STEP-BY-STEP 2.12

1. In the **Meeting2** file, select all of the text in the text box containing the quotation.

2. Using the appropriate dialog box or menu, set the leading or line spacing to 18 points. You may have to type the unit of measure (such as *pt*, which is the abbreviation for point) in order to switch from lines to points. Setting the spacing to 18 points decreases the amount of space between lines.

3. Deselect the text and then position the insertion point anywhere within the quotation.

STEP-BY-STEP 2.12 Continued

4. Set the spacing before the paragraph to 3 points and the spacing after the paragraph to 6 points. You may have to type a unit of measure in a Control palette box such as p3 or p6 to set the spacing in points. When you are finished, the text box should look similar to the one in Figure 2-14.

FIGURE 2-14
Adjusted line and paragraph spacing

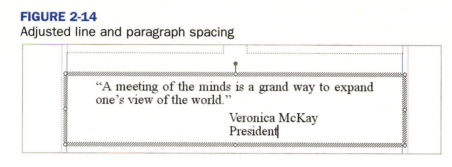

> "A meeting of the minds is a grand way to expand one's view of the world."
>
> Veronica McKay
> President

5. Save changes and leave the **Meeting2** file open to use in the next exercise.

Set Margins in a Text Box

To control the amount of space between text and the text box border, set the text box margins, which are sometimes called the *frame inset*. Your program probably has a narrow default text box margin size, such as 0.04 inch. You can increase a margin by increasing the width, or decrease a margin by decreasing the width. Each margin can be set independently of the other margins. In most programs, the text box margins are set in a dialog box. You can set the margins for one text box or for selected text boxes at the same time.

STEP-BY-STEP 2.13

1. In the **Meeting2** file, select the two text boxes containing the lists. To select both boxes at the same time, select one, press and hold Shift, and then select the other.

2. Open the dialog box in which you can set text box margins. For example, click **Format** on the menu bar, click **Text Box**, and then click the **Text Box** tab.

3. Set the left, right, top, and bottom margins to 0.1 inch, and then click the **OK** button in the dialog box. The margins in the text boxes increase, as shown in Figure 2-15.

FIGURE 2-15
Increase text box margins

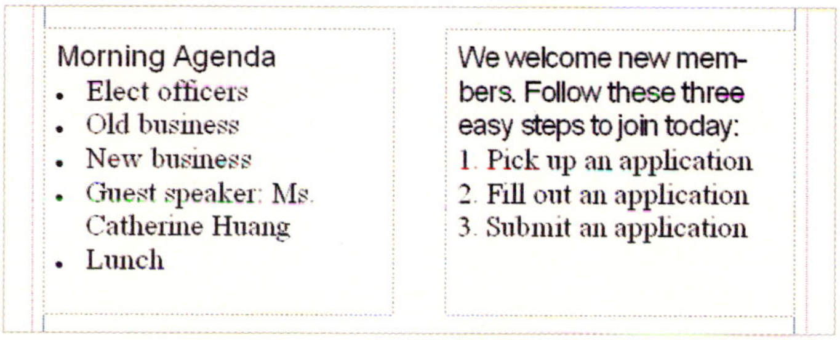

Morning Agenda
- Elect officers
- Old business
- New business
- Guest speaker: Ms. Catherine Huang
- Lunch

We welcome new members. Follow these three easy steps to join today:
1. Pick up an application
2. Fill out an application
3. Submit an application

4. Save changes and leave the **Meeting2** file open to use in the next exercise.

Copy, Move, and Import Text

To save yourself the trouble of rekeying, you can easily copy, move, or import text into a desktop publishing document. The Copy, Cut, and Paste commands are used in all Windows programs to copy and move text as well as objects from one location to another. The copied or cut items are stored temporarily on the *Clipboard*, which is a temporary storage area in your computer's memory. When you select the Paste command, the item is inserted at the current location. A cut item is removed from the original location, while a copied item remains in both the original and new locations. Cut, Copy, and Paste commands are available as toolbar buttons or on the Edit menu.

> **Note** ☑
>
> In some programs, if you include the paragraph mark at the end of a paragraph when you copy or move text, you include the paragraph formatting, too.

Using the Clipboard, you can copy or move selected text within a text box or from one text box to another. You can also copy or move an entire text box and its contents. You can even copy and move text from one document to another, even if the documents are different types. For example, you can copy a chart from a spreadsheet into a publication document, or a paragraph from a word processing document into a text box in a publication.

When you want to import an entire text file into your desktop publishing document, you use the Insert Text File command or the File Place command. Locate and select the file you want to insert, and then click OK. Depending on your program, you may be able to insert text-only files, or you may be able to import and preserve text that has been formatted in a word processing document. When you insert a file, all of the file is inserted into a text box.

> **Extra for Experts**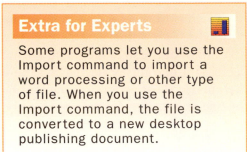
>
> Some programs let you use the Import command to import a word processing or other type of file. When you use the Import command, the file is converted to a new desktop publishing document.

When copying or importing text, you may find that the text box or frame is not large enough to hold all text. If a text box cannot show all text, it usually displays a symbol near the bottom, such as A... or a red triangle in the bottom handle of the frame. If you see such a symbol, adjust the size of the text box or frame until it disappears to make sure you have all text showing.

STEP-BY-STEP 2.14

1. In the **Meeting2** file, select the text *Guest speaker: Ms. Catherine Huang* in the bullet list. Try not to include the paragraph mark at the end of the line. You want to copy this text into the headline text box at the top of the page.

2. Use the **Copy** button or command to copy the text to the Clipboard. Position the insertion point at the end of the headline text in the text box at the top of the page, and press **Enter** to start a new paragraph.

3. Use the **Paste** button or command to paste the text at the insertion point location. If you copied the paragraph mark, too, the line will retain its bullet list formatting. Simply click the **Bullets** button on the toolbar to remove the bullet. You may also need to center the text horizontally.

STEP-BY-STEP 2.14 Continued

4. Click the **Text Box** or rectangular frame tool on the toolbar and insert a new text box between the headline text box and the text boxes containing the lists. Size the box to fill the open area—about 6.3 inches by 1.2 inches.

5. Select all the text in the quotation text box, including the speaker's name and title. Use the **Cut** button or command to cut the selection to the Clipboard. Then click in the new text box and use the **Paste** button or command. The text moves to the new text box. If a dialog box is displayed asking if you want to use AutoFlow, click No to continue. Don't worry if some of the text is hidden. You can adjust the size of the box later. The top part of your document should look similar to Figure 2-16.

FIGURE 2-16
Copy and move text in a document

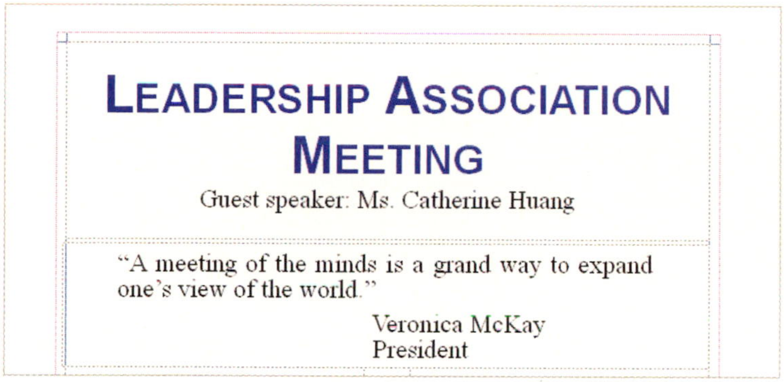

LEADERSHIP ASSOCIATION MEETING
Guest speaker: Ms. Catherine Huang

"A meeting of the minds is a grand way to expand one's view of the world."

Veronica McKay
President

6. Position the insertion point in the text box where the quotation originally appeared. This box should be empty now.

7. Select the command to insert a text file. For example, click **Insert** on the menu bar, and then click **Text File**. Locate and select **DP Step 2-14** from the data files, and then click **OK**. The text is inserted into the empty text box. If you are using Adobe PageMaker, first select the empty frame, then click **File**, click **Place**, and locate and open the data file.

8. Select the inserted text and change the font to **Arial**.

9. If your program has a copy fitting option, select the command to automatically size the text to fit in the text box. If not, set the font size to **14** points.

10. Set the left and right indents to **0.25** inches.

11. Justify the horizontal alignment.

STEP-BY-STEP 2.14 Continued

12. Display the document in Print Preview, if that option is available, or change the zoom to display the entire page. It should look similar to Figure 2-17. If some of the text is hidden, adjust the size and position of the text boxes until all text is displayed.

FIGURE 2-17
Completed publication

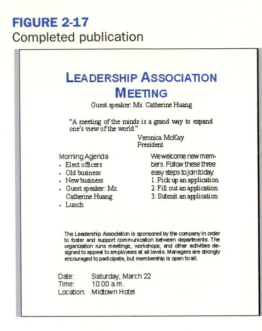

13. Print one copy of the file. Close the Print Preview window if necessary.

14. Save changes and close the **Meeting2** file. Leave your desktop publishing program open to use in the next exercise.

> **Note** ✅
>
> In some programs, such as PageMaker, you cannot insert columns in a text box. Instead, use text blocks to constrain text to the width of a column on the page.

Control Text Flow

In some desktop publishing programs, you can control the way text flows within a text box by dividing the text box into newsletter-style columns. In newsletter-style columns, text flows from the bottom of a column to the top of the next column to the right. With newsletter-style columns, the columns are fixed within the size and position of the text box, so you do not have a great deal of flexibility when it comes to arranging the text in the publication.

To provide more flexibility, some programs let you connect text boxes so text that does not fit in the first text box automatically flows into the next connected text box. When you use connected text boxes, you can size and position each text box independently. You can even connect text boxes on different pages.

> **Extra for Experts** 📊
>
> Most desktop publishing programs have features for controlling hyphenation and the way words break from one line to the next. You can usually use options in the Hyphenation or Type dialog box to insert *discretionary* and *manual hyphens*, change the width of the *hyphenation zone*, and turn automatic hyphenation off or on. You can also insert *em dashes* rather than double hyphens for punctuation, and *en dashes* in place of the words to or through.

Divide a Text Box into Columns

If your program offers a feature for dividing a text box into columns, you use a columns dialog box usually accessed by clicking a button in the Format Text Box dialog box. Key the number of columns you want to apply, and then specify the amount of space to leave between columns. When you type in the text box, text is entered in the left-most column. When you reach the bottom of the left-most column, the text automatically wraps to the top of the next column to the right.

If your program does not have a feature for dividing text boxes into columns, save the data file as instructed in the exercise below and then go on to the next section.

STEP-BY-STEP 2.15

1. In your desktop publishing program, open **DP Step 2-15** from the data files.

2. Save the file as **Reminder**.

3. Increase the zoom to at least 75%, and then select the second text box from the top.

4. Open the Columns dialog box. For example, click **Format** on the menu bar, click **Text Box**, click the **Text Box** tab, and then click the **Columns** button.

5. Key **2** in the Columns box and key **0.25** in the Spacing box. Click the **OK** button in the Columns dialog box, and then click the **OK** button in the Format Text Box dialog box. The text box is formatted into two newsletter-style columns, with 0.25 inches of space between the columns.

> ### Extra for Experts
>
> Some desktop publishing programs have Paragraph Specifications commands for keeping paragraphs and lines together on a page or in a column. Options include keeping lines together, keeping a paragraph with the next paragraph, and controlling widows and orphans—words or short lines of text displayed at the top or bottom of a column or page.

6. Save changes and leave the **Reminder** file open to use in the next exercise.

Connect Text Boxes

In most programs, you connect text boxes by selecting the first text box, clicking a linking tool such as Create Text Box Link, and then clicking the next text box to connect. Or you may be able to simply click the bottom *windowshade* handle of one frame and then click in the next frame with the link pointer. The box to connect must be blank, but the first box may contain text. Repeat the procedure to connect additional boxes. The text will flow from one box to the next in the order in which you connect the boxes. To break the link connecting boxes, click in the box and then use a tool such as Break Forward Link.

> ### Note
>
> Some programs display icons to indicate whether text boxes are connected and whether they contain overflow text, or more text than can fit within the box. Rest the mouse pointer on the icon to see what it means.

If your program does not offer support for connected text boxes, skip the following exercise, close your program, and continue with the Lesson Review.

STEP-BY-STEP 2.16

1. In the **Reminder** file, click in the text box containing the text *Register now or you'll miss the following*.

2. Display the Connect Frames toolbar or the toolbar in your program that has the buttons for connecting text boxes, and then click the **Create Text Box Link** button. If you are using Adobe PageMaker, click in the bottom windowshade handle.

3. Click the next blank text box. The two boxes are now connected.

4. Click back in the previous text box and position the insertion point at the end of the text *Register now or you'll miss the following:*, and press **Enter** to start a new line. Notice that the insertion point jumps to the connected text box.

5. Key the following lines:
   Guest speaker Catherine Huang
   Election of officers
   Lunch

6. Press **Enter**, and key **Call 555-5555 to register now!** Notice that the last line does not fit in the text box.

7. Link the current text box to the next blank text box. The overflow text displays in the newly connected box.

8. Select the text box that contains the text entered in step 5, and increase the width slightly so that the name Catherine is not hyphenated.

9. Display the document in Print Preview. It should look similar to Figure 2-18.

FIGURE 2-18
Completed document

STEP-BY-STEP 2.16 Continued

10. Print one copy of the document.

11. Save changes and close the **Reminder** file. Close your desktop publishing program. You have completed the exercises in this lesson.

SUMMARY

In this lesson, you learned:

■ When you want to create a publication from scratch, create a blank publication.

■ You can create new text boxes at any time, and delete text boxes you no longer need.

■ Apply font formatting to enhance the appearance of a publication and make the text easier to read.

■ Horizontal alignment controls the position of text relative to the left and right text box margins, and vertical alignment controls the position of text relative to the top and bottom text box margins.

■ Set indents to create temporary margins for a paragraph in a text box.

■ Set tabs to position text along a single line.

■ Lists are an effective way to communicate important points of information. Use bullet lists when order doesn't matter, and use numbered lists when order matters.

■ You can change the spacing between characters, lines, and paragraphs to make your text easier to read and to control the amount of white space in a document.

■ The Clipboard is the easiest way to copy and move text and objects, but you can also insert an entire text file into a text box.

■ You can control text flow by creating columns within a text box or, in some programs, connecting text boxes.

VOCABULARY *Review*

Define the following terms:

Clipboard	Indents	Sans serif font
Color scheme	Insertion Point	Serif font
Font	Kerning	Tabs
Font effects	Leading	Tracking
Font size	Margins	Vertical alignment
Font style	Points	White space
Horizontal alignment		

REVIEW *Questions*

TRUE / FALSE

Circle T if the statement is true or F if the statement is false.

T   F   **1.** Set a left tab when you want to align all of the text in a text box with the left margin.

T   F   **2.** The default font is always 12-point Arial.

T   F   **3.** Use tracking to control the spacing between all characters in a selection.

T   F   **4.** Use kerning to control the spacing between pairs of characters.

T   F   **5.** Use a quotation or double indent to indent a paragraph from both the left and right margins.

T   F   **6.** Font size is usually measured in inches.

T   F   **7.** Keyed text is inserted to the right of the insertion point

T   F   **8.** Drag a corner handle to resize the height and width of a text box at the same time.

T   F   **9.** Use a numbered list when the order of items in the list doesn't matter.

T   F   **10.** Connect text boxes to place the overflow from one text box into the next text box.

WRITTEN QUESTIONS

Write a brief answer to the following questions.

1. How many fonts should you use in a publication?

2. What are some reasons for creating a blank publication instead of using a publication design or template?

3. What is the difference between kerning and leading?

4. What are the four types of horizontal alignment?

5. List at least three instances when you could use lists in a publication.

FILL IN THE BLANK

Complete the following sentences by writing the correct word or words in the blanks provided.

1. In some desktop publishing programs, you can control the way text flows within a text box by dividing the text box into _____.

2. Items that are cut or copied are stored in the _____ until you paste them in a new location.

3. You can control the amount of white space between text and the text box border by changing the text box _____.

4. The amount of space allotted for the width of each character is determined by the _____ set.

5. Font size is measured in _____.

6. Lists are usually formatted using a(n) _____ indent.

7. Tab _____ are characters such as dots that are repeated on the line preceding the tab stop.

8. Font _____ are attributes applied to characters.

9. When you connect text boxes, the first box may contain text, but the box to connect must be _____.

10. _____ fonts have short lines and curlicues at the ends of the lines that make up each character.

PROJECTS

PROJECT 2-1

1. Launch your desktop publishing program and create a new blank document with 1-inch margins.

2. Save the file as **Sale**.

3. Insert four text boxes or frames as follows:
   A. Draw one text box starting in the upper-left corner of the document, where the left and top margins meet. Size the box approximately 2 inches high and 6.5 inches wide (the width of the page from margin to margin).
   B. Start the second text box immediately below the first (with no space between the boxes), and size it to approximately 2.5 inches high and 6.5 inches wide.
   C. Repeat step B above to draw a third text box immediately below the second.
   D. Draw the fourth text box immediately below the third, sizing it to fill the remaining area at the bottom of the document—approximately 2 inches high by 6.5 inches wide.
   E. If you are using Adobe PageMaker, change the margins of each frame to 0.05 on all sides and set the stroke for each frame to None.

4. Click in the first text box at the top of the page, and key and format text as follows:
   A. Select a sans serif font such as Gill Sans MT in 48 points and key **Hip Hop Music**.
   B. Press **Enter**, change the font size to **36**, and key **Grand Opening Sale**.
   C. Center the text horizontally and vertically in the text box.
   D. Select the text in the text box and apply the Small caps font effect.

5. Click in the next text box down, and key and format text as follows:
   A. Using the same sans serif font you used in step 4, in 26-point font size, key the text **Join in the Excitement**, and then press **Enter** to start a new line.
   B. Change to a serif font such as Georgia in 18 points and set a left indent of 2 inches.
   C. Key the following five lines of text, pressing **Enter** after each line:
   Contests
   Food
   Live music
   Giveaways
   Special guests
   D. Select all five lines and apply bullet list formatting. (In some programs you may want to adjust the space between the bullet and the text.).
   E. Center the first line of text in the text box, then select it and apply bold, italics, and an underline.
   F. Set the paragraph spacing to leave 12 points of space after the selected paragraph.
   G. Select the *E* and the *x* in the word *Excitement* and expand the kerning to add space, then select the *x* and the *c* and collapse the kerning to remove space.

6. Click in the third text box, and key and format text as follows:
   A. Using the same sans serif font you used in step 4, in 26-point font size, key the text **Enter to Win**, and then press **Enter** to start a new line.
   B. Change to a serif font such as Georgia in 18 points. Set a left indent of 1.25 inches and a right indent of 1 inch.
   C. Key the following three lines of text, pressing **Enter** after each line:
   Fill out an entry form
   Drop it off at any Hip Hop Music store
   Wait for the call announcing you're the winner!
   D. Select all lines but the first and apply number list formatting. You may need to adjust the hanging indent in PageMaker.
   E. Center the first line of text in the text box, then select it and apply bold, italics, and an underline.
   F. Set the paragraph spacing to leave 12 points of space after the selected paragraph.

7. Click in the last text box, and key and format text as follows:
   A. Set a left indent at 1.5 inches.
   B. Using the same serif font you used earlier, in 18-point font size, key the text **Hip Hop Music** and then press **Enter**.
   C. Change the font size to **16** points, and then key **5151 South City Turnpike**. Press **Enter**, key **West Hill, NH 03300**, and then press **Enter** to start a new line.
   D. Remove the left indent (set the indent to 0), and then set a left tab stop at 2.5 inches on the horizontal ruler.
   E. Change the font size to **14** points and key the text **Monday – Saturday**. Press **Tab** and key the text **10:00 a.m. until 9:00 p.m.** Press **Enter** to start a new line.
   F. Key the text **Sundays**, press **Tab**, and key the text **12:00 p.m. until 9:00 p.m.** Press **Enter** to start a new line.
   G. Delete the left tab stop and set a right tab stop at 5.7 inches on the horizontal ruler. Key the text **For information contact**, press **Tab**, and key **Jay Hewitt, Store Manager**. Press **Enter** to start a new line.
   H. Press **Tab** and key **555-555-5433**.
   I. Click anywhere on the line with the city, state, and ZIP code, and set spacing to leave 6 points of space after the current paragraph.
   J. Set the vertical alignment in the text box to bottom.

8. Check the spelling in the document and make corrections as necessary. If necessary, adjust text box size and position to display all text.

9. Print one copy of the document.

10. Save changes and close the **Sale** file, but leave your desktop publishing program open to use in Project 2-2.

PROJECT 2-2

1. In your desktop publishing program, create a new blank full-page document with 1-inch margins.

2. Save the file as **Invite**.

3. Insert a text box the full size of page 1.

4. Select a decorative font, such as Comic Sans MS in 36 points, change the font color to blue, set the horizontal alignment to center, and key the text **Hip Hop Music is having a Grand Opening Sale!**

5. Press **Enter** to start a new line, change the font color to black, the font size to 26 points, and key the following lines of text. (Press **Enter** at the end of each line.)

   You're Invited!
   Friday April 10
   4:30 p.m.

6. On a new line, change the font size to 20 points and key the following lines:

   5151 South City Turnpike
   West Hill, NH 03300

7. Select all text in the document and, if necessary, set the horizontal alignment to center, and set the line spacing to leave 6 points of space before and after each paragraph.

8. Start a new line, and then insert **DP Project 2-2** from the data files into the text box.

9. Select the newly inserted text and change the font to a casual script, such as Freestyle Script in 24 points, and justify the alignment.

10. Set line spacing to leave 36 points of space before the paragraph.

11. Check the spelling in the document and then print it. Fold the printed page into an invitation.

12. Save changes and close the **Invite** file. Close your desktop publishing program.

SCANS WEB PROJECT

For a project on China, use the Internet to research the Chinese alphabet. See if you can find information about different characters and what they mean, and which are considered lucky or unlucky. Then see if you can find a Chinese character font that you can download for free to use in a publication. For example, you may design a poster or banner using the Chinese characters. If you have trouble locating a Chinese character font, see if you can find an English-language font that is designed to simulate Chinese characters.

SCANS TEAMWORK PROJECT

As a group, plan and design a publication announcing an upcoming event at your school or in your community. For example, you may want to create a flyer, banner, or poster to announce a concert or play, a sporting event, a parade, or a meeting. You can work together on each stage of creating the flyer, or you can assign tasks.

Write the text you want on the flyer, and then create a mock-up of the flyer so you can determine the page size and how you want the text positioned on the page. For example, determine whether all the text should be in one text box, or if you should split it into multiple text boxes, and then indicate spacing and alignment on the mock-up as well. Decide which text should be large and which should be smaller, and discuss the types of fonts you want to use. You can use your desktop publishing program to test different fonts, font sizes, and font effects. Try to find a combination of two or three fonts that you think work well together, and print sample text to see how they look when printed. Finally, create the flyer document.

You can start with a blank document, or use a template or design that matches your mock-up. Apply font formatting, spacing, and alignment to make the flyer look appealing and be easy to read. When you are finished, check the spelling and then print the flyer.

CRITICAL*Thinking*

ACTIVITY 2-1

Use your desktop publishing program to create a business card for yourself. Create a mock-up so you can size and position all the information you want to include. You can use your actual information, or make up a job you would like to have. Include at least your name, address, phone number, and e-mail address. When you are ready, start with a blank document, or use one of your program's templates or designs. Use text boxes to position the text the way you planned on the mock-up. Use two fonts, and any colors, styles, and effects that you think enhance the card. Try different alignments and spacing. When you are finished, check the spelling and print one copy. If you are happy with the result, you can purchase blank cards and print additional copies.

FORMATTING PAGES

OBJECTIVES

Upon completion of this lesson, you should be able to:

- Set up pages.
- Set guides.
- Use master pages.
- Insert page numbers.
- Add and delete pages.
- Create a template.
- Select a color scheme and font scheme.
- Use styles.

Estimated Time: 2 hours

VOCABULARY

Binding

Color scheme

Facing pages

Field

Font scheme

Footer

Gutter

Header

Layout guides

Master page

Mirrored pages

Page layout

Paper size

Style

Two-page spread

Good page formatting uses the basic principles of design, including *contrast*, *balance*, and *consistency*, to capture a reader's attention. Your desktop publishing program has many tools to help you use these principles when you format your publication. When you create a document using a template or design, your desktop publishing program automatically applies page formatting options suitable for the publication type. The formatting includes a *page layout* that controls settings such as page size, margin width, the number of pages in the publication, and the page orientation. You can also format pages on your own by selecting options manually. For example, you may set a custom page size for a brochure, change the orientation for a booklet, or add pages to a catalog. That way, you can customize built-in designs, and you can create your own designs from scratch. You can even save your own designs as a template for creating future documents. In this lesson, you learn how to format pages by applying layouts and other options.

Set up Pages

Page setup options usually include the *page size*, *margins*, and *page orientation*. As you learned in earlier lessons, the page size is the height and width of the printed page, the margins are the space between the edges of the page and the content, and the page orientation is the position of the paper in relation to the content. You may also be able to set other options, such as the *paper size*, which is the size of the actual sheet of paper on which the publication is printed. Paper size is sometimes called the sheet size.

Margins are usually set for the top, bottom, left, and right of a page. If you are going to bind or fold a publication, you need to leave extra space along the inside page edges, or *gutter*—usually, the left edge of right-hand or odd-numbered pages, and the right edge of left-hand, or even-numbered pages. *Binding* is the way pages or sections of a book or booklet are secured together using stitching, staples, or glue. Sometimes, depending on the program and publication type, the left and right margin settings are actually called inside and outside margins. "Inside" refers to the edge that may be bound or folded, and "outside" refers to the edge opposite the binding or fold.

In all desktop publishing programs, you can change these settings manually. In some programs, you can select built-in options in a task pane or dialog box to automatically apply the changes.

Change Page Setup Options Manually

Often, page setup options depend on the publication type and are set automatically when you select a template or design, or when you select the publication type in a Document Setup or Page Setup dialog box similar to the one in Figure 3-1. The Document Setup dialog box in your program may also have options for setting the number of pages in the publication, specify-

> **Note** ☑
>
> If the margin settings are not in the Page Setup dialog box, you set them by adjusting the margin guides. Working with guides is covered in the next exercise.

ing *double-sided printing*, and creating a *two-page spread*. A two-page spread consists of two *facing pages* that are sometimes called *mirrored pages* because their layout and margins are not identical, but reversed.

FIGURE 3-1
Page Setup dialog box

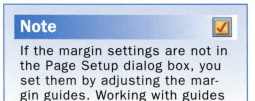

STEP-BY-STEP 3.1

1. Launch your desktop publishing program, and if necessary click the **New** button on the toolbar to create a new document. If the Document Setup dialog box opens, skip step 2. (If the Template dialog box opens, close it.)

2. Click **File** on the menu bar, and then click **Page Setup** or a similar option, such as or **Document Setup** to open the appropriate dialog box.

3. Set the orientation to Landscape, or Wide.

4. Click **Custom** in the publication type or page size list and then set the page size dimensions to 7 inches wide by 5 inches high.

5. If the margin settings are in the dialog box, set them to 1 inch on all sides, and clear all other options. Don't worry if there are no margin setting options in the dialog box. You learn how to set margins using guides later in this lesson.

6. Click the **OK** button in the dialog box. The publication should look similar to the one in Figure 3-2.

FIGURE 3-2
Custom page size

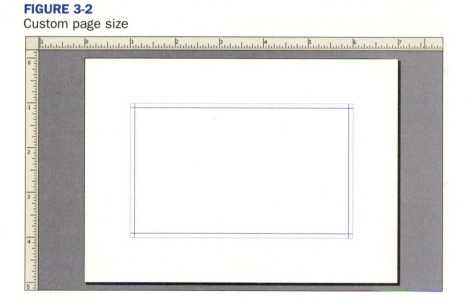

7. Save the file as **Notice**.

8. Open the Page Setup or Document Setup dialog box again.

9. Click **Postcard** in the Publication type list, and then click ¼ **page Letter** in the Page size list. Alternatively, set the custom page size to 5.5 inches wide by 4.25 inches high.

10. Click the **OK** button. The changes are applied to the document layout.

11. Save changes and leave the **Notice** file open to use in the next exercise.

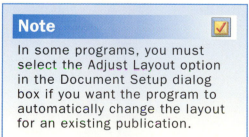

Note ☑

In some programs, you must select the Adjust Layout option in the Document Setup dialog box if you want the program to automatically change the layout for an existing publication.

Apply Built-In Options

In some programs, you can apply built-in options to change the appearance of pages. The options are usually displayed in the task pane. They change depending on the current publication type, and sometimes even depending on the current page. To apply a built-in option, open the task pane and select the type of option you want to change, or select the type of option directly from the Format menu. Then, click the option to apply it. Again, the available options depend on the type of publication you are working on and possibly, even the current publication page.

For example, if you want to include a customer address on the back of a catalog publication, click Catalog Options in the task pane or on the Format menu. Then, click Include in the customer address section. Your program automatically changes the layout and design of the back page of the catalog to include the address. To remove the address, click None. To change a catalog page from two columns of all text to one column with graphics, click Page Content in the task pane or on the Format menu, make the page you're planning to modify active, and then click the option to apply it.

Not all programs offer built-in options. For example, Adobe PageMaker does not. If your program does not, skip this exercise, close the Notice file, but leave your desktop publishing program open to use in the following exercise.

STEP-BY-STEP 3.2

1. In the **Notice** file, click **Format** on the menu bar, and then click **Quick Publication Options**.

2. In the task pane, click the **No picture** layout. It may be the second choice from the bottom in the middle row. Rest your mouse pointer on each layout option to display a description of it.

3. Click the **No heading** layout in the task pane. The publication changes to reflect the selection.

4. Close the task pane. The file should look similar to the one in Figure 3-3.

FIGURE 3-3
Apply a built-in layout option

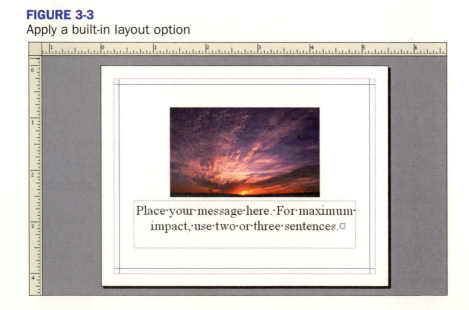

5. Save changes and close the **Notice** file. Leave your desktop publishing program open to use in the next exercise.

Set Guides

Page layout, or the way you organize and arrange objects and white space on a page, significantly affects the overall impact of a publication. Page layout involves the use of alignment, size, and position to lead the reader's eye across the page and makes it easy for the reader to locate and absorb information. All desktop publishing programs have *layout guides* or nonprinting gridlines that can be displayed on the screen while you work to help you position and align objects.

Different programs use different terms to identify guides. Your program may use column guides or grid guides to define columns and rows; margin guides to define the top, bottom, left, and right margins; and ruler guides to define any point along the vertical or horizontal ruler. Usually, each type of guide is displayed in a different color so you know differentiate them. In most programs, you set column, grid, and margin guides for the entire publication, but you can set ruler guides on any page. In the next section, you learn about creating guides on master pages to make sure they are consistent on every page. Figure 3-4 shows different guides in a desktop publishing document.

Note

If you select a layout option that has more or fewer pages than the current publication, your program displays a dialog box asking you to confirm the insertion or deletion of additional pages. Click Yes to apply the option and continue.

Note

In programs that have text blocks as well as text frames, you must use text frames if you want to overlap defined columns. Text blocks are constrained within the column borders.

FIGURE 3-4
Color-coded guides in a blank publication

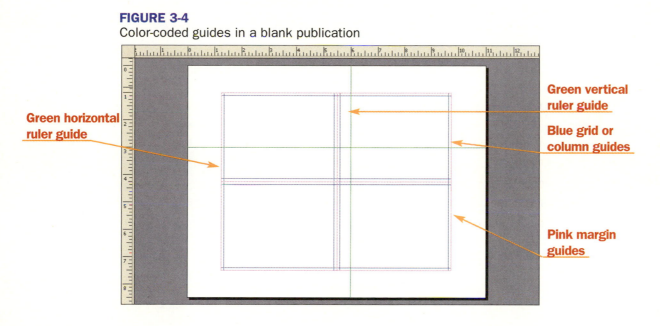

Green horizontal ruler guide

Green vertical ruler guide

Blue grid or column guides

Pink margin guides

To set guides, you usually use a dialog box such as Column Guides or Layout Guides, shown in Figure 3-5. In some programs, you set margins in the Document Setup dialog box, as you learned earlier. Some guides you toggle on or off using a menu, and then move them into the desired position by pressing Shift and dragging the line with the mouse. To remove a guide, change the settings or select a menu command to clear the guides.

Hot Tip

In some programs, you insert ruler guides simply by clicking or Shift-clicking on the ruler and then dragging the guide into to the document window.

FIGURE 3-5
Layout Guides dialog box

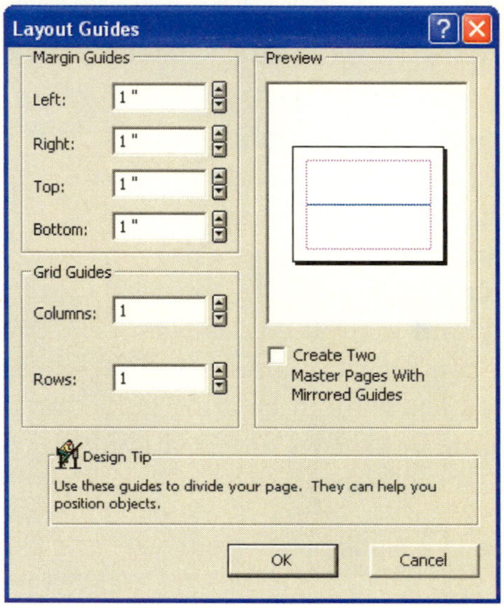

STEP-BY-STEP 3.3

1. In your desktop publishing program, click the **New** button and create a new blank 8.5-inch by 11-inch single-page document. If you are using a program that prompts you for document setup options, clear the **Facing pages** and **Double-sided** options.

2. Save the file as **Safety**.

3. Select the command to open the dialog box for setting margin guides. For example, click **Arrange** on the menu bar, and then click **Layout Guides**.

4. In the margins section, key **1.25** in the Left (Inside), Right (Outside), Top, and Bottom boxes and then click the **OK** button. This sets the margin guides to 1.25 inches from the edge of the page on all sides.

5. Select the command to open the dialog box for setting grid or column guides. This may be the same dialog box that you used in step 3, or you may have to click **Layout** on the menu bar and then click **Column Guides**. Key **2** in the Columns box, and then click the **OK** button.

Note

If guides are not displayed on your screen, you may have selected the command to toggle them off. Click View on the menu bar, and then click the command to show guides.

STEP-BY-STEP 3.3 Continued

6. Select the command to display a horizontal ruler guide, or press and hold **Shift** and then click and drag a guide off the horizontal ruler. If necessary, zoom in to at least 66% to get a closer look at the page.

7. Move the horizontal ruler guide so it is 3 inches below the top of the page. Depending on your program, either drag or Shift-drag the guide to move it. The pointer might change to a double-headed arrow and include the word *Adjust*.

8. Insert a text box or text frame between the top margin and the horizontal ruler guide, sized to the width of the page. If you are using Adobe PageMaker, set the stroke for the frame to None and change the frame margins to 0.05 inches on all sides. Select a sans serif font such as Arial; set the font size to 48; apply boldface; and set the horizontal alignment to center.

9. Key the text **New Security Rules**. The file should look similar to the one in Figure 3-6.

FIGURE 3-6
Text added to Safety file

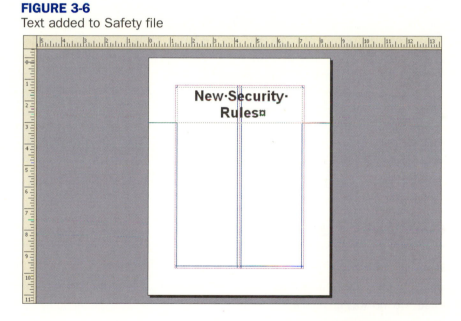

10. Save changes and leave the **Safety** file open to use in the next exercise.

Did You Know?

You can change the unit of measure in most desktop publishing programs to inches, centimeters, *picas*, or points.

Use Master Pages

Most desktop publishing programs include some form of *master page* to help you maintain consistency through a multipage publication, but these features may be used differently depending on your program. For example, in Microsoft Publisher, a master page is used to store objects that are repeated on every page of a publication, such as page numbers, a *watermark*, or a logo that you want in the corner of every page. In Adobe PageMaker, master pages are used like layout templates to help you maintain consistent formatting throughout a publication. They store basic page setup options as well as objects.

To understand master pages, imagine a background that displays standard and consistent elements on every page in a publication. On each page of the publication, you overlay a sheet of tracing paper. You can see through the tracing paper to the background elements, but you can insert different content on the tracing paper to customize the foreground of each page.

No matter which program you use, changes that you make to a master page affect every page formatted with that master, while changes that you make to the foreground page affect only that page. To modify a master page, you must switch to that page. Otherwise, the changes are applied to the foreground page only.

In programs that use simple master pages to store objects to be displayed on every page, you can have a single master page for an entire document. You can also have a master page spread, which creates a left page master page and a right page master page suitable for publications that have facing pages or two-page spreads, such as booklets. You create a master page spread by selecting the option in the Layout Guides dialog box. To work on master pages in these programs, simply switch to Master Page view by choosing Master Page on the View menu, and then apply the settings and objects you want on the page.

In programs that use master pages to control layout, you can have one master page (called a *document master*) for an entire publication, or you can have different master pages for different pages. In these programs, a document master is created automatically using the default document setup options when you create a new document. If you change the page setup, the changes are automatically applied to the master. You can also create additional master pages using the options in the Master Page palette. To work on a master page in these programs, select the specific master page by selecting it from a list on a shortcut menu, on the Layout menu, or in the Master Page palette. Some programs always display a Master Page icon on the horizontal scroll bar. Click the icon to switch to the master page. Other programs display the Master Page icon only when you are in Master Page view. The Master Page icons are usually in a different color from the regular page icons, and probably display an L for left or an R for right.

STEP-BY-STEP 3.4

1. In the **Safety** file, switch to Master Page view. For example, click **View** on the menu bar and then click **Master Page,** or click the Master Page icon if it is available. Elements that you entered on the foreground page are no longer displayed, while elements on the master document, such as margin guides and, in some programs, column guides, are.

STEP-BY-STEP 3.4 Continued

2. Insert a text box or frame along the bottom margin. (Don't forget to remove the stroke, if necessary.) Select a sans serif font such as Arial, set the font size to **18**, and the horizontal alignment to **Center**. Key the text **These rules will be strictly enforced at all times.** If necessary, set the vertical alignment to bottom so the text runs across the bottom margin. The page should look similar to Figure 3-7.

FIGURE 3-7
A master page

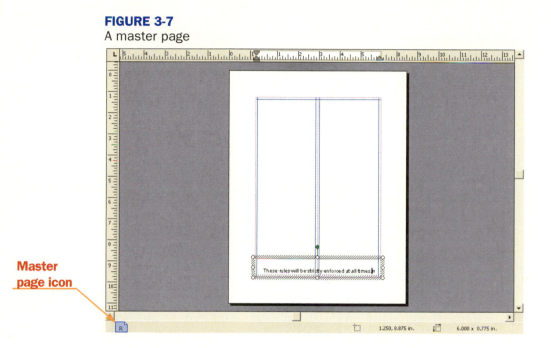

Master page icon

3. Change back to regular page view. The content on the master page and the foreground page appears.

4. Save changes and leave the **Safety** file open to use in the next exercise.

Insert Page Numbers

Page numbers are an important feature of multi-page documents. For example, page numbers in a catalog help readers locate specific items and may also be used for ordering. In most desktop publishing programs, page numbers are inserted on a master page as a *field* or marker. A field is a code instead of an actual number so the page number updates if you add, delete, or move pages within the publication. Usually, page numbers are inserted in either the page *header* or *footer*. A header displays information repeated at the top of every page in the area between the top margin and the top edge of the page, and a footer repeats information at the bottom of every page in the area between the bottom margin and the bottom edge of the page.

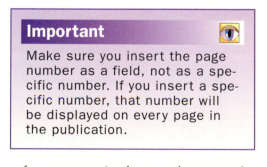

Important

Make sure you insert the page number as a field, not as a specific number. If you insert a specific number, that number will be displayed on every page in the publication.

To insert page numbers, switch to the master page and then select the Page Numbers command on the Insert menu. Most programs display a page numbers dialog box similar to the one in Figure 3-8 in which you can select options such as the location of the number on the page, the number format, and whether a number should appear on the first page.

FIGURE 3-8
Page Numbers dialog box

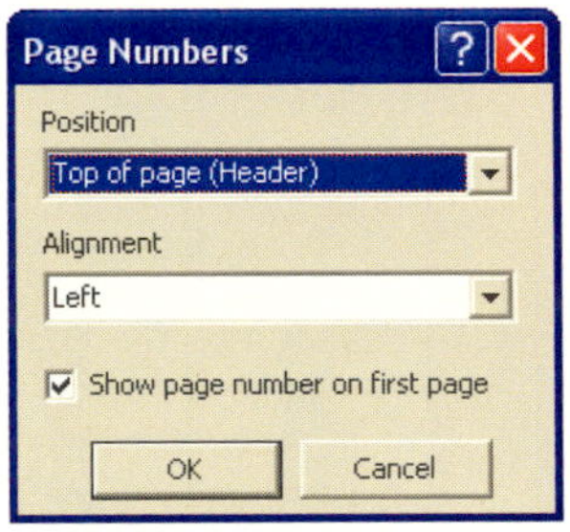

If there is no page number command on the Insert menu, you may be able to key the code for inserting page numbers directly on the page by clicking the text tool in the toolbox, clicking on the page where you want the numbers displayed, and then keying the code for your program or pressing a shortcut key combination such as Ctrl + Alt + P or Ctrl + Shift + N. Use the Document Setup dialog box to set numbering options.

You can insert any information that you want on every page into a header or footer. You can always create headers and footers manually by inserting the data in that part of the document, but some programs have commands you can use to quickly create headers and footers. To use a command to create a header or footer, select the Header and Footer command on the View menu. Key data into the text boxes, or use the toolbar buttons described in Table 3-1.

TABLE 3-1
Header/footer toolbar buttons

ICON	BUTTON NAME	CLICK TO
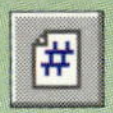 [#]	Insert Page Number	Insert automatically updating page numbers.
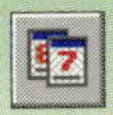 [📅]	Insert Date	Insert current date.
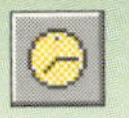 [🕐]	Insert Time	Insert current time.
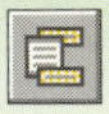 [⊡]	Show Header/Footer	Switch between the header and footer areas.
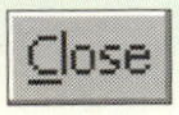 [Close]	Close	Click to close the toolbar and return to the previous document view.

STEP-BY-STEP 3.5

1. In the **Safety** file, change to Master Page view.

2. Insert page numbers in the center of the footer. For example, click **Insert** on the menu bar, and then click **Page Numbers**. In the Page Numbers dialog box, select **Bottom of page (Footer)** from the Position list, and select **Center** from the Alignment list. Make sure the option to display numbers on the first page is selected, and then click the **OK** button. If you are using PageMaker, click the text tool in the toolbox, select a 10 point font size, click at the horizontal center of the page in the footer area, and then press **Ctrl + Alt + P**.

3. Zoom in on the bottom of the page to at least 100% magnification. It should look similar to Figure 3-9. Because you are in Master Page view, the code is displayed instead of the actual page number.

FIGURE 3-9
Page number in Master Page view

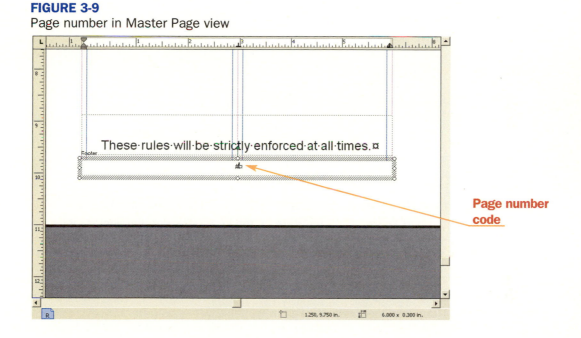

Page number code

STEP-BY-STEP 3.5 Continued

4. Change to regular page view. The footer area should look similar to Figure 3-10.

FIGURE 3-10
Page number in regular page view

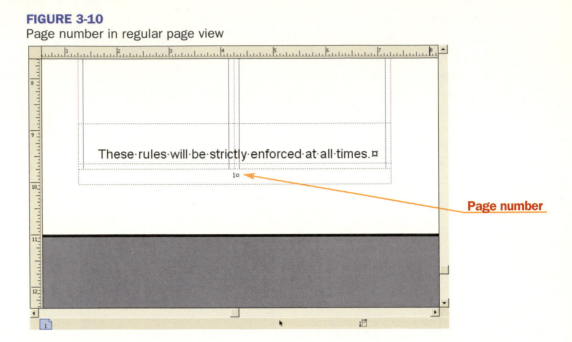

Page number

5. Change back to Master Page view.

6. Create a header with the current date left aligned. For example, click **View** on the menu bar, and then click **Header and Footer**. Click the **Date** button on the Header and Footer toolbar, and then click the **Close** button on the **Header and Footer** toolbar. If your program does not have a Header and Footer feature, simply use the text tool to key the date in the header area.

7. Change to regular page view.

8. Save changes and leave the **Safety** file open to use in the next exercise.

Insert and Delete Pages

A fundamental way to change the layout of a publication is to change the number of total pages. In most programs, you can easily insert new pages or delete pages you don't need. To insert a new page, use the Page command on the menu bar or the Insert Pages command on the Layout menu. Usually, a dialog box

> **Note** ☑
>
> Keep in mind that if you change the number of pages in a book-style publication by an odd number, it affects the layout of the entire document. For example, left-hand pages, which are usually even-numbered, may become right-hand pages, which are usually odd-numbered.

similar to the one in Figure 3-11 displays, in which you select options such as how many pages to insert, where to insert them, and whether to create content on the new page(s). In some programs, you also select the master page to apply to the new pages. To delete a page, make it active and use a command such as Delete Page on the Edit menu or Remove Pages on the Layout menu. Usually, but not always, a dialog box appears that asks you to select options or to confirm the deletion. Be careful deleting pages, because all the content on the page is deleted at the same time.

FIGURE 3-11
Insert Page dialog box

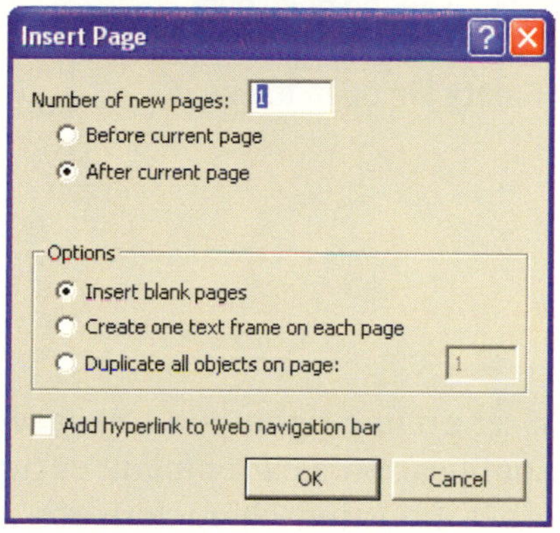

Insert Page

Number of new pages: 1

○ Before current page
● After current page

Options
● Insert blank pages
○ Create one text frame on each page
○ Duplicate all objects on page: 1

□ Add hyperlink to Web navigation bar

OK   Cancel

S TEP-BY-STEP 3.6

1. In the **Safety** file, make sure you are in regular page view, and then select the command to insert one blank page after the current page. The new page is displayed on the screen. It should look similar to Figure 3-12. Notice that all the content you inserted on the master page is on the new page, but the content you inserted on the foreground page is not.

FIGURE 3-12
New page 2

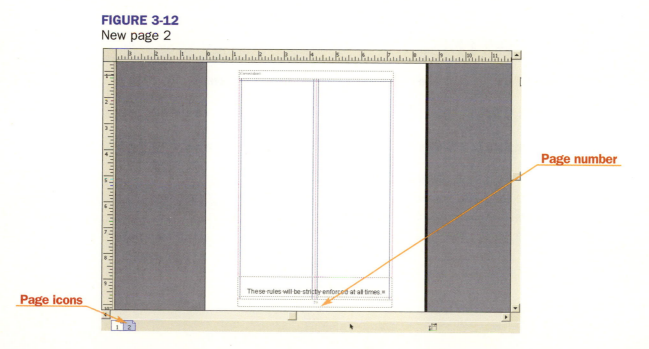

Page number

Page icons

These rules will be strictly enforced at all times.

STEP-BY-STEP 3.6 Continued

2. Insert another new blank page. Now, the publication has three pages. Try deleting a page.

3. Switch to page 2, and then select the command to delete it. For example, click **Edit** on the menu bar, and then click **Delete Page**. If necessary, click the **OK** button in any confirm dialog boxes to complete the deletions.

4. Save changes and leave the **Safety** file open to use in the next exercise.

> ### Extra for Experts
>
> In some programs, you can reposition pages within a document by dragging the page icons. However, in many programs, the only way to move a page is to insert a new blank page, then copy and paste the content from the original page to the new blank page.

Create a Template

Once you have a publication set up just right, you can save it as a template so you can base future documents on it. Saving a publication as a template ensures that new documents are created with uniform page setup and formatting characteristics. In addition, your template can include elements that you want to be the same in every new document, such as page numbers, disclaimer text, and even a corporate logo.

Save a Publication as a Template

Save a publication as a template using the familiar Save As command. In the Save As dialog box, key a template name and select the template file type from the Save as type drop-down list. In some programs, the template file is automatically stored in the Templates folder with other publication templates. In other programs, you can store the template file in any folder.

STEP-BY-STEP 3.7

1. In the **Safety** file, click **File** on the menu bar, and then click **Save As**. The Save As dialog box opens.

2. Key **2 Page Rules** in the File name box. It is a good idea to use a name that describes the template.

3. Click **Template** or a similar option, such as *Program Name* **template**, from the Save as type list.

4. If necessary, select the location where you want to store the template. For example, select the location where you have been saving all your files.

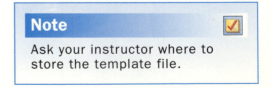

> ### Note
>
> Ask your instructor where to store the template file.

STEP-BY-STEP 3.7 Continued

5. Click the **Save** button in the Save As dialog box. The file is saved as a template.

6. Close the **2 Page Rules** file, and leave your desktop publication program open to use in the next lesson.

Create a Publication Based on a Custom Template

There are two basic ways to create a new document based on a custom template, depending on your program. In some programs, you open the New Publication task pane or dialog box and then click *From template* to open the Open Template dialog box, which should look similar to the one in Figure 3-13. Click the template you want to use, then click the Create New button. In other programs, you click Open on the File menu to display the Open dialog box. You locate and select the template file; make sure the Copy option button is selected; and then click the Open button in the dialog box. Your program opens a copy of the template that you can save as a new file with a new name. If you click the Original option button instead of the Copy button, your program opens the original template file, which you can edit.

FIGURE 3-13
Open Template dialog box

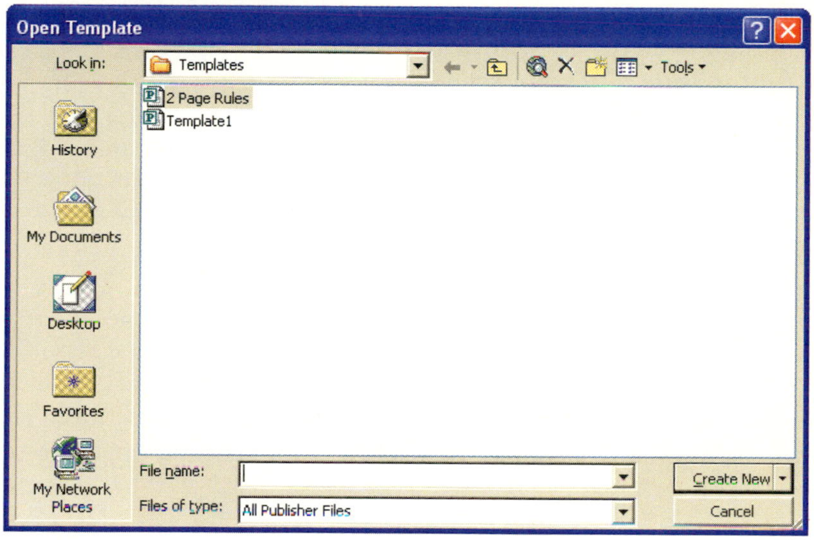

STEP-BY-STEP 3.8

1. In your desktop publishing program, select the command to open the dialog box that lists templates. For example, in Publisher, click **View** on the menu bar, click **Task Pane**, and then click **From template**. In PageMaker, click **File** on the menu bar, and then click **Open**.

2. If necessary, change to the location where you stored the 2 Page Rules template file.

3. Select the **2 Page Rules** template file, and then open it as a new publication file. For example, click the **Create New** button, or click the **Copy** option button and then click the **Open** button. A new file based on the template is created and displayed.

4. Save the file as **Safety2**. This file is a publication file, not a template file.

5. Close the **Safety2** file, and leave your desktop publishing program open to use in the next exercise.

Apply a Color Scheme and Font Scheme

As you have already learned, publications based on a template or design are created with a particular *color scheme* and *font scheme*. The color scheme is a set of coordinated colors used in the publication and is sometimes called the *color library*. A font scheme is a set of coordinated fonts applied to text. In many programs, you can change the font scheme or color scheme simply by picking a new scheme in a dialog box, task pane, or palette.

> **Note** ☑
>
> Not all programs have options for applying font schemes and color schemes. For example, PageMaker does not.

Change the Color Scheme

Most color schemes have three or more colors that are automatically applied to different elements of a document. Usually, the main color is used for text, and additional colors are used for accents such as bullets, lines, and shading. To select a color scheme, open the color task pane or palette and click the scheme you want to apply. You can find the Color Schemes command on the Format menu. The Color Schemes task pane looks similar to the one in Figure 3-14.

FIGURE 3-14
Color Schemes task pane

Don't worry if your program doesn't support color schemes. You learn more about working with color in Lesson 5, including how to define colors, modify colors, create custom color schemes, and import colors.

> **Did You Know?**
>
> If your program uses color schemes, when you open a color palette such as Font Color or Line Color, only the colors in that scheme are displayed. In Lesson 5, you learn how to add colors to a color palette.

STEP-BY-STEP 3.9

1. In your desktop publishing program, open **DP Step 3-9** from the data files. This is a version of the Postcard file you created in an earlier lesson.

2. Save the file as **Postcard2**. If your program does not offer color schemes, leave this file open and go on to the next exercise.

3. Open the Color Schemes task pane or palette. For example, click **Format** on the menu bar, and then click **Color Schemes**.

4. Scroll through the list of color schemes. Click a color scheme that has bright colors, such as **Wildflower**.

5. Scroll through the list of color schemes and click one that includes only shades of blue, such as **Dark Blue**.

STEP-BY-STEP 3.9 Continued

6. Close the task pane or palette. The file should look similar to the one in Figure 3-15.

FIGURE 3-15
Postcard2 with the Dark Blue color scheme

7. Save changes and leave the **Postcard2** file open to use in the next exercise.

Change the Font Scheme

If your program has built-in font schemes, they usually include two fonts: a main font for headings and a minor font for body text. To select a font scheme, display a task pane or dialog box such as the Font Schemes palette. The Font Schemes task pane looks similar to the one in Figure 3-16. Click the scheme you want to apply.

FIGURE 3-16
Font Schemes task pane

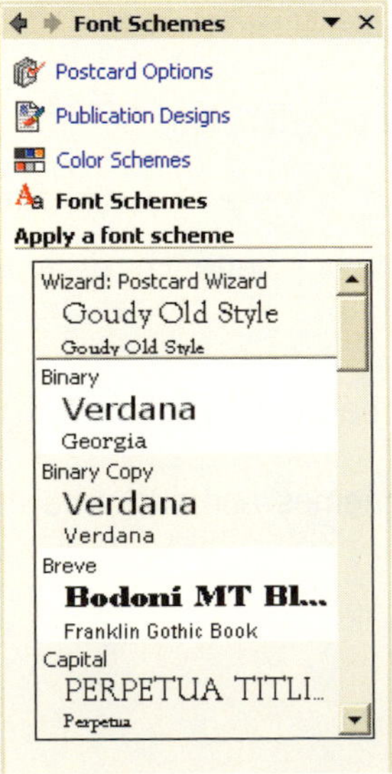

If your program does not have font schemes, you can still experiment with the fonts available on your system. You can change the font, font style, font size, and font color to give your publication a different look.

STEP-BY-STEP 3.10

1. In the **Postcard2** file, open the Font Schemes task pane or palette. For example, click **Format** on the menu bar, and then click **Font Schemes**. If your program does not have font schemes, apply the fonts manually.

2. Scroll through the list of font schemes. Click a font scheme that combines two versions of a similar font, such as **Foundry**, which uses Rockwell Extra bold as the main font and Rockwell as the minor font.

3. Scroll through the list of font schemes and click one that seems sophisticated, such as **Monogram**, which uses Edwardian Script ITC as the major font and TW Cen MT as the minor font.

4. Close the task pane or palette. The file should look similar to the one in Figure 3-17. Remember, if your program does not have font schemes, you can manually apply the fonts to make your publication look similar to the figure.

FIGURE 3-17
Postcard2 with the Monogram font scheme

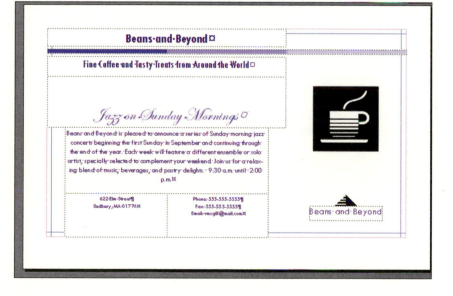

5. Save changes and leave the **Postcard2** file open to use in the next exercise.

Use Styles

A *style* is a collection of formatting settings that you can apply to text and, in some programs, to objects all at once. For example, a style might include the font, the font size, the alignment, and the font effect. Most programs include a list of styles for formatting text, headings, lists, and other parts of a publication. Styles can be very useful in helping you maintain consistent formatting throughout a document, and they can save you time. To apply a style, click in the paragraph to format, or select the text to format, and then open the Styles task pane or palette. For example, click Format on the menu bar and click Styles and Formatting, or click Window on the menu bar, click Show Styles, and then click the style to apply. You can also select a style and then key new text.

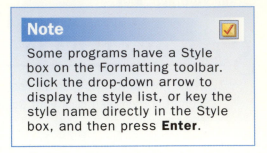

Note

Some programs have a Style box on the Formatting toolbar. Click the drop-down arrow to display the style list, or key the style name directly in the Style box, and then press **Enter**.

S TEP-BY-STEP 3.11

1. In the **Postcard2** file, open the task pane or palette that lists styles. For example, in Publisher, click **Format** on the menu bar, and then click **Styles and Formatting**. In PageMaker, click **Window** on the menu bar, and then click **Show Styles**.

2. Click anywhere in the company name text *Beans and Beyond* in the lower-right corner of the document, and then scroll through the list of styles. In some programs, such as PageMaker, you must click the text tool before you click the text. Click the first body text style in the list. It may be called Body Text or simply Body. The style is applied to the text.

3. Scroll through the list of styles and click the second organization or company name style or the Subhead 2 style. (In some programs, such as PageMaker, you may also want to apply the Subhead 2 style to the *Beans and Beyond* text at the top of the card.)

STEP-BY-STEP 3.11 Continued

4. Click in the headline *Jazz on Sunday Mornings*, and then click the second organization or company name style again, or the Headline style. The document should look similar to the one in Figure 3-18.

Note ✅

You may notice that even though the same style is used to format different text, the font sizes vary. This is because the AutoFit option is set to automatically size the text to fit in the text boxes.

FIGURE 3-18
Text formatted with styles

5. Save changes without modifying the personal information, and then print the publication.

6. Close the **Postcard2** file and your desktop publication program.

SUMMARY

In this lesson, you learned:

- Page formatting controls the layout and organization of objects on a page.

- The basic page setup options include page size, margins, and page orientation.

- There are three types of guides in most desktop publishing programs: column or grid guides, margin guides, and ruler guides.

- Guides help you arrange and position objects on a page.

- Master pages help you maintain consistency in multipage documents.

- In some programs, master pages store objects that are the same on every page, and in other programs they store page layout and formatting settings for the publication.

- You should insert page numbers on a master page.

- You can insert and delete pages at any time.

- You can save a document as a template so that you can create new documents based on it.

- Some programs have color schemes and font schemes you can quickly apply to any publication.

- Use a style to quickly apply a set of formatting characteristics to text in a publication.

VOCABULARY *Review*

Define the following terms:

Binding	Footer	Mirrored pages
Color scheme	Gutter	Page layout
Facing pages	Header	Paper size
Field	Layout guides	Style
Font scheme	Master page	Two-page spread

REVIEW *Questions*

TRUE / FALSE

Circle T if the statement is true or F if the statement is false.

T F **1.** Changes you make to a master page affect all pages that use that master page.

T F **2.** A header is the area between the top margin and the top edge of the page.

T F **3.** Page numbers inserted as a field are updated when pages are added or deleted.

T F **4.** A font scheme is a collection of formatting settings you can apply to text all at once.

T F **5.** Page size is the term used for the height and width of the printed page.

T F **6.** If you plan to bind or fold a publication, be sure to leave extra space along the outside edges of the pages.

T F **7.** If you don't want guides to print, you must delete them from your publication.

T   F   **8.** To save a file as a template, use the Save As command.

T   F   **9.** Use ruler guides to set up columns on a page.

T   F   **10.** To modify a master page, you must switch to Master Page view.

WRITTEN QUESTIONS

Write a brief answer to the following questions.

1. What is the primary benefit of using master pages?

2. Name one principle of design that can be applied to page layout, and then list some of the desktop publishing features that help you use that principle.

3. Why are left and right margins sometimes called inside and outside margins?

4. How many fonts are included in a typical font scheme?

5. What are some of the formatting settings frequently included in a style?

FILL IN THE BLANK

Complete the following sentences by writing the correct word or words in the blanks provided.

1. Some programs have one master page called a(n) _____ master that is used for the entire publication.

2. The _____ is the space along the inside page edges.

3. Create a two-page _____ when you want to set up facing pages.

4. Another term for sheet size is _____ size.

5. Page numbers are usually inserted as a(n) _____ or marker so they are updated if you add, delete, or move pages.

6. The area between the bottom margin and the bottom edge of the page is called the _____.

7. Save a file as a(n) _____ so you can base future documents on it.

8. A(n) font _____ is a set of coordinated fonts.

9. A(n) _____ is a collection of formatting settings that you can apply to text.

10. You can set _____ guides to define any horizontal or vertical point in a publication.

PROJECTS

PROJECT 3-1

Before beginning this project, create a mock-up of a two-sided 8.5-inch × 11-inch newsletter with two columns on both pages and a *banner headline* that extends across the top of the first page. You need space for four articles on each page, but the articles may not be of equal length.

A. Use a ruler and a pencil to draw columns on both sides of a letter-sized sheet of paper.

B. Use a ruler and a pencil to draw horizontal rules indicating the location of the banner headline on page 1 and possible divisions for positioning the four articles on each page.

1. Launch your desktop publishing program and open **DP Project 3-1** from the data files. This file contains all the content you need to create a two-sided newsletter, already formatted and divided into text boxes. However, you must size and position the text boxes to create a layout that is appealing and easy to read.

2. Save the file as **CNONews**.

3. Increase the zoom to at least 75% and take some time to examine the content. Look at both pages. Notice that some of the text boxes are overflowing with text. At least one is overlapping the margins.

4. Zoom out to show the whole page and divide both pages into two columns of equal width.

5. Make page 1 active and move all text boxes except the one at the top of the page out into the scratch area (the gray area around the outside of the page).

6. Format the page as follows:
   A. Set horizontal ruler guides at 2.25, 2.5, and 6.75 inches on the vertical ruler. You can check the position of your ruler guides using the coordinates in the status bar or Control palette.

   > **Hot Tip**
   >
   > If you have trouble selecting a guide to move it, try positioning the mouse pointer on the guide in the margin area.

   B. Size and position the remaining text box to fit vertically between the top margin and the first ruler guide, and horizontally across the width of the page.
   C. Size and position the text box containing the date and volume number vertically between the first and second ruler guides, and horizontally across the width of the page.
   D. Now move the second ruler guide down 0.25 inch, to the 2.75 inch mark on the vertical ruler.
   E. Size and position the text box with the headline *Annual Fundraiser* vertically between the second and third ruler guides and horizontally within the left column.
   F. Move the third ruler guide down 0.25 inch to the 7 inch mark on the vertical ruler. Size and position the text box with the headline *Volunteer News* vertically between the third ruler guide and the bottom margin, and horizontally within the left column. Notice that there is still overflow text.
   G. Insert a new blank text box or frame sized and positioned vertically between the second and third ruler guides and horizontally within the right column. If you are using Adobe PageMaker, remove the stroke from the text frame and change the frame's margins to 0.05 inches on all sides. Connect the text box at the bottom of the left column with the blank text box at the top of the right column. The overflow text should flow into the new text box. If necessary, improve the appearance of the publication by increasing the tracking in the last paragraph in the left column to force additional lines to the top of the right column.
   H. Size and position the remaining text box vertically between the third ruler guide and the bottom margin, and horizontally within the right column. Page 1 is now complete.

7. Make page 2 active and drag all of the text boxes into the scratch area.

8. Format the page as follows:
   A. Insert a horizontal ruler guide at 5 inches on the vertical ruler.
   B. Size and position the text box with the headline *Officer Nominations* to fit vertically between the top margin and the horizontal ruler guide, and horizontally within the left column.
   C. Size and position the text box with the *masthead* list of editors and officers to fit vertically between the ruler guide and the bottom margin, and horizontally within the left column.
   D. Move the ruler guide up to 2.5 inches on the vertical ruler, and then size and position the text box containing the text *Don't Forget!* to fit vertically between the top margin and the ruler guide and horizontally within the right column.
   E. Move the ruler guide down to the 2.75 inch mark on the vertical ruler, and then size and position the remaining text box within the remaining space.

9. Print both pages, either on separate sheets of paper or on a double-sided sheet.

10. Save changes and close the **CNONews** file, but leave your desktop publishing program open to use in Project 3-2.

PROJECT 3-2

Before beginning this project, create a mock-up of a side-fold card using a blank letter-sized sheet of paper:
A. Fold the sheet in half top to bottom, then in half again left to right.
B. Mark the front, back, and two inside pages, and then unfold the sheet. Note that the sheet is divided into four pages and that only one side of the sheet of paper will display content.

1. Create a new blank document in your desktop publishing program. In the Page Setup dialog box, set options to create a Side-fold card with pages sized 4.25 inches wide by 5.5 inches high in Portrait orientation. If necessary in your program, set margins to 0.25 inches on all sides; make sure the Facing pages option is selected; and set the number of pages in the document to 4.

2. If your program asks permission to add pages, click the **OK** button.

3. Save the file as **CNOInvite**.

4. Increase the inside margin to 0.75 inches.

5. Change to Master Page view and set up the pages as follows:
A. Insert two horizontal ruler guides. Position one across the top of the sheet at the 0.5 inch mark on the vertical ruler, and position the other across the bottom of the sheet at the 5 inch mark on the vertical ruler.
B. Draw four text boxes—one at the top of each page between the ruler guide and the top margin and one at the bottom of each page, between the ruler guide and the bottom margin. (If you are using Adobe PageMaker, you may want to use text blocks instead of text frames. In that case, skip this step and proceed with the next step.).
C. Using the default font in 8 points in both top text boxes, key **Community Network Organization**. Left-align the text on the left page and right-align the text on the right page. Drag the text block if necessary so the bottom border of the box aligns with the ruler guide.
D. Using the same font and font size in both bottom text boxes, key **Page**, leave a space, and then insert the page number field. Again, left-align the text on the left page and right-align the text on the right page.

6. Change to regular page view and make page 1 active if necessary. Set up the page as follows:
A. Insert three horizontal ruler guides positioned at 1.5, 2.5, and 3.5 inches on the vertical ruler.
B. Draw two text boxes sized to fit between the inside and outside margins—one between the first and second ruler guides you just added and one between the second and third ruler guides. If necessary, remove the stroke and set frame margins to 0.05 on all sides.

7. Enter and format text in the text boxes as follows:
A. Display the Font Schemes list and select a decorative but sophisticated font scheme such as **Etched,** which uses Copperplate Gothic and Garamond. If your program does not offer font schemes, use Copperplate Gothic for all headings and Garamond for lists and other text in the rest of this exercise.

B. In the top text box that you just created, key **CNO**. Display the Styles list and apply the **Title** style to the text. If the title style is not available, apply a style such as **Headline** style. If necessary, set the font size to **48**, and adjust the frame size to accommodate the text.

C. In the bottom text box that you just created, key **Needs Your Help**. Apply the **Title 5** style to the text. If the Title 5 style is not available, apply a style such as **Subhead 1**. Change the font size to **22**.

D. Center the text in both text boxes horizontally and vertically.

8. Display pages 2 and 3 and insert two vertical ruler guides. Position one 1 inch from the left edge of page 2 and the other 1 inch in from the right edge of page 3. (In some programs, that is at 1 inch and 7.5 inches on the horizontal ruler. In other programs, it is 3.25 inches on each page.)

9. On page 2, insert a text box sized to fit between the text boxes on the top and bottom and the vertical ruler guide on the left and the margin on the right (inside). If necessary, remove the stroke and change frame margins to 0.05 on all sides. Enter and format text as follows:

A. Apply the **Heading 7** style (or use a 12-point font) and key **Entertainment provided by:** and then press **Enter** to start a new line.

B. Apply the first **List Bullet** style, or if that style is not available, use a **Hanging indent** and then apply bullets to each line, but change the font size to 14 points and key the following list:

The Davis Brothers
Lisa Dianne
The Shindig Dancers
Comedy by George

C. Center the text vertically in the text box.

10. On page 3, insert a text box sized to fit between the text boxes on the top and bottom, the margin on the left (inside), and the vertical ruler guide on the right. If necessary, remove the stroke and set the frame margins to 0.05. Enter and format the text as follows:

A. Apply the **Title 5** style (or use a 14-point font) and key **Please join us at our annual fundraising drive on October 11.**

B. Press **Enter** to start a new line and change to the **Normal** or **Hanging indent** style, but increase the font size to 16 points.

C. Key **Tickets in advance**, press **Tab**, and key **$25**. Press **Enter**, key **Tickets at the door**, press **Tab**, and key **$35**.

D. Click in the first paragraph on the page and set the spacing after the paragraph to 24 points.

E. Center the text vertically in the text box.

11. Make page 4 active and draw a text box sized to fit between the top and bottom and left and right margins. If necessary, modify the stroke and margin settings as usual. Enter and format text as follows:

A. Apply the **Heading 1** style (or use a 16-point font), key **Special Thanks To**, and then press **Enter** to start a new line.

B. Apply the **List Bullet** style, or if that style is not available, apply a **Hanging indent.** Then, add a bullet to the list items, but increase the font size to 12 points; set the line spacing to leave 12 points of space before and no space after; and key the following list:

> Main Street Cleaners
> Bumpy's Breakfast Cafe
> Center Karate Studios
> The Mayor
> Auto Mile Gas and Service Station
> Electrical Supply
> Midtown Hotel

C. Center the text vertically in the text box.

12. Check the spelling of the document and then print it. Fold the printed page into an invitation.

13. Save changes and close the **CNOInvite** file and your desktop publishing program.

Note ☑

Your program may automatically apply an accent mark to the word Cafe.

WEB PROJECT

Use the Internet to research desktop printers. Look up types of printers, such as ink jet, bubble jet, and laser, and the features they offer. Are some designed for a specific purpose? Do some offer features that make them more suitable for desktop publishing than others? Take note of specifications such as resolution and speed. Pick three to five printers and make a comparison chart. You can use a spreadsheet program if you have one, or write the chart by hand. When you have compiled all of the information you need, decide which printer you think is the best value.

TEAMWORK PROJECT

As a group, plan and design a newsletter for your class or for a school or community organization. You should decide the page setup, including the number of pages, and whether you will print the newsletter double-sided or single-sided. Make a mock-up so you have a general idea of the size, layout, and appearance, and any objects you want displayed on all pages. If so, plan to use master pages. Assign articles to each member of the team, then research the topics, and write enough text to fill the publication.

When you are ready, use your desktop publishing program to create the publication. Use the page setup tools to organize it, including layout and ruler guides. Take turns entering and positioning the text on the page. Select a font scheme, and use styles to format the headings and the body text. You can modify the formatting if you want to change the alignment, indents, or font formatting. When you are finished, check the spelling and then print the newsletter. With your instructor's permission, print enough copies to distribute to the class.

CRITICAL *Thinking*

ACTIVITY 3-1

Use your desktop publishing program to create a side-fold card as an invitation, greeting card, or thank you card. Create a mock-up so you can size and position all of the information you want to include. Remember that page 1 is the front cover, pages 2 and 3 are facing pages in a two-page spread, and page 4 is the back cover, and design the publication accordingly. Look at cards you have received for ideas. When you are ready, start with a blank document, or use one of your program's templates or designs. Use layout guides and ruler guides to set up the pages, and then insert text boxes to enter the content. Use a font scheme, or select any fonts you want to use. Don't forget to use text formatting such as alignment, lists, and color to enhance the publication. When you are finished, check the spelling and print one copy.

WORKING WITH OBJECTS

OBJECTIVES

Upon completion of this lesson, you should be able to:

- Identify types of objects.
- Draw shapes.
- Modify fills and strokes.
- Acquire objects.
- Size and crop objects.
- Position and arrange objects.
- Set text wrap.

Estimated Time: 2 hours

VOCABULARY

Bitmap

Crop

Distribute

Download

Embed

Fill

Flip

Floating object

Group

Link

Object

Picture frame

Pixels

Rotate

Scale

Scanner

Stack

Stroke

Vector

*O*bjects are the text boxes, charts, shapes, pictures, and other elements you insert in a publication to provide information, organize a page, and improve visual appeal. You can draw objects such as shapes and text boxes directly in a publication file, or you can import objects from a variety of sources, including digital cameras, graphics programs, and scanners. Once an object is placed in a publication, you use your desktop publishing program to size, position, and enhance it on the page. For example, you can crop a photograph to eliminate unnecessary content, or you can increase the size of a shape to make it a focal point. Most desktop publishing programs provide many tools for working with objects. In this lesson, you learn how to insert objects in a publication, how to acquire objects from different sources, and how to size and position the objects on a page.

Identify Types of Objects

*Y*ou have already learned how to create text box objects in a publication, how to insert a picture file, and how to insert a text file. Depending on your program, you may have worked with picture or text frame objects as well. These are only a few of the types of objects you can include in a desktop publishing document. For example, you can create *drawing objects*,

Microsoft Excel worksheet objects, or Adobe Table objects. You can also insert graphics files and possibly, other types of files as objects. In general, you can create new or import existing objects in any format that is *compatible* with your program.

When you work with graphics files, keep a few basic concepts in mind. The two types of graphics used in computer applications are **bitmap** and **vector**. Vector graphics consist of lines and curves—called *vector paths*—that are defined by mathematical objects called vectors. Shapes you draw with the drawing tools are usually vectors. Bitmaps, which are sometimes called *raster images*, use colored dots—called **pixels**—arranged in a grid to define an image. Digital photographs are usually bitmaps.

In addition, there are different types of graphics file formats. Three of the most common are:

- Tagged Image File Format (.tif or .tiff). *TIFF* files are used for storing bitmap images and are frequently used in desktop publishing because they support transparency and reproduce well when printed.

- Joint Photographic Experts Group (.jpg or .jpeg). *JPEG* files are used for photographs and other images that incorporate a great many colors. JPEG files can be compressed to save disk space, but they do not support transparency.

- Graphics Interchange Format (.gif). *GIF* files can contain up to 256 colors and support transparency. They are frequently used for cartoons, logos, and animations on the World Wide Web.

Draw Shapes

You can use your program's drawing tools to draw basic shapes such as rectangles, ovals, lines, and arrows. To use a drawing tool, click on it to select it. The mouse pointer changes to a crosshair. Hold down the mouse button and drag in the publication window to create the shape. The shape is inserted with a thin black **stroke** and no **fill**. The stroke is the line used to draw a shape, and the fill is the area inside a shape. You learn about changing the stroke and fill later in this lesson. New shapes are selected by default and have sizing handles around their edges. In some programs, a rotation handle may be displayed as well.

In some programs, you use a polygon tool to draw a multisided shape, but other programs offer a special tool for quickly inserting complex shapes that are sometimes called AutoShapes. Use AutoShapes to easily insert whimsical shapes such as lightning bolts and smiley faces and to quickly draw outlines for banners, stars, and *callouts*.

To draw an AutoShape, click the AutoShape tool on the toolbar, click the category of shape, and then click the shape you want to insert. Drag in the document to draw the shape. To draw a polygon, first set options such as the number of sides and star angle insets in a dialog box. For example, click Element on the menu bar, and then click Polygon Settings. Key the settings, then click OK. Click the Polygon tool in the toolbox and drag to draw the shape.

Hot Tip

Hold down the Shift key while dragging to constrain the shape. For example, use the Shift key with the Ellipse or Oval tool to draw a perfect circle. Use it with the Rectangle tool to draw a perfect square. Use it with the Line tool to draw lines at 45-degree angles.

S TEP-BY-STEP 4.1

1. Launch your desktop publishing program, and open **DP Step 4-1** from the data files.

2. Save the file as **Eyes**. This publication is a reminder postcard that already contains two text box objects. You are going to draw basic shapes to create a picture of eyeglasses.

3. Click the **Oval** tool and then click and drag in the white space in the upper-left corner of the page to draw an oval shape approximately 0.5 inches high and 1 inch wide. When you release the mouse button, the shape is inserted. It should look similar to Figure 4-1. (Not all programs display a rotation handle.)

FIGURE 4-1
Oval shape in the publication

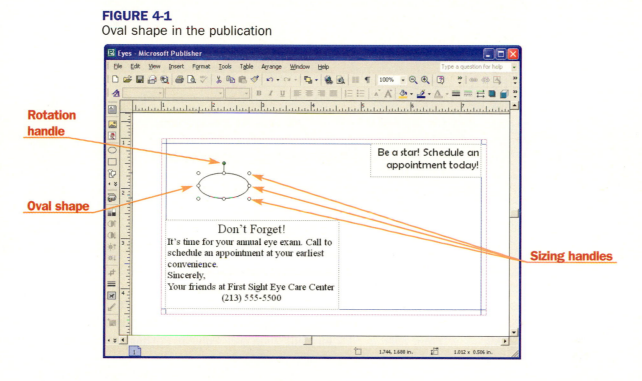

4. If necessary, click the **Oval** tool again, click about 0.25 inches to the right of the first shape, and draw another oval shape of approximately the same size.

5. Click the **Line** tool and draw a line between the ovals.

6. Click the **Line** tool again and draw a diagonal line about 0.5 inches long starting from the left end of the oval on the left side of the page and heading toward the upper-left corner of the page.

STEP-BY-STEP 4.1 Continued

7. Click the **Line** tool again and draw another diagonal line about the same angle and length as the first, starting from the right end of the oval on the right side of the page. The file should look similar to Figure 4-2. Now insert a star shape.

FIGURE 4-2
Basic shapes combine to make a picture

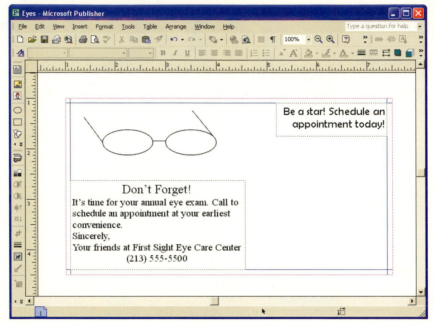

8. Select the tool for drawing a 5-pointed star with 50-degree angles or star insets. For example, click the **AutoShapes** tool, click **Stars and Banners**, and then click the **5-Point Star**. In a program such as Adobe PageMaker, you may need to click **Element**, then click **Polygon Settings** to specify a 5-sided shape with 50-degree star insets, and then click the **Polygon** tool.

FIGURE 4-3
Star shape added to the postcard

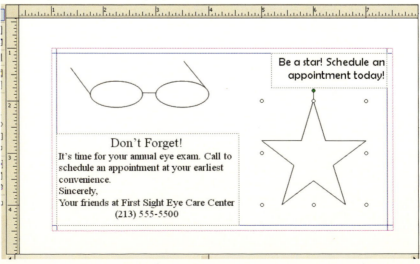

STEP-BY-STEP 4.1 Continued

9. Click and drag to draw the shape approximately 2 inches high and 2 inches wide in the white space in the lower-right corner of the page. The file should look similar to Figure 4-3.

10. Save changes and leave the **Eyes** file open to use in the next exercise.

Modify Fills and Strokes

By default, when you draw a shape, it is displayed with no fill and a thin black stroke. Some objects, such as text boxes, have no fill and no stroke. In most programs, you can modify the fill and stroke by changing the color or style using the options in a dialog box, such as Format AutoShape, which is shown in Figure 4-4, or Fill and Stroke. You may also be able to select the options from a menu or palette. For example, click the Line/Border Style tool or click Element and then click Stroke to display a palette of stroke options.

> ### Did You Know?
> You can usually change the stroke around inserted objects as well, and you may be able to change the background fill of certain types of pictures.

FIGURE 4-4
Stroke and fill options in a dialog box

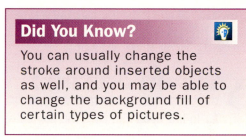

Usually, you can apply a solid or pattern fill color and set the transparency or tint. For strokes, you can usually select a color and a weight—or width—and sometimes you can select a style, such as a double line or a dotted line.

To make changes to an object, you must first select it. To select a shape, click the selection pointer on the

> ### Note
> By default, only colors in the current color scheme or palette are available. You learn more about creating custom colors in Lesson 5.

toolbar, and then click the shape. The selection pointer usually looks like a black or white pointing arrow. To select more than one object at a time, select the first object, press and hold Shift, and select another object. Or, just drag the selection pointer around all the objects you want to select. To cancel a selection, click a blank area of the drawing.

In certain desktop publishing programs, commands for modifying objects are found in a dialog box accessed from the Format menu or from a right-click shortcut menu. The names of the command and the dialog box change depending on the selected object. For example, if you right-click a text box, you click Format Text box on the menu to open the Format Text Box dialog box. If you right-click an AutoShape and then click Format AutoShape on the menu, the Format AutoShape dialog box opens. The options in the dialog boxes are basically the same. Note that when you see Format *Object* dialog box in the following exercises, it is referring to this dialog box.

Extra for Experts

For some objects, such as text boxes, you may be able to select on which sides you want to have a line or border.

STEP-BY-STEP 4.2

1. In the **Eyes** file, click the pointer tool and then, if necessary, click the star shape to select it.

2. Open the dialog box that lists fill and stroke options for the shape. For example, right-click the shape and then click Format AutoShape; or right-click the shape and then click Fill and Stroke. If necessary, click the Colors and Lines tab to display fill and stroke options.

3. Click the **Fill Color** list and then click yellow. If necessary in your program, select the Solid fill option.

4. Set the line weight to 2 points.

5. Click the **OK** button in the dialog box. The changes are applied to the star.

6. Select the lines and ovals that make up the eyeglasses, and then open the dialog box that lists fill and stroke options for the shape. Change to the Colors and Lines tab if necessary.

7. Click the **Fill Color** list and then click blue, and then set the line weight to 1 point, if necessary.

8. Click the **OK** button in the dialog box. The changes are applied to the selected shapes.

9. Select the two text boxes in the publication, and then open the dialog box again. Set the fill color to gray, the line color to black, and the line weight to 0.70 points. If your program doesn't offer a gray fill color, apply a 20% tint of black—select black as the color and then change the tint or transparency to 20%.

STEP-BY-STEP 4.1 Continued

10. Click the **OK** button in the dialog box. The changes are applied to the text boxes. (You may need to adjust text box size to show all text after making these changes.) When you deselect the text boxes, the file should look similar to Figure 4-5.

FIGURE 4-5
Fills and strokes added to the postcard file

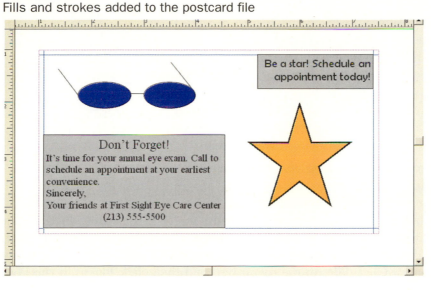

11. Print one copy of the **Eyes** file.

12. Save changes and close the **Eyes** file. Leave your desktop publishing program open to use in the next exercise.

Acquire Objects

Frequently, objects you want to include in your desktop publishing documents already exist in one form or another. Luckily, there are many ways to acquire objects for use in your publications. For example, you can insert clip art pictures, scan printed material, or transfer files from a digital camera. You can copy and paste objects created in other programs, such as a chart stored in a spreadsheet file, or a table from a word processing document.

> **Did You Know?**
>
> If you have a graphics tablet and the appropriate software installed on your computer, you can draw or trace pictures that are converted into graphics files.

Before you can use a *hardware device* such as a scanner or digital camera to acquire data, the device must be correctly attached to your computer—or your computer network—and installed. That means you must physically connect the cables from the device to your computer, although some devices, such as internal modems, connect to slots inside the computer itself, and some devices use optical or other wireless connections. In addition, you must install the software that comes with the device, including the *device driver*. The device driver is a software program that enables your computer to communicate with the hardware device. The driver usually comes on a CD with the device, or you can download it from the manufacturer's Web site. Your operating system may include drivers for common devices. When you set up and install new hardware, make sure you read and follow all instructions, or consult a professional.

Insert Graphics Files

In Lesson 1, you learned how to replace sample clip art in a publication with a different picture file. In fact, you can insert any graphics file from any storage device attached to your computer, including hard drives, network drives, removable drives, and connected devices such as digital cameras.

In some programs, you insert a file into a *picture frame*. A picture frame is a placeholder object used to define the area in the file where you want an object displayed. Usually, you can define the frame as part of the steps for inserting the file. In some programs, if you don't define a frame, the file is inserted as a *floating object* in its default size and shape. A floating object can be sized and positioned anywhere on the page.

In some programs, the first step in inserting a graphics file is drawing a picture frame. In other programs, drawing the frame is the last step. For example, if your program has a Picture Frame tool on the toolbar, click it and drag on the page to draw the frame. When you release the mouse button, the Insert Picture dialog box opens. Locate and select the file to insert, and then click the Insert button to insert the file into the frame. If your program does not have a Picture Frame tool, you may have to use the Place command. Click File on the menu bar, and then click Place. In the Place dialog box, locate and select the file to insert and then click Open. Click and drag the insertion pointer to draw the frame. When you release the mouse button, the picture is inserted in the frame.

Computer Ethics

COPYRIGHT LAWS

Although many sources allow you to download or scan images for your personal use, in other cases, acquiring images without permission is illegal. Copyright laws protect artists and photographers just as they protect authors. In addition, even your own original photographs may cause problems if other people or other people's property appear in the picture. You may need to obtain permission from the people in the photograph or the owners of the property in your photograph in order to legally use the image in a publication or on a Web site. For images from other sources, sometimes you can obtain permission to use them by writing or e-mailing the owner. In some cases, you may be asked to pay a fee. Even when you obtain permission, you should always cite the source of the image. You can do this by adding a caption to the image or by creating a list of sources similar to a bibliography. You should include the name of the artist; the title of the image; the source where you obtained the image; the copyright date, which is the date the image was originally published; and the date you downloaded or acquired the image.

STEP-BY-STEP 4.3

1. In your desktop publishing program, open **DP Step 4-3a** from the data files. This is a version of the Eyes publication you used in the previous exercise.

2. Save the file as **Eyes2**.

3. Insert **DP Step 4-3b** from the data files into a picture frame in the white space in the upper-left corner of the page. Draw the frame about 1.25 inches wide, starting at the 2 inch mark on the horizontal ruler and about 0.25 inches down from the top margin. If the height doesn't adjust automatically, set it to 1 inch. The publication should look similar to Figure 4-6. Don't be surprised if the frame size and position adjust automatically to fit the proportions of the picture.

FIGURE 4-6
Picture inserted in frame

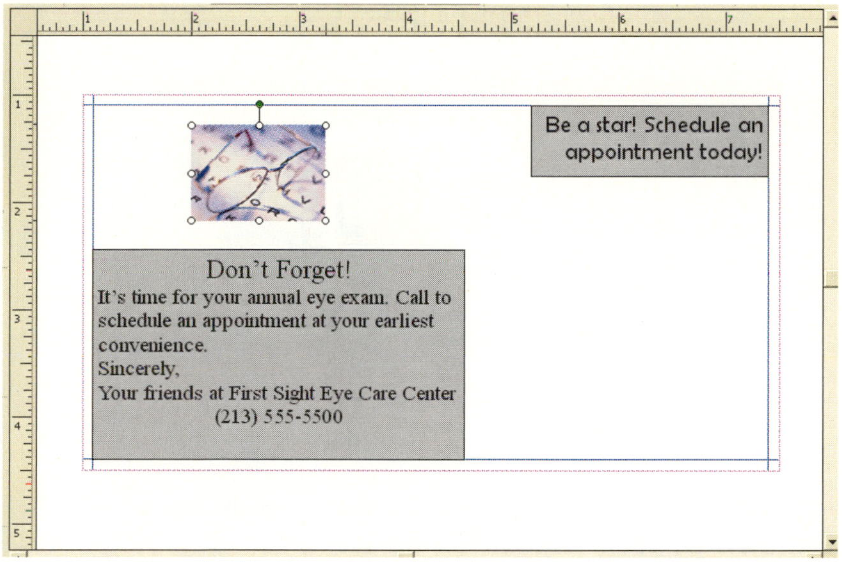

Be a star! Schedule an appointment today!

Don't Forget!
It's time for your annual eye exam. Call to schedule an appointment at your earliest convenience.
Sincerely,
Your friends at First Sight Eye Care Center
(213) 555-5500

4. Deselect the image and then save changes. Leave the **Eyes2** file open to use in the next exercise.

Insert Clip Art

Virtually all desktop publishing programs come with collections of clip art, or you can buy clip art on a disk or CD. The steps for inserting clip art in a document vary depending on the program you are using, but usually you select an image from a palette or task pane similar to the one in Figure 4-7.

FIGURE 4-7
Clip art task pane

To open the clip art task pane or palette, click Insert on the menu bar, click Picture, and then click Clip Art. Or click Window on the menu bar, click Plug-in Palettes, and then click Show Picture Palette. Alternatively, click the Clip Art or Picture Palette button on the toolbar.

In some programs, you search for clip art by key word. Simply key the text in the Search text box, and then click the Search button. Clip art matching the search text is displayed in the task pane or palette. Sometimes the clip art is sorted by category. Select a category to display the clip art in that category. Once you locate the image you want to use, click it to insert it in the document, or select it and then click the command to insert it into the current document. If necessary, drag the insertion pointer to define the size and location where you want to place the file.

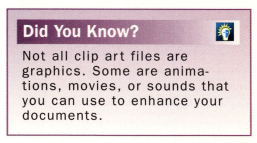

Did You Know?

Not all clip art files are graphics. Some are animations, movies, or sounds that you can use to enhance your documents.

STEP-BY-STEP 4.4

1. In the **Eyes2** file, click the appropriate toolbar button to display the clip art task pane or palette.

2. If a Search text box is available, key **stars**, and then click **Search**. Clip art matching the key word *stars* is displayed. If your program has clip art sorted by category, try looking for an image named *Stars* in the Decorations and Borders or Special Occasions category.

3. Scroll down the list to see the available images. Locate the one shown in Figure 4-8, or a similar image, and insert it into the file.

> **Note**
> You may be prompted to insert a CD or to browse for the location where the images are stored.

FIGURE 4-8
Clip art in the publication

4. Deselect the clip art image, save changes, and leave the **Eyes2** file open to use in the next exercise.

Download Clip Art from the Internet

There are many Web sites that offer free clip art. You simply locate the image you want on the site and then *download* it. Downloading saves a copy of the image file on your computer. You must have access to the Internet to locate and download clip art files. That means your computer must be connected to the Internet, and you must have an account with an Internet Service Provider (ISP).

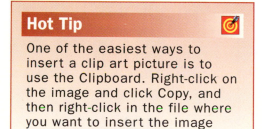

> **Hot Tip**
> One of the easiest ways to insert a clip art picture is to use the Clipboard. Right-click on the image and click Copy, and then right-click in the file where you want to insert the image and click Paste.

Some desktop publishing program manufacturers provide links from the program to a clip art site. For example, at the bottom of the Clip Art task pane in Microsoft Publisher, there is the *Clips Online* link to Microsoft's Design Gallery Live clip art Web site. Click the link to go to the site. If you know the address of a clip art site, you can also key the address directly in your Web

browser's Address bar. Then press Enter or click a button such as Go to jump to that site. Alternatively, you can use a *search site* and search for the *key word* "clip art." A search site is a Web site that helps you locate a Web page even if you don't know the page's address. A key word is a word or phrase that you believe identifies the Web site. After you search for a key word, the search site lists Web addresses of sites that match your term. Click on the Web address or the site name to jump directly to that site.

Some clip art sites ask you to register by entering your name and e-mail address, but many sites let you browse freely until you find a file you want to download. Some sites have download procedures for copying clip art files to your hard disk, or you can use your

browser's Save Picture As command to save the image as a graphics file on your computer. In some cases, you can use the Copy and Paste commands to copy the object to your publication.

> **Net Tip**
>
> You can use the Save As command to download virtually any image from a Web page to your computer. However, it is important to know the source of any file you download from the Internet. Some files may be copyrighted material that you need permission to use, while some files may have viruses that could infect your computer and other computers on the same network.

STEP-BY-STEP 4.5

1. Sign in to your Internet Service Provider and launch your Web browser.

2. Key **clipartconnection.com** in your browser's Address bar and then click **Go** or press **Enter**. The Web page that opens should look similar to Figure 4-9.

FIGURE 4-9
Clipartconnection.com Web page

STEP-BY-STEP 4.5 Continued

3. In the Search box near the top of the page, key **glasses** and then click the **Search** button.

4. Click the image in the middle of the first row to select it, right-click on it to display a shortcut menu, and then click **Save Picture As** on the shortcut menu. A Save Picture dialog box opens.

5. Key the filename **Glasses.jpg** in the File name box. Select the location where you want to store the file from the Save in list, if necessary, and then click **Save**. By default, the file is saved in JPEG format.

6. Close your Web browser and disconnect from the Internet.

7. In the **Eyes2** file, insert the **Glasses** file into the lower-right corner of the page, as shown in Figure 4-10.

FIGURE 4-10
Downloaded picture inserted in the publication

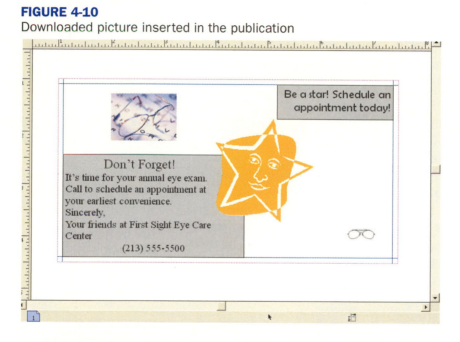

8. Print one copy of the **Eyes2** file.

9. Save changes and close the **Eyes2** file. Leave your desktop publishing program open to use in the next exercise.

Scan Printed Material

Use a *scanner* to convert printed material into a graphics file. A scanner is a hardware device that uses light to capture a digital version of printed or hand-written data, which is then stored as a graphics file on your computer. You can scan any printed data, including pictures, photographs, maps, charts, graphics, and even text.

Note ✅

Keep copyright laws in mind when selecting images for scanning. Make sure you have the owner or artist's permission to use the image before you insert it into a document or file. Refer to the section on Computer Ethics on page 100 for more information.

Most scanners come with software that lets you select where you want to store the imported images and also determines the file format. However, most desktop publishing programs support scanning and *TWAIN*, which is the software language used to control scanners, so you can probably use your program to scan the image directly into your desktop publishing program. Some programs insert the scanned image directly into the document as an object, while some create and save a graphics file and then import the image from the file.

Like any hardware device, the scanner must be correctly connected and installed on your computer to work. In addition, you must place the printed material correctly in the scanner. For example, make sure the top of the material is at the top of the scanner and that the entire page is within the scan area.

The steps for scanning directly into a document vary depending on the program you are using. Usually, you click Insert on the menu bar, click Picture on the Insert menu, and then click From Scanner on the submenu. In other programs, you might find the Scan command directly on the Insert menu or on the File menu. In some programs, you use the Acquire command on the File menu.

> ### Did You Know?
>
> Most programs let you preview a picture before you scan it. This is useful for making sure you have the printed page positioned correctly and have selected the options you need.

Once you select the command, a submenu or dialog box offers you a choice of scanning the image or selecting the specific scanning device you want to use. Some programs automatically save the scanned image as a graphics file, so you may be prompted to enter a filename. You then select options in a dialog box similar to the one in Figure 4-11. The options depend on the type of scanner you are using and your graphics program, but usually include settings for scanning in color, black and white, or grayscale, as well as for scanning text. When the scan is complete, the image is displayed as a new, unnamed file in the program window.

> ### Hot Tip
>
> Some programs have an Insert from Scanner toolbar button you can click to quickly access the Insert Picture from Scanner dialog box.

FIGURE 4-11
Scan dialog box

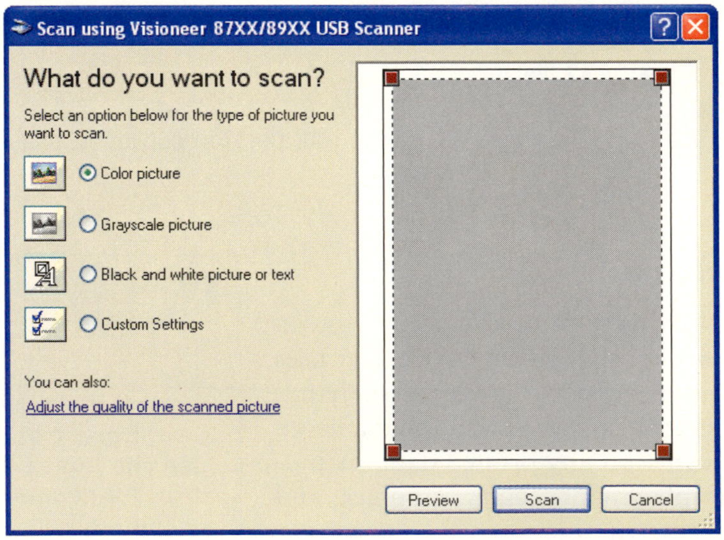

STEP-BY-STEP 4.6

1. On a blank sheet of white paper, draw a picture of a 5-pointed star, sized about 2 inches square. Use any style or colors that you want.

2. In your desktop publishing program, open **DP Step 4-6** from the data files. This is a version of the same file you have been working with.

3. Save the file as **Eyes3**.

4. Make sure your scanner is connected and switched on, then position the picture on the scanner glass.

5. Select the command to acquire an image from the scanner. If prompted, save the file as **Star1**.

6. Select options to scan a color picture. If necessary, drag the insertion pointer to draw a frame in the lower-right corner of the page. Alternatively, drag the scanned image into the lower-right corner. Depending on the scanned picture, the file should look similar to Figure 4-12.

FIGURE 4-12
Scanned image in the publication

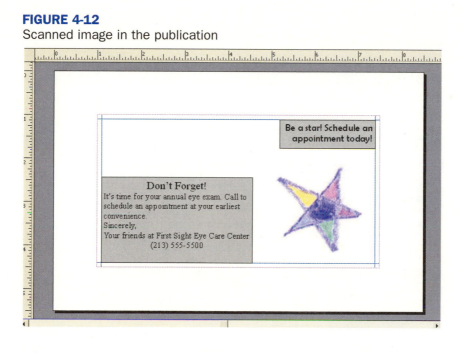

7. Save changes and leave the **Eyes3** file open to use in the next exercise.

Transfer Files from a Digital Camera

Digital cameras make it easy to take original photographs that you can then transfer as files to your computer. In most cases, the photographs are stored as files in the camera's internal memory or on a storage device attached to the camera, such as a disk, memory stick, or memory card. When a digital camera is correctly connected to a computer, most operating systems read the camera as just another disk drive, which means you can use the Copy and Paste commands to transfer the files from the camera to a storage device on your computer, such as a hard disk. Then, you use the Insert or Place command to insert the picture into a publication.

The software that comes with your camera may automatically transfer the files from the camera as soon as the camera is connected. The following steps provide information on how to transfer the pictures manually. Before you begin, make sure the camera has been installed for use with your computer.

> **Note** ☑️
>
> Usually, cameras store pictures in JPEG format, but some high-end cameras use TIFF. JPEG compresses the pictures, so they take less space on the storage device than TIFF files, but some quality may be lost in the compression process.

S TEP-BY-STEP 4.7

1. Use your digital camera to take one or more portraits of people wearing glasses, and then correctly attach the camera to your computer system.

2. Open the **My Computer** window from the desktop. My Computer displays the storage devices installed on your computer system, including the camera, as shown in Figure 4-13.

FIGURE 4-13
Digital camera listed as a storage device in My Computer

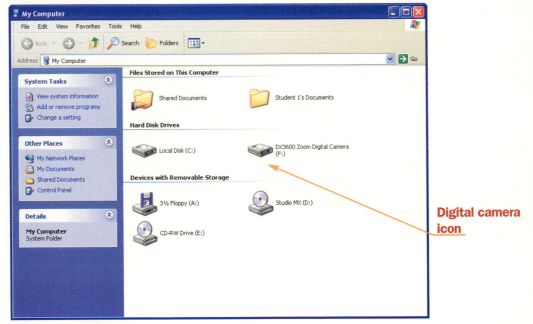

Digital camera icon

3. Double-click the icon representing the camera. A window displaying the contents of the camera opens. If necessary, double-click the specific location where the files are stored, such as internal memory or a storage device.

4. Select the file(s) you want to transfer.

> **Hot Tip** 🎯
>
> To select more than one file at a time, press and hold Ctrl and click the additional files.

STEP-BY-STEP 4.7 Continued

5. Click **Edit** on the window's menu bar, and then click **Copy**.

6. Open the **My Documents** window, or the window that contains the folder where you want to store the image file.

7. Click the **My Pictures** folder icon, or the icon representing the folder where you want to store the image file.

8. Click **Edit** on the window's menu bar, and then click **Paste**. Your operating system copies the image file into the selected folder.

9. Right-click the transferred file and click **Rename**, then key **Eyepic1** and press **Enter**. Rename additional transferred files consecutively. For example, name the next file Eyepic2, then Eyepic3, and so on.

10. Close all open windows.

11. In the **Eyes3** desktop publishing file, insert one or more of the transferred photo files into the white space in the upper-left corner of the page. The publication should look similar to Figure 4-14.

FIGURE 4-14
Photos inserted in the publication

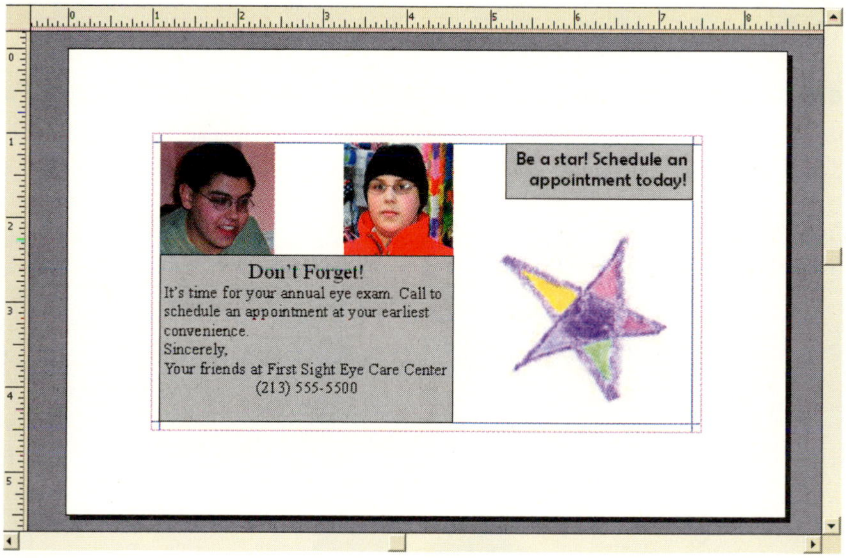

12. Print one copy of the **Eyes3** file.

13. Save changes and close the **Eyes3** file. Leave your desktop publishing program open to use in the next exercise.

Copy and Paste Objects

Use the Clipboard to quickly copy and paste any object from any location into a publication. Right-click the object, click Copy, right-click the location on the publication page where you want to insert the object, and click Paste. You can also use the Copy and Paste commands on the Edit menu, or the Copy and Paste buttons on the toolbar.

By default, pasted objects are embedded in the publication. When you *embed* an object, the object is not connected in any way to the original file. You can also use the Paste Special command to *link* an object in the publication. A linked object maintains a connection to its original file. You can update the object if changes are made to the original.

STEP-BY-STEP 4.8

1. In your desktop publishing program, open **DP Step 4-8a** from the data files.

2. Save the file as **Eyead**.

3. Locate and open **DP Step 4-8b** from the data files. The shapes used to draw the glasses have been grouped into one unit, so the Ungroup button may be displayed in the middle of the document window. You learn about grouping later in this lesson.

4. Right-click the glasses, and then click **Copy** on the shortcut menu. Close **DP Step 4-8b** without saving any changes.

5. In the **Eyead** file, right-click in the white space at the bottom of the page and click **Paste** on the shortcut menu. The picture is pasted into the file. The bottom half of the page should look similar to Figure 4-15. If necessary, drag the glasses into the white space at the bottom of the page as shown.

FIGURE 4-15
Picture pasted into publication

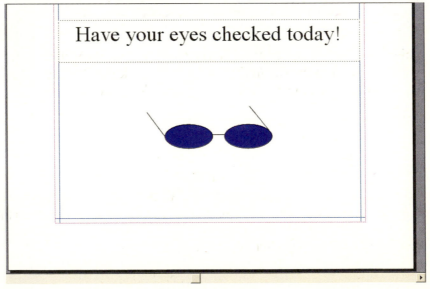

6. Save changes and leave the **Eyead** file open to use in the next exercise.

Insert Embedded Objects

As mentioned earlier, an embedded object is one that is created using its original program—called the *source*—then copied and pasted into a different program file—called the *destination*. There is no link between the source file and the destination file. You can use the Insert Object dialog box shown in Figure 4-16 to create new embedded objects or embed objects already created and stored in a file. Use a menu command to open the dialog box. For example, click Insert on the menu bar and then click Object, or click Edit on the menu and then click Insert Object. To create a new object, click the Create New button, click the object type, and then click OK. The source program opens so you can create the object. When you are finished, close the file to insert the object in the publication.

> **Note** ☑
>
> You must know how to use the source program to create the object.

FIGURE 4-16
Insert Object dialog box

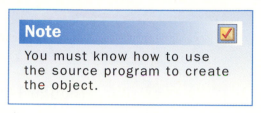

To create an object from an existing file, click the Create from File button in the Insert Object dialog box, then enter the path to the file in the File box, or click the Browse button to locate and select the file. When you click OK in the Insert Object dialog box, the object is inserted in the publication.

STEP-BY-STEP 4.9

1. In the **Eyead** file, click in the white space in the top half of the page, and then choose the command to open the Insert Object dialog box. For example, click **Insert** on the menu bar, and then click **Object**.

2. Click the **Create from File** option button.

3. Click the **Browse** button to open the Browse dialog box. Locate and select **DP Step 4-9** in the data files. This is a Microsoft Excel worksheet file that contains a chart object. Click the **Open** or **OK** button in the Browse dialog box.

STEP-BY-STEP 4.9 Continued

4. Click the **OK** button in the Insert Object dialog box. The chart object is inserted into the publication file. It should look similar to Figure 4-17. If necessary, drag the object into position as shown.

FIGURE 4-17
Chart object in the publication

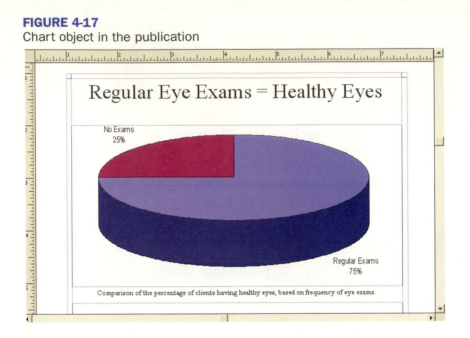

5. Save changes and leave the **Eyead** file open to use in the next exercise.

Size and Crop Objects

Once an object is inserted in a publication file, you can easily change its size to integrate it on the page. There are basically three ways to change an object's size. You can simply resize the object to change its height and/or width. You can *scale* the object, which means to change its size by a percentage of its original size. Or, you can *crop* the object, which means to remove one or more of its outer edges.

Resize or Scale an Object

To resize an object quickly, simply drag a sizing handle in or out. Drag a top or bottom handle to change the height, drag a side handle to change the width, or drag a corner handle to change the height and width at the same time.

To set a precise size or scale for an object, use the options in a dialog box such as the Format *Object* dialog box or a palette such as the Control palette. Key the dimensions or scale percentage in the appropriate boxes, and then click the OK or Apply button.

S TEP-BY-STEP 4.10

1. In the **Eyead** file, select the picture of the glasses near the bottom of the page.

2. Drag the sizing handle at the lower-left corner of the object to the corner where the left and bottom margins meet, and then drag the sizing handle at the upper-right corner of the object to the corner where the right margin and the lower text box meet. This increases the size of the object significantly. Try scaling the object.

3. Click the object to select it, and then choose the command to open the dialog box or palette where you set precise dimensions. For example, click **Format** on the menu bar and then click **Object**. If necessary, click the **Size** tab.

4. In the Size section, click in the **Height** box and key **2.5**, and then click in the **Width** box and key **4.75**. Click the **OK** or **Apply** button to apply the change. The bottom half of the page should look similar to Figure 4-18. If necessary, drag the object into position as shown.

FIGURE 4-18
Resize the object precisely

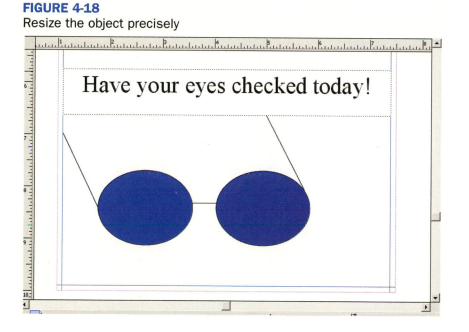

5. Save changes and leave the **Eyead** file open to use in the next exercise.

Crop an Object

When you want to remove the outer portions of an object, you crop it. To crop an image in most programs, click the Crop tool on the Picture toolbar or in the toolbox to display cropping handles around the object. Drag the handles to define the area you want to remove. For example, drag a top handle down to remove the upper edge of the object. To crop by a precise amount, use the options in the Format *Object* dialog box or the Control palette.

STEP-BY-STEP 4.11

1. In the **Eyead** file, click the chart object to select it. From the location of the sizing handles, you can see that the object has a lot of extra space around it. Try cropping the object to remove the extra space.

2. Click the **Crop** tool on the toolbar or in the toolbox. You may need to display the Picture toolbar to locate the Crop tool.

3. Drag the upper-middle crop handle down about 2.25 inches, or until the top edge of the object is located just above the text *No Exams*. When you release the mouse button, the object is cropped.

4. Drag the left crop handle to the right until the left edge of the object is just to the left of the edge of the chart, then drag the right crop handle to the left until the right edge of the object is just to the right of the text *Regular Exams*. Finally, drag the lower crop handle up about 2 inches so the bottom edge of the object is just under the text *75%*. The top half of the page should look similar to Figure 4-19. If necessary, resize the object and drag it into position as shown.

FIGURE 4-19
Cropped object

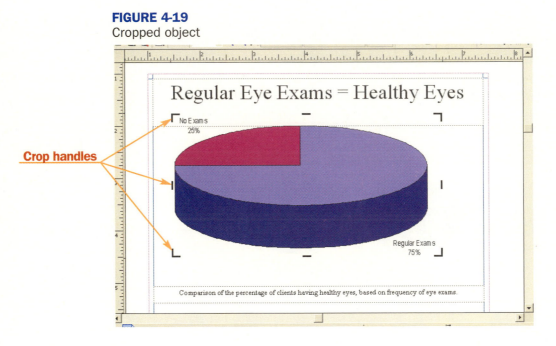

5. Deselect the object, save changes, and leave the **Eyead** file open to use in the next exercise.

Position and Arrange Objects

As you have already learned, the way you position and arrange objects on the page is one of the most important factors in creating a successful publication. The easiest way to position an object is to select it and then drag it to a new location, but most programs include tools for fine-tuning position, including alignment options, precise positioning, and layering, or stacking.

In most programs, objects are modified based on a *reference point*, which is a fixed spot used as a control for moving and modifying objects. The default reference point depends on the program you are using, but it is often the center of the object or the upper-left corner. While many programs do not let you move the reference point, some programs do, and it can greatly affect modifications made to the object. For example, if you set the precise position of two identical objects to 2 inches horizontal and 2 inches vertical, and then set one reference point at the center of an object and the other in the upper-left corner of the object, the objects will be positioned in different places on the page. The following exercises assume that the default reference points have not been moved.

Position an Object Precisely

To position an object precisely in some programs, you use the Format *Object* dialog box to specify the horizontal and vertical location relative to either the upper-right corner, the upper-left corner, or the center of the page. In other programs, you set the horizontal (X) and vertical (Y) *coordinates* in a palette such as Control. The coordinates are specific points laid out in an invisible grid that starts in the upper-left corner of the page, with the coordinates of 0, 0. As you move an object to the right, the X coordinate increases. As you move down, the Y coordinate increases.

S TEP-BY-STEP 4.12

1. In the **Eyead** file, select the chart object if it is not already selected.

2. Choose the command to open the dialog box or palette where you enter values to position an object. For example, click **Format** on the menu bar, and then click **Object**. Click the **Layout** tab if necessary.

3. Click in the **Horizontal** or **X** box and key **1.75**. If necessary, click the **From** box and select **Top Left Corner**.

4. Click in the **Vertical** or **Y** box and key **2.24**. Again, if necessary click the **From** box and select **Top Left Corner**.

5. Click the **OK** button or the **Apply** button. The object moves to the specified position. If the object does not appear to be centered in the space, you may have to drag it into position.

6. Save changes and leave the **Eyead** file open to use in the next exercise.

Align Objects

You have already learned how to use guidelines to visually align objects on a page. Most desktop publishing programs also have tools for making sure objects are precisely aligned. You can toggle on the Snap to feature if you want objects to automatically align to the guides. You can use the Nudge command or the arrow keys to move an object up, down, left, or right in small increments. In some programs, you can align an object to adjust its position horizontally relative to the left and right margins, and vertically relative to the top and bottom margins.

If you are using a program such as Adobe Page-Maker that does not have options for aligning or distributing individual objects, you can complete the following exercise by dragging the objects or setting the X and Y coordinates.

Extra for Experts

Many programs also have a *distribute* command you can use to space multiple objects evenly between either the top and bottom margins or the left and right margins.

S TEP-BY-STEP 4.13

1. In the **Eyead** file, click the picture of the glasses on the bottom half of the page.

2. Select the command to center align the object between the left and right margins. For example, click **Arrange** on the menu bar, click **Align or Distribute**, and then click **Align Center**. The object is centered horizontally between the margins. If necessary, drag the object into position, or set the X and Y coordinates.

3. Select the command to align the object with the bottom margin. For example, click **Arrange** on the menu bar, click **Align or Distribute**, and then click **Align Bottom**.

4. Use the Nudge command to nudge the object up so it is even with the bottom layout guide. For example, click **Arrange** on the menu bar, click **Nudge**, and then click **Up**. Repeat the command nine more times, or press the Up arrow key on the keyboard nine times. The publication should look similar to the one in Figure 4-20.

FIGURE 4-20
Objects aligned in publication

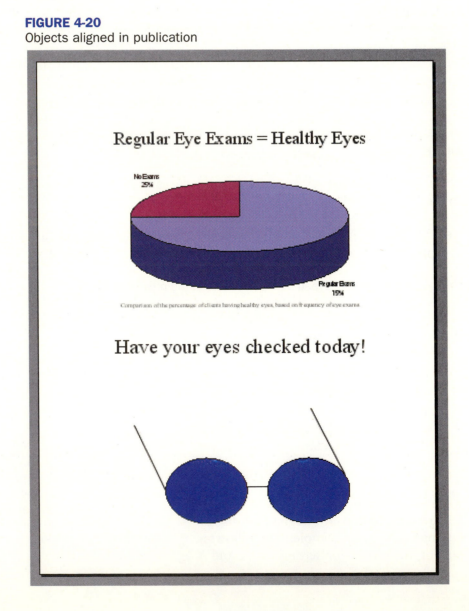

STEP-BY-STEP 4.13 Continued

5. Print one copy of the **Eyead** file.

6. Save changes and close the **Eyead** file. Leave your desktop publishing program open to use in the next exercise.

> **Note** ☑️
>
> If the commands on the Align or Distribute menu are dimmed, click the Relative to Margin Guides command to activate them.

Group and Reorder Stacked Items

When you want to apply the same changes to more than one object at once, you can select all of the objects and then apply the changes. Alternatively, you can *group* multiple objects. Grouped objects can be selected and modified as one unit. That way, you don't have to worry about selecting all items each time you want to make changes.

To create a group, simply select the objects you want to include and then click the Group button, or click the Group command on a menu such as Arrange or Element. Selection handles surround the entire group, rather than the individual objects in the group. Use the Ungroup button or command to turn off grouping so you can work with the individual objects again.

As you insert objects, they *stack* in the document, even if they do not actually overlap each other. The first object is at the bottom or back of the stack, and the most recent object is at the top or front of the stack. You sometimes need to rearrange the stacking order of objects to make sure that an object is displayed properly or to create overlapping effects.

The command to rearrange the stacking order varies depending on the program you are using. It may be the Arrange command on the Element menu, or the Order command on the Arrange menu. There may even be an Order button on the tool-bar. Once you locate the command and select it, a menu of stacking options is displayed. Most programs give you four options for adjusting stacking order: Send to Back, Send Backward, Bring Forward, and Bring to Front. Send to Back moves an object behind all other objects, while Bring to Front positions an object in front of all other objects. Send Backward and Bring Forward move objects forward or backward one position at a time. To change the stacking order, select the object you need to change and then select a command.

> **Extra for Experts** 📊
>
> Do not confuse the stacking order with layers. Some programs have a Layers feature you can use to separate a document into individual transparent planes. Layers are used for creating complex publications and certain special effects.

S TEP-BY-STEP 4.14

1. In your desktop-publishing program, open **DP Step 4-14** from the data files. This is another version of the original reminder postcard.

2. Save the file as **Eyes4**.

STEP-BY-STEP 4.14 Continued

3. Select all of the shapes that comprise the picture of the glasses. Sizing handles are displayed around each shape, and in some programs the Group button is displayed.

4. Click the **Group** button, or select the command to group the objects. For example, click **Arrange** on the menu bar, and then click **Group**. The objects are grouped into a single unit. Notice that sizing handles are displayed around the entire group. In some programs, the Group button changes to the Ungroup button.

5. Resize the entire group to about 1 inch high by 3 inches wide, if necessary.

6. Select the large blue star and position it horizontally 5 inches and vertically 2 inches from the upper-left corner of the page.

7. Set the stacking order for the large blue star to send it to the back. For example, select the star, click **Arrange** on the menu bar, click **Order**, and then click **Send to Back**.

8. Position the four smaller stars relative to the top left corner as follows:

Black star: horizontally 6 inches and vertically 1.75 inches

Yellow star: horizontally 4.5 inches and vertically 1.75 inches

Orange star: horizontally 6 inches and vertically 2.75 inches

Purple star: horizontally 4.5 inches and vertically 2.75 inches

9. Select the black star and change its stacking order to send it to the back.

10. Select the purple star and change its stacking order to send it to the back. The publication should look similar to the one in Figure 4-21.

FIGURE 4-21
Grouped and stacked objects

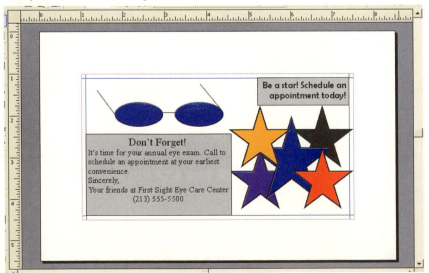

STEP-BY-STEP 4.14 Continued

11. Print one copy of the **Eyes4** file.

12. Save changes and close the **Eyes4** file. Leave your desktop publishing program open to use in the next exercise.

Rotate and Flip

Two other methods of changing the way an object is positioned on the page are rotating and flipping, which is sometimes called *reflecting*. When you *rotate* an object, it pivots around its reference point. When you *flip* an object, you reverse the image either horizontally (left to right) or vertically (top to bottom).

In some programs, such as Microsoft Publisher, a rotation handle is displayed with certain shapes when an object is selected. Simply drag the rotation handle to rotate the object around a center reference point. In other programs, such as Adobe PageMaker, you must first click the Rotate or Free Rotate tool in the toolbox or select the Free Rotate command from a menu to display rotation handles. Drag any handle to rotate the object. In some programs, the handle you drag becomes the reference point. Some programs also have a menu command for rotating an object in 90-degree increments left or right, and most programs also let you rotate an object by a precise amount by entering a specific value for the rotation in a dialog box such as Format *Object* or a palette such as Control.

To flip an object, choose either the Flip Horizontal or Flip Vertical command on a menu such as Arrange, or click the Reflect button on a toolbar or in a palette such as Control.

STEP-BY-STEP 4.15

1. In your desktop publishing program, open **DP Step 4-15** from the data files.

2. Save the file as **Eyes5**.

3. Select the purple star and rotate it to the right until the top point is pointing to the upper-right corner of the page (approximately 35 degrees).

4. Select the black star and drag the rotation handle about 0.25 inches to the left (approximately −25 degrees).

5. Select the orange star and drag the rotation handle about 0.25 inches to the right (approximately 25 degrees).

6. Select the lightning bolt and flip it horizontally.

STEP-BY-STEP 4.15 Continued

7. Flip the lightning bolt vertically. The publication should look similar to Figure 4-22. If necessary, adjust the position of the objects.

FIGURE 4-22
Objects rotated and flipped

8. Save changes and leave the **Eyes5** file open to use in the next exercise.

Set Text Wrap

Y ou can set text wrap to adjust the width, shape, and position of white space between text and objects on a page. You have already learned that text automatically wraps within a text box from the end of one line to the beginning of the next line. Most desktop publishing programs also have a selection of text wrap styles and options you use to control the way text wraps to make room for objects. Most programs offer five wrapping styles, as described in Table 4-1.

TABLE 4-1
Text wrap styles and options

BUTTON	STYLE NAME	DESCRIPTION
	Square	Wraps text evenly around four sides of an object.
	Tight	Wraps text along the contours of an object.
	Through	Continues lines of text through transparent backgrounds of objects.
	Top and Bottom	Wraps text evenly on the top and bottom of an object.
	None	Does not wrap text. Instead, text is stacked behind or in front of the object.

In most programs, the text wrapping options are listed in a dialog box, such as Format *Object* or Text Wrap. Simply select the object, and then open the dialog box and select the style you want to apply. Alternatively, click the Text Wrap button on a toolbar such as Picture, and then click the style on the pop-up palette that is displayed. Depending on the style you select and your program, you may also be able to set text flow options to control the way text flows around the object. For example, if you select Square, Tight, or Through, you can select whether to wrap the text on both sides of the object, only the left side, only the right side, or just on the largest side of the object. If you select the Square wrapping style, you can enter the specific distance you want to maintain between the object and any of its four sides, sometimes called the *standoff*.

S TEP-BY-STEP 4.16

1. In the **Eyes5** file, select the lightning bolt shape and set the wrapping style to **Tight**. For example, click the shape, click the **Text Wrap** button on the toolbar, and then click **Tight**. You may need to display the Picture toolbar to locate the Text Wrap button.

2. Select the orange star and set the wrapping style to **Square**.

3. Select the black star and set the wrapping style to **Square**.

STEP-BY-STEP 4.16 Continued

4. Select the purple star and set the wrapping style to **Tight**. The publication should look similar to Figure 4-23. If necessary, adjust the size and position of objects. If your program has Standoff settings, you may have to adjust the measurements to a value such as 0.01 all around.

FIGURE 4-23
Text wrapped around objects

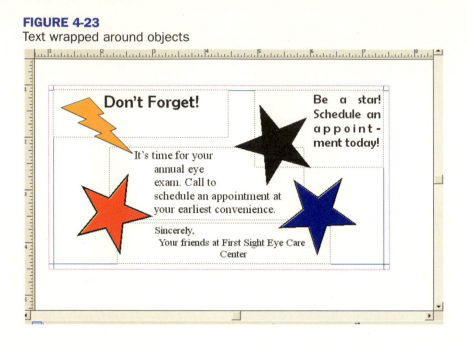

5. Print one copy of the **Eyes5** file.

6. Save changes and close the **Eyes5** file and your desktop publishing program.

SUMMARY

In this lesson, you learned:

■ There are many types of objects you can insert in desktop publishing documents.

■ Most desktop publishing programs have drawing tools you can use to draw basic shapes.

■ You can insert many types of graphics files in a desktop publishing program.

■ Use a scanner to convert printed material into an object or graphics file.

■ You can transfer files from a digital camera to a computer, and then insert them into a publication.

■ Most desktop publishing programs come with clip art, or you can download clip art from the Internet.

■ It is important to obey copyright laws and to cite sources of material you acquire from other sources.

■ One of the easiest ways to insert an object in a publication is to use the Copy and Paste commands.

■ You can modify objects by changing the color and style of fills and strokes.

■ You can resize, crop, and position objects using precise values or by dragging handles with the mouse.

■ To integrate objects with text, you can select from several text wrapping styles.

VOCABULARY *Review*

Define the following terms:

Bitmap	Floating object	Rotate
Crop	Group	Scale
Distribute	Link	Scanner
Download	Object	Stack
Embed	Picture frame	Stroke
Fill	Pixels	Vector
Flip		

REVIEW *Questions*

TRUE / FALSE

Circle T if the statement is true or F if the statement is false.

T F **1.** By default, when you draw a shape, it is displayed with no fill.

T F **2.** An ISP is a Web site that helps you locate a Web page even if you don't know the page's address.

T F **3.** Use a scanner to convert a graphics file into a printed document.

T F **4.** By default, pasted objects are linked to a publication.

T F **5.** When you want to move an object up, down, left, or right by a very small amount, use the Nudge command.

T F **6.** Scale an object to remove one or more of its outer edges.

T F **7.** Bitmap graphics use colored dots arranged in a grid to define an image.

T F **8.** To select more than one object at a time, press and hold Shift and then click each object.

T F **9.** When you rotate an object, you reverse the image.

T F **10.** Select a text wrap style to control the way text makes room for objects on the page.

WRITTEN QUESTIONS

Write a brief answer to the following questions.

1. Name at least two hardware devices you can use to acquire graphics objects.

2. What are some of the modifications you can make to a shape's stroke or fill?

3. What is the benefit to using a frame when you insert a picture?

4. Name at least two graphics file formats and list some characteristics of each.

5. What is the difference between linking an object and embedding an object?

FILL IN THE BLANK

Complete the following sentences by writing the correct word or words in the blanks provided.

1. Select the _____ text wrapping style to wrap text along the contours of an object.

2. _____ graphics consist of lines and curves that are defined by mathematical objects.

3. The _____ is the area inside a shape.

4. The _____ is the line used to draw a shape.

5. You can align _____ relative to the left and right margins.

6. To position an object so it _____ other objects, change its stacking order to Bring to Front.

7. _____ an object to change its size by a percentage of its original size.

8. Use a(n) _____ to convert printed material into a graphics file.

9. _____ are colored dots arranged in a grid to define an image.

10. Some programs have a(n) _____ feature you can use to quickly draw whimsical objects such as lightning bolts and smiley faces.

PROJECTS

PROJECT 4-1

1. Launch your desktop publishing program and open **DP Project 4-1a** from the data files. This file is a version of the CNO newsletter you worked with in Lesson 3. You are going to enhance it by inserting pictures and shapes.

2. Save the file as **CNONews2**.

3. Insert the graphics file **DP Project 4-1b** from the data files into a frame in the upper-left corner of page 1 to complement the newsletter title.
   A. Size the frame to about 1.25 inches high by 1.5 inches wide, if necessary. You can do this before inserting the picture, or you can resize the picture after you insert it in the publication.
   B. Position it along the left margin (about 1.1 inches from the top left corner horizontally and vertically).
   C. If the text and the picture overlap, set the text wrap for the picture to Square.

4. Locate a clip art picture of wrapped presents. You may look in the clip art collection that came with your program or in other clip art you have on a CD or installed on your system, or you may want to download a picture from the Internet.

5. Insert the clip art to illustrate the story with the headline *Holiday Helpers Needed* in the lower-right corner of page 1. Format the picture as follows:
   A. Size the picture to about 0.75 inches high by 0.75 inches wide.
   B. Set the text wrap for the clip art to **Tight** or adjust the standoff as necessary to allow for tight wrapping.
   C. Position the clip art to the left of the headline, overlapping the column guides. Fine-tune the position as necessary so that all of the text fits in the text box.

6. Change to page 2 and draw a smiley face on the page near the letter to the editor. You may draw the face using an AutoShape, or by using basic shapes.
   A. Size the smiley face to 0.5 inches by 0.5 inches.
   B. Fill the shape with the color yellow.
   C. Set the text wrap to **Square**.
   D. Position the shape to the left of the text *Dear Editor*, then fine-tune the position so all of the text fits in the text box.

7. Print both pages, either on separate sheets of paper or on a double-sided sheet.

8. Save changes and close the **CNONews2** file. Leave your desktop publishing program open to use in Project 4-2.

PROJECT 4-2

1. In your desktop publishing program, open **DP Project 4-2a** from the data files. This is a version of the invitation you worked with in Lesson 3.

2. Save the file as **CNOInvite2**.

3. On page 1, insert the graphics file **DP Project 4-2b** from the data files and format the object as follows:
   A. Resize the object to about 3 inches wide by 2.75 inches high.
   B. Position it in the white space on the bottom half of the page.
   C. Center it horizontally between the margins.

4. On page 2, insert a picture of entertainment. You may acquire the picture from any source you want. For example, insert clip art, a scanned picture, a picture acquired from a digital camera, or a picture you draw on a graphics tablet. Format the object as follows:
   A. Size and position the object to fit in the white space at the top of page 2.
   B. Try flipping or rotating the object to create an interesting effect.

5. On page 3, insert a different picture of entertainment. You may want to use a different source from the one you used in step 4 to acquire the image. Format the object as follows:
   A. Size and position the object to fit in the white space at the bottom of page 3. This balances the object on page 2.
   B. Apply a similar effect to the object that you used for the object on page 2. This provides consistency.

6. On page 4, insert objects to decorate the white space along the outside margin and the bottom of the page. For example, insert shapes, such as stars or hearts, or clip art, or a drawing that you scan or create with a graphics tablet. Use color to highlight the objects, and rotate and position them to create interesting angles and juxtapositions. Create a pattern by repeating the shapes, or by grouping shapes and repeating the group. Try overlapping the objects and changing the stacking order to make the page exciting and festive.

7. When you are satisfied with page 4, print the publication and fold it into an invitation.

8. Save changes and close the **CNOInvite2** file and your desktop publishing program.

SCANS ## WEB PROJECT

The copyright laws that govern the use of material found on the Internet may be complex, but you can find Web sites that list the dos and don'ts in simple, straightforward language. Use the Internet to find some basic rules to keep in mind when you download information such as a picture from a Web site. See if you can find information about the proper way to request permission for using a picture, and then use a word processing program to write such a letter. Finally, look up different ways to cite sources for Internet data. Ask your instructor which method he or she prefers, and then use that method to cite sources.

TEAMWORK PROJECT

As a group, plan and design a flyer or brochure about a historic or famous site in your community. You need to agree on the site and then research it so you have the correct information to include in the publication. If possible, use a digital camera to take pictures of the site to include in the document. Alternatively, find pictures that have already been printed that you can use. As with other publications, you should decide the page setup, including how many pages to include, and whether you will use double-sided or single-sided printing. Then, mock up the publication so you have a general idea of its size, layout, and appearance.

When you are ready, use your desktop publishing program to create the publication document. Insert all text and objects, and position them on the pages so the document is appealing and easy to read. When you are finished, check the spelling and then print the publication.

CRITICAL *Thinking*

ACTIVITY 4-1

Enhance one of the publications you created in a previous lesson by inserting objects. For example, add clip art pictures or digital photos to the side fold card, and/or draw basic shapes. Open the file and save it with a new name so you can make the changes without affecting the original publication. Insert graphics files, or create the objects directly in the publication. Once you insert the objects, use the tools in your desktop publishing program to adjust the size and position for the best impact. For example, scale the objects to make them larger or smaller, or crop out parts you don't need. You can rotate or flip the images and change the stroke and fill if you want. Adjust the text wrap to control the white space around the pictures. When you are finished, check the spelling and print one copy.

ENHANCING PUBLICATIONS

Upon completion of this lesson, you should be able to:

- Work with color.
- Enhance objects.
- Enhance text.
- Insert horizontal rules.
- Apply border art.
- Create a watermark.
- Use design objects.

Estimated Time: 1.5 hours

VOCABULARY

CMYK

Color system

Dot leader

Dropped capital

Gradient

Horizontal rule

Hue

Letterhead

Logo

Masthead

Pattern

Process color

RGB

Shadow

Spot color

Table of contents

Texture

Tint

Transparency

Watermark

Maybe you can't judge a book by its cover, but an exciting, attractive book jacket can certainly capture a potential reader's attention. When you add visual details and enhancements to a document, you make the publication more appealing. You can also use enhancements to create *brand recognition*. For example, if you repeat a color or shape in print—think of the blue and yellow of a Blockbuster Video sign or the black and white cow print of the boxes Gateway computers come in—people associate certain colors or shapes with specific organizations. In this lesson, you learn how to use desktop publishing tools to enhance publications with special effects and color. You can add shadows and 3-D effects to objects to make them stand out on a page. You can apply borders and rules to visually separate elements on a page, and you can add borders and watermarks to pages as decoration or part of an overall publication design. You can even use text as a decoration by turning it into a graphics object or starting a paragraph with a dropped capital letter.

Work with Color

Color, also called *hue*, is frequently the first thing a reader sees and responds to. While some publications, such as some newspapers, use only two colors—black and white—many incorporate at least one additional color for emphasis and effect, and some use a wide spectrum of colors for reproducing photographs and other full-color images.

You have already learned how to select a color scheme and apply standard colors to text, fills, and strokes. You can also define custom colors. The options available for working with color vary depending on your desktop publishing program, but in general you select the element you want to color, and then open a dialog box where you can select or define a custom color. The custom color is then added to the palette so you can apply it to other elements in the publication.

Understand Color Systems

When you work with color in a desktop publishing program, the most important thing to keep in mind is that the way colors are displayed on your computer screen is not necessarily the way they will look when printed. Many factors affect the way colors appear on your screen and in print, including the specific printer model, the specific monitor model, and your software program. But the most important factor is that printers and monitors use different *color systems*. A color system is a method for defining standard colors. It may also be called a *color model*.

The color system used for displaying colors on a monitor is called **RGB**. The RGB system creates colors by combining different values of red, green, and blue. The main color system used for defining colors in print is called **CMYK** (or CMY). The CMYK system creates colors by combining percentages of cyan (blue), magenta (red), yellow, and black. These colors—often called *process color*—are the colors of the ink used in four-color printing. Process color is usually used for publications that contain many colors, such as brochures that include photographs or high-definition graphics.

When a publication designer wants to use a specific color of ink instead of mixing the color during printing, he or she can select a *spot color* from a color system or library such as the *Pantone Matching System*. A spot color is ink that is premixed before the printing process. You use spot colors when it is necessary to have an exact color such as matching a client's logo color, or when printing with only one or two colors, or when using special inks for emphasis. You can use both spot colors and process colors in the same publication. Spot color printing on its own is usually less expensive than process color printing.

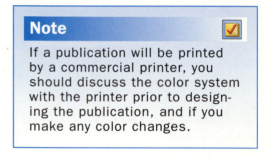

Note

If a publication will be printed by a commercial printer, you should discuss the color system with the printer prior to designing the publication, and if you make any color changes.

Create Custom Colors

There are two basic methods for defining a custom color, both of which use a color dialog box similar to the one in Figure 5-1.

FIGURE 5-1
Create custom colors

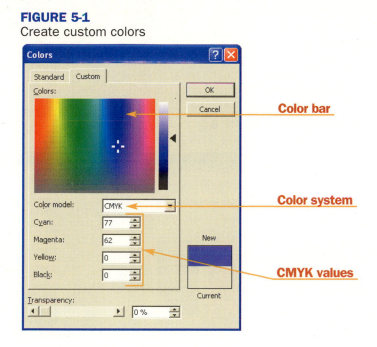

The first method, which may not be available in all programs, is to simply select a color from a *color bar*. A color bar displays a spectrum of colors across a rectangle from left to right. To apply a custom color using a color bar, start by selecting the element to color and opening the standard color scheme palette. Select the option to open the colors or custom colors dialog box, click the color you want to apply, and then click OK.

The other method for defining a custom color is to key the color system values for a particular color in the dialog box. To apply a custom color by keying a color system value, select the element to color and open the standard color scheme palette. Select the option to open the custom colors dialog box, select the color system from a drop-down list, and key values for each color. Units used for values differ by system. For example, RGB values usually range from 0 to 255, but CMYK values use percentages.

In some programs, you simply click OK to apply the color to the element, while in other programs you must key a name for the custom color, save it, and then apply it from the standard color scheme palette. In either case, the custom color is added to the color palette for that publication.

Net Tip

Look on the Web to find color system tables listing values for the entire range of colors. Such a table can save you time in experimenting with color values to find the one you want.

Some programs come with color charts for particular color systems that you can use to select a specific color. When you select the color system from the drop-down list in the custom color dialog box, a color chart dialog box similar to the Pantone Colors dialog box shown in Figure 5-2 opens. Click the color you want to use, and then click OK.

> **Did You Know?**
>
> RGB, CMYK, and the Pantone Matching System are not the only color systems. Other common process color systems include HSL (Hue, Saturation, Lightness) and Grayscale, which uses percentages of black to create shades of gray. Other spot color systems include Toyo Color Finder and DIC Color Guide.

FIGURE 5-2
Pantone color chips

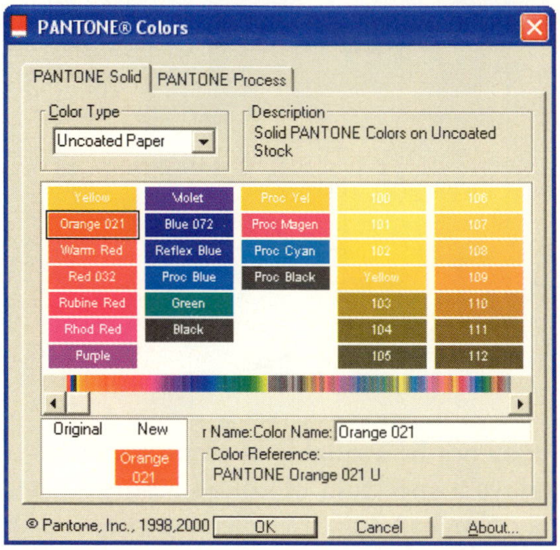

You can also usually modify a color by changing its *tint* and/or *transparency*. Tint, which is sometimes called *brightness*, is the range of a color from black to white. When you add white to a color, you increase its brightness. Add black to shade or decrease the brightness. Transparency, which is sometimes, called opacity, measures the degree to which you can see through a color. To make a color completely opaque, set the transparency to 0%. To see through a color, increase the transparency. The options for changing tint and/or transparency may be found in the Colors dialog box or palette.

> **Extra for Experts**
>
> You can make colors in some bitmap graphics and clip art files transparent so they do not show when printed. Select the Set Transparent Color tool or command in your desktop publishing program, and then click the color in the image.

STEP-BY-STEP 5.1

1. Launch your desktop publishing program, and open **DP Step 5-1** from the data files.

2. Save the file as **Coffee**. This publication is a flyer announcing coffee tasting at the Beans & Beyond coffee shop.

STEP-BY-STEP 5.1 Continued

3. Insert an 8-point star shape in the upper left of the publication. (Set the star inset to 17% if necessary.) Size the shape to 3 inches high by 3 inches wide, and position it horizontally 1.25 inches from the upper-left corner and vertically 1 inch from the upper-left corner. If necessary, rotate the shape so one point of the star is vertical.

4. With the star shape selected, open the Fill color custom colors dialog box. For example, click the **Fill Color** tool on the toolbar, click **More Fill Colors**, and then click the **Custom** tab.

5. Select the CMYK color system and key the following values: Cyan: **70**; Magenta: **30**; Yellow: **5**; Black: **0**. If necessary, name the color Star Blue.

6. Click the **OK** button as many times as necessary to close all dialog boxes and apply the color to the shape. If necessary, click the new color in the color palette to apply it. The shape should look similar to Figure 5-3.

> ### Extra for Experts
>
> In some programs, you can modify color schemes by defining new colors. Select the scheme, and then define the standard or custom colors for each scheme element. Click OK to change the current scheme, or click the Save Scheme button and key a name to create a new color scheme.

FIGURE 5-3
Custom color fill

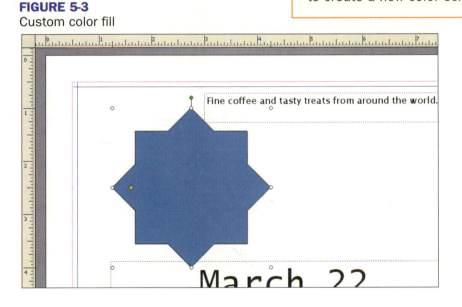

Fine coffee and tasty treats from around the world.

March 22

7. Save changes and leave the **Coffee** file open to use in the next exercise.

Enhance Objects

Many programs provide options for formatting objects with special effects such as shadows, 3-D, textures, gradients, and patterns. Patterns, textures, and gradients are applied as fill or stroke effects, while shadows and 3-D effects are used to format entire objects. The methods for applying special effects to objects vary depending on your program, and not all programs offer all types of effects. In programs that offer only basic effects such as patterns, you select a fill or stroke effect from a menu or in the Stroke and Fill dialog box as you learned in Lesson 4. In programs that offer many special effects, you use the appropriate dialog box or toolbar button.

To apply fill effects such as gradients, textures, or patterns, you usually select the object to format, open the basic fill color palette, then click Fill Effects to open the Fill Effects dialog box. There may be multiple tabs in the dialog box, each one offering options for applying specific fill effects. Locate the effect you want to use, click it, and then click OK. To apply a stroke pattern, you usually select the object to format, open the basic stroke color palette, and then click Patterned Lines to open the Patterned Lines dialog box. Locate the pattern you want to use, click it, and then click OK.

Apply Patterns, Textures, and Gradients

Patterns are simply repetitive designs such as grids or hatchmarks. By default, they are black on white, but you can usually select a foreground color and a background color. Patterns may be applied to both fills and strokes. *Textures* are bitmap graphics files used as fills. You can select from a list of built-in textures, or select a picture file to use as a texture.

Gradients are a blend of colors that gradually change in brightness or tint. You usually select one or more colors to include in the gradient, and then select a pattern or style. For example, a *radial gradient* blends colors out from a central point, while a *linear gradient* blends the colors horizontally. There may be other gradient options available in your program as well, such as variations of the selected style or a list of preset colors and styles. Shadows and 3-D effects are applied to an entire object.

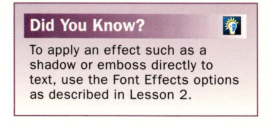

Did You Know?

To apply an effect such as a shadow or emboss directly to text, use the Font Effects options as described in Lesson 2.

S TEP-BY-STEP 5.2

1. In the **Coffee** file, select the star shape if it is not already selected.

2. Open the dialog box that contains options for applying texture fill effects. For example, click the **Fill Color** tool on the toolbar, click **Fill Effects**, and then click the **Texture** tab. If you are using a program such as PageMaker that does not offer texture effects, open the dialog box or menu for applying fill patterns.

3. Click a blue, heavy texture, such as Denim. Click the **OK** button as many times as necessary to apply the effect to the shape. It should look similar to Figure 5-4. If your program does not offer texture effects, select a large grid pattern.

STEP-BY-STEP 5.2 Continued

FIGURE 5-4
Texture fill effect

Fine coffee and tasty treats from around the world.

March 22

4. Open the dialog box that contains options for applying gradient fill effects. For example, click the **Fill Color** tool on the toolbar, click **Fill Effects**, and then click the **Gradient** tab. If your program does not offer gradient effects, open the dialog box or menu for applying fill patterns.

5. Click a radial gradient style that shades one color from the center out. Click the **OK** button as many times as necessary to apply the effect to the shape. If your program does not offer gradient effects, select a small grid pattern.

6. Open the dialog box or menu for applying stroke pattern effects. For example, click the **Line Color** button on the toolbar, click **Patterned Lines**, and then click the **Pattern** tab.

7. Click a dark horizontal line pattern, and then click the **OK** button as many times as necessary to apply the effect to the shape. The shape should look similar to Figure 5-5. If your program does not support patterned lines, select a 3-point dashed line as the stroke.

STEP-BY-STEP 5.2 Continued

FIGURE 5-5
Gradient fill and patterned line effects

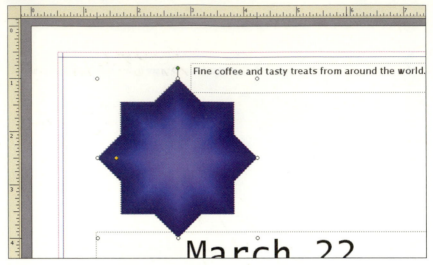

8. Save changes and leave the **Coffee** file open to use in the next exercise.

Apply Shadows and 3-D Effects

A *shadow* adds shading on one side of the outer edge of an object to create the illusion of depth and highlights. A 3-D effect also creates the illusion of depth by adding or extending shapes along one or two sides of an object. To apply a shadow, select the object to format, and then select the command to open a palette of available styles. For example, click the Shadow Style button on the toolbar. Click the style you want to apply. You may also be able to use toolbar buttons to adjust options such as the position, color, and size of shadows.

The procedure for applying 3-D effects is basically the same. Select the object to format, then click the button to open a palette of 3-D styles. For example, click the 3-D Styles button on the toolbar. Click the style you want to apply. You also may be able to use toolbar buttons to adjust options such as the depth, direction, tilt, and lighting of the 3-D effect.

Usually, you cannot combine shadows and 3-D effects on the same object. Not all desktop publishing programs have features for applying shadows and 3-D Effects. If you are using a program such as PageMaker that does not, skip the following exercise.

S TEP-BY-STEP 5.3

1. In the **Coffee** file, select the star shape and then open the dialog box or menu for applying a shadow. For example, click the **Shadow Style** button on the toolbar.

STEP-BY-STEP 5.3 Continued

2. Click the style that applies a long shadow extending from the bottom of the shape up and to the right. For example, select shadow style 12. It should look similar to Figure 5-6.

FIGURE 5-6
Shadow effect

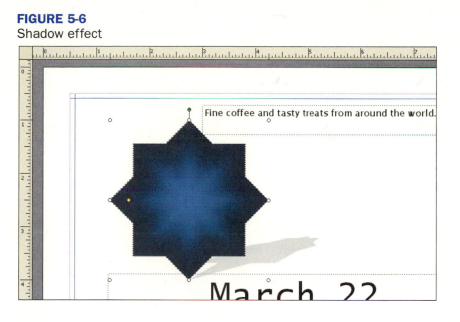

3. Open the dialog box or menu for applying 3-D effects. For example, click the **3-D Style** button on the toolbar.

4. Click the style that tilts the face of the object down and to the right, and extends the top and left sides of the object up and to the left. For example, select 3-D style 18. It should look similar to Figure 5-7.

FIGURE 5-7
3-D effect

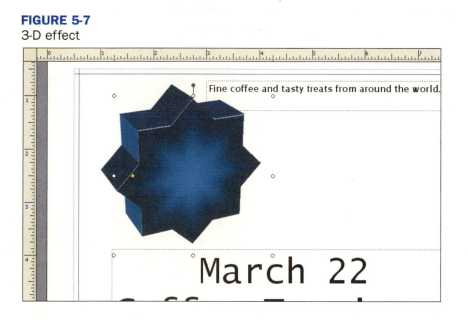

5. Save changes and leave the **Coffee** file open to use in the next exercise.

Enhance Text

In addition to formatting text with fonts and font formatting, many desktop publishing programs provide tools for creating sophisticated effects using text. Most programs have a feature for creating a *dropped capital*—sometimes called a *drop cap*—a decorative effect in which the first character in a paragraph is larger than the other characters. The drop cap may be offset to the left of the lines of text in the paragraph or inset to the right. Some programs offer a utility that lets you create text objects that include special effects formatting such as shadows and 3-D, and some programs let you simply add text to shapes.

Create Dropped Capitals

Dropped capital letters are often used to dress up the first paragraph of a chapter in a book or for emphasizing the first paragraph in a newsletter or magazine article. When you apply a dropped capital, the first letter in the paragraph is scaled to the specified size, which is usually measured in lines. In some programs, you can select additional options for formatting the dropped capital, including whether you want the character to drop down into the paragraph or extend up above the paragraph. You may also be able to select more than one character to drop and to change the font formatting. Some programs come with a selection of built-in dropped capital styles.

To apply a dropped capital, position the insertion point in the paragraph to format, and then open the Drop Cap dialog box. For example, click Format on the menu bar, and then click Drop Cap, or click Utilities on the menu bar, click Plug-ins, and then click Drop cap. Some Drop Cap dialog boxes have a tab displaying a list of built-in styles as well as a Custom Drop Cap tab

Note ☑

To remove a dropped capital, click in the formatted paragraph, open the Drop Cap dialog box, and click the Remove button.

that displays formatting options. Key the number of lines you want the character to drop, or select alternative formatting options, and then close the dialog box to apply the formats.

S TEP-BY-STEP 5.4

1. In the **Coffee** file, position the insertion point in the paragraph of text beginning with *The baristas*.

2. Open the Drop Cap dialog box. For example, click **Format** on the menu bar, and then click **Drop Cap**. Click the **Custom Drop Cap** tab, if necessary.

STEP-BY-STEP 5.4 Continued

3. Key **2** for the number of lines to drop the capital. Click the **OK** or **Apply** button to apply the dropped capital to the paragraph. It should look similar to Figure 5-8.

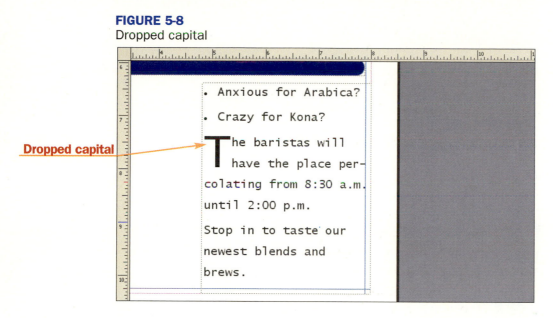

Dropped capital

4. Save changes and leave the **Coffee** file open to use in the next exercise.

Create Text Art

Some desktop-publishing programs, such as Publisher, have a feature that lets you turn your text into graphics objects. Creating an object from text characters lets you remove the constraints of the text box and adds flexibility in terms of formatting, sizing, and positioning the text. For example, you can format the object with special effects such as fills and shadows, scale it, and position it anywhere on the page. However, not all desktop publishing programs include a feature for creating text art. If you are using a program such as PageMaker that does not, you may be able to create a text art object in a different program and insert it into your publication.

To create a text art object, start the utility provided with your program. For example, click Insert on the menu bar, click Picture, and then click WordArt. Alternatively, click the appropriate toolbar button to start the utility. In most cases, you then select a style and click OK. Key the text you want included in the object and select font formatting. Click OK to create the object.

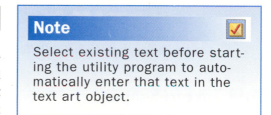

Note

Select existing text before starting the utility program to automatically enter that text in the text art object.

You can use standard techniques to format the entire object, such as scaling, moving, and rotating. In addition, buttons on a toolbar enable you to modify the text art itself. For example, you may be able to change the shape, edit the text, or select a different style for the text. Other options may include changing to vertical text, adjusting character height and spacing, and selecting an alignment.

STEP-BY-STEP 5.5

1. In the **Coffee** file, delete the text box that contains the text *March 22 Coffee Tasting*.

2. Start the utility for creating text art. For example, click the **Insert WordArt** button on the toolbar. If your program does not support text art, locate and insert **DP Step 5-5** from the data files into the **Coffee** file and then continue with step 5 below.

3. Click a style that displays simple black text in a shape that arcs up in the middle, and then click the **OK** button.

4. Key the text **Coffee Tasting** to replace the sample text, and then click the **OK** button. Your program creates the text object and inserts it in the publication.

5. Resize the object to 1.25 inches high by 6.5 inches wide.

6. Position the object vertically 4.25 inches from the upper-left corner and horizontally 1 inch from the upper-left corner (centered between the left and right margins). It should look similar to Figure 5-9.

FIGURE 5-9
Text as a graphics object

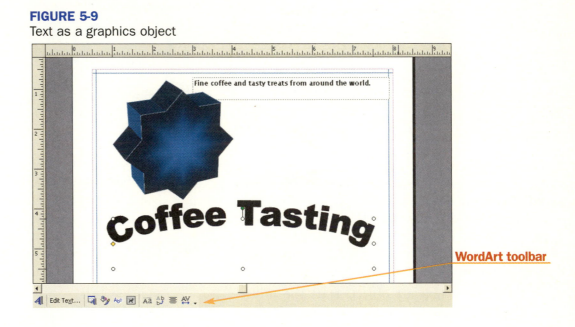

WordArt toolbar

7. Save changes and leave the **Coffee** file open to use in the next exercise.

Add Text to Shapes

In some programs, such as Publisher, you can add text to shapes inserted in a publication. Simply select the shape and key the text. The program automatically inserts a text box that is sized and positioned to constrain the text within the shape. You can key and format the text as you would in any text box. Not all programs—including PageMaker—have a feature for adding text to shapes, but you may be able to create the same effect by layering a text box on top of the shape.

S TEP-BY-STEP 5.6

1. In the **Coffee** file, select the star shape.

2. Key the text **March 22**. If your program does not support adding text to shapes, insert a text box or frame sized to fit within the star. Format the text box with no fill and no stroke, and then key the text in the text box.

3. Select the text and format it as follows: Use a serif font such as Times New Roman. Set the font size to 36 points and set the font color to white. (If the text does not show up well in white, use black.) Center-align the text vertically and horizontally in the text box. It should look similar to Figure 5-10.

FIGURE 5-10
Text added to a shape

4. Save changes and leave the **Coffee** file open to use in the next exercise.

Insert Horizontal Rules

Horizontal rules are printing lines that can be inserted before or after a paragraph of text. In most programs, you apply a rule using a dialog box such as Horizontal Rules or Paragraph Rules. First, position the insertion point in the paragraph to be formatted. Next, open the dialog box for applying rules and select the option to apply a rule before the paragraph and/or after the paragraph. For example, click Format on the menu bar, and then click Horizontal Rules. Or, click Type on the menu bar, click Paragraph, and then click the Rules button. Select formatting options for each rule. For example, select the line weight, the line style, and the line color. You can also specify to indent the rule from the left and/or right text box margin, and you may be able to specify how much space to leave between the text and the rule. Click OK to apply the rule. To remove a rule, open the dialog box and deselect the option for applying the rule before and/or after the paragraph.

STEP-BY-STEP 5.7

1. In the **Coffee** file, click in the first bullet item, and then open the dialog box for applying horizontal rules.

2. Select options to apply a 2-point, single-line rule before the paragraph. Change the line color to the custom blue you created earlier in this lesson, then click the **OK** button as many times as necessary to close all dialog boxes and apply the rule.

3. Position the insertion point in the last paragraph of text in the same text box and open the dialog box for applying horizontal rules.

4. Select options to apply a 2-point, single-line rule after the paragraph. Change the line color to the custom blue you created earlier in this lesson, and then click the **OK** button as many times as necessary to close all dialog boxes and apply the rule. When deselected, the text box should look similar to Figure 5-11.

FIGURE 5-11
Horizontal rules applied before and after paragraphs

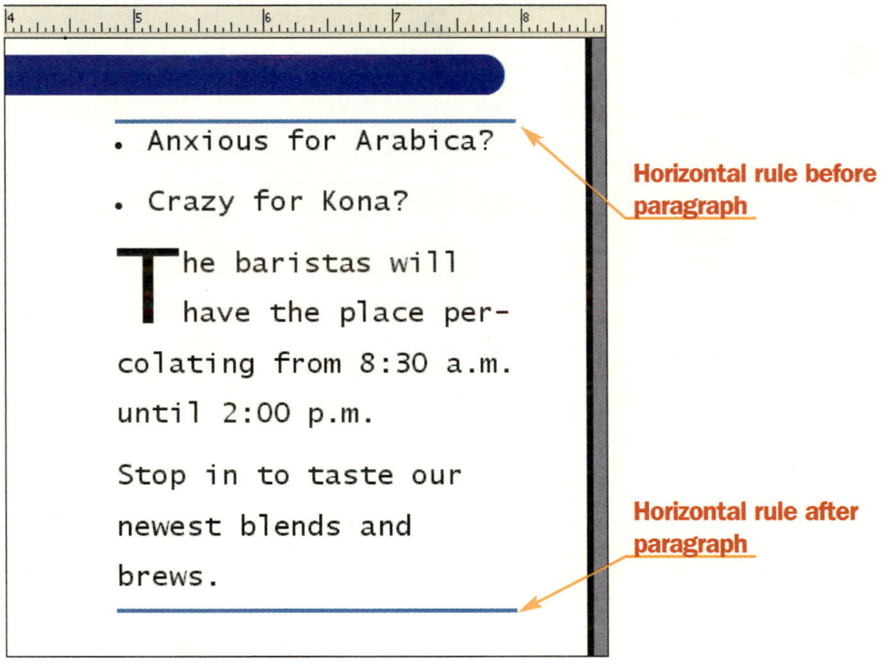

- Anxious for Arabica?

- Crazy for Kona?

Horizontal rule before paragraph

The baristas will have the place percolating from 8:30 a.m. until 2:00 p.m.

Stop in to taste our newest blends and brews.

Horizontal rule after paragraph

5. Save changes and leave the **Coffee** file open to use in the next exercise.

Apply Border Art

Some desktop-publishing programs, such as Publisher, come with a collection of built-in border art pictures you can apply around rectangular objects such as text boxes and squares. To apply border art, select the object, and then open the Format *Object* dialog box. Click the Border Art button to open the Border Art dialog box. Click the border you want to apply, and then click OK. Click OK again to close the Format *Object* dialog box and apply the border.

In some programs, you can create a custom picture border. Simply click the Create Custom button in the Border Art dialog box and then click the Select Picture button. Locate and select the picture file you want to use, and then click OK. Key a name for the new border and then click OK again. The new border is added to the list of available borders.

> **Note** ☑
>
> To create a page border, draw a text box the size of the margins on the master page, and then apply a border to it. The border then appears in the background on all pages in the publication.

S TEP-BY-STEP 5.8

1. In the **Coffee** file, select the text box containing the slogan at the top of the page.

2. Open the Border Art dialog box. For example, click **Format** on the menu bar, click **Text Box**, click the **Colors and Lines** tab, and then click the **Border Art** button. If you are using a program such as PageMaker that does not have a feature for applying border art, apply a blue 6-point triple line stroke on all sides of the object, and then skip to step 4.

3. Select the **Classical Wave** border, and then click the **OK** button as many times as necessary to close all dialog boxes and apply the border. If the Classical Wave border is not available, select any border.

4. Center-align the text horizontally in the text box. If the text appears too close to the border, align it vertically in the text box as well, or resize the text box if necessary.

5. Select the star shape and align it on the left, relative to the left and right margins. The page should look similar to Figure 5-12.

FIGURE 5-12
Border art around a text box

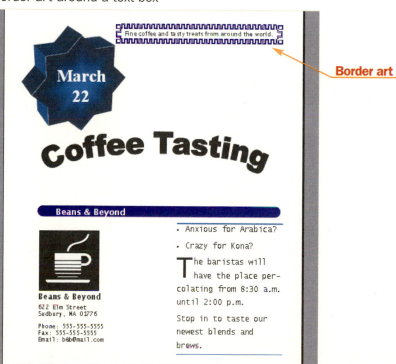

6. Save changes and leave the **Coffee** file open to use in the next exercise.

Create a Watermark

A *watermark* is a semitransparent image usually inserted in the background of printed publications. Watermarks can be found on many types of publications but are often used on stationery, business cards, and even currency and checks, as they are difficult to forge and can be proof of authenticity. In most programs, watermarks must be created from a picture file. You insert the picture file on the page and adjust its size and position. Then, adjust the image control settings to make the picture semitransparent. The image control settings may be in a dialog box or on a toolbar, such as the Picture toolbar. Send the image to the back of the stacking order so it is layered behind all other objects on the page.

Some programs have options that automatically adjust the color and transparency to settings appropriate for a watermark. For example, in some programs you click the Color button on the Picture toolbar and then click Washout. In other programs, you must manually adjust the settings to at least 70%. For example, click Element on the menu bar, click Image, and then click Image Control. Increase the lightness and contrast settings as necessary (click Apply to see the change without closing the dialog box), and then click OK.

Most programs let you control the transparency of any image, but some programs, such as Adobe PageMaker, provide image control only for black and white or grayscale bitmaps. In that case, you may need to convert an image to grayscale in a different program and then insert it into your publication.

> **Extra for Experts**
>
> If you want to use an object that is not a picture file, you can save it as a picture. Right-click the object and click Save as Picture on the shortcut menu to open the Save As dialog box. Key a name, select a storage location, and then click the Save button.

> **Note**
>
> If you want a watermark to appear on every page of a publication, insert it on a master page.

STEP-BY-STEP 5.9

1. In the **Coffee** file, delete the picture of the cup of coffee near the lower-left corner of the page.

2. Change to Master Page view.

3. Insert the picture file **DP Step 5-9** from the data files on the master page.

4. Resize the picture to approximately 7.5 inches high by 7.5 inches wide, and center it horizontally and vertically relative to the page margins.

STEP-BY-STEP 5.9 Continued

5. Set the image control to washout, or set the lightness to 85% and the contrast to somewhere between 20% and 50%, then click the **OK** button.

6. Switch back to regular page view. The page should look similar to the one in Figure 5-13.

FIGURE 5-13
Watermark in the background

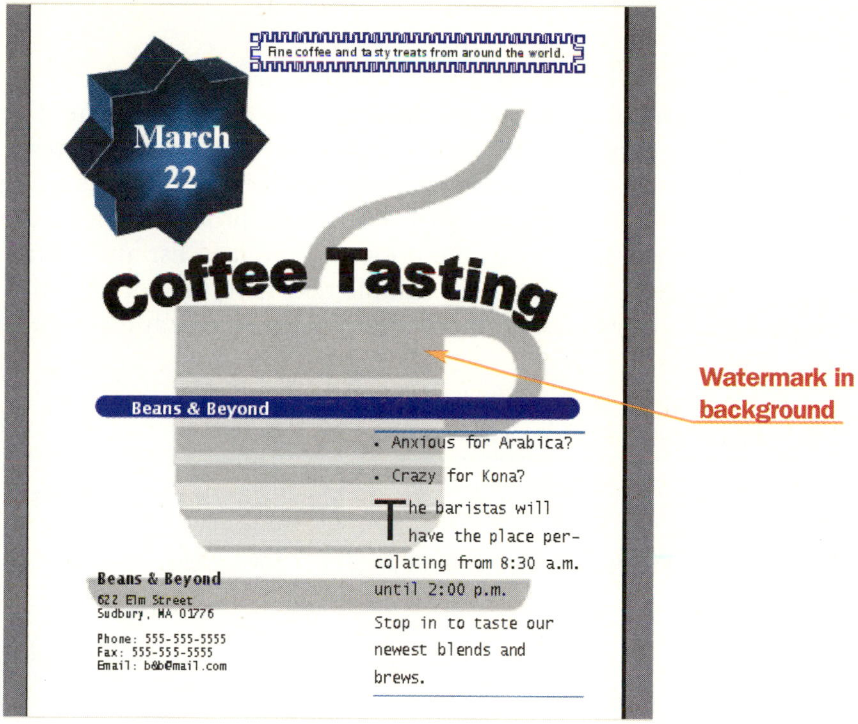

Watermark in background

7. Print one copy of the **Coffee** file.

8. Save changes and close the **Coffee** file. Leave your desktop publishing program open to use in the next exercise.

Use Design Objects

Many desktop-publishing programs, including Publisher, come with tools for automatically setting up and formatting elements of a publication that otherwise have to be created manually. For example, you may be able to quickly insert such features as tables of contents, logos, forms, pull-quotes, and mastheads. Unfortunately, not all desktop publishing programs include tools for automating the creation of these features. If you are using a program such as PageMaker that does not, you can manually insert and format text and graphics and design these features on the page.

If your program includes pre-designed publication elements, they are probably listed in a design gallery or dialog box. To open the gallery, click the Design Gallery Object button on the toolbar, or click Insert on the menu bar, and then click a command such as Design Gallery Object. In the gallery, click the category of the element you want to create, click the design you want to use, and then click Insert. The element is inserted as an object, or a group of objects, in the publication. You can customize the object by replacing sample text and graphics, by sizing it and positioning it on the page, and even by changing formatting. For example, you can change the font or color scheme or apply special effects.

Mastheads

A *masthead* is simply the information displayed across the top of a newsletter or newspaper, including, but not limited to, the title, the date, and the volume number. A masthead usually includes graphics elements such as borders or rules. Some include quotes, slogans, color, and pictures. You can set up a masthead manually by positioning text boxes and graphics across the top of the page and applying formatting. However, if your program can automatically set up a masthead, you can easily select one from the program's built-in list and insert it in your publication. To customize the masthead, replace the sample text with the correct information and make any formatting changes you want, such as modifying the color or font scheme.

S TEP-BY-STEP 5.10

1. In your desktop publishing program, open **DP Step 5-10** from the data files.

2. Save the file as **Brew**. This is the front page of a newsletter.

3. Open the gallery or dialog box that lists available design objects. For example, click **Insert** on the menu bar and then click **Design Gallery Object**.

> **Note** ✅
>
> If your program does not offer design objects, you can set up the masthead yourself using text boxes and formatting. Ask your instructor for more information.

4. Select the **Masthead** category, and then click the **Accessory Bar** masthead design. Click the **Insert Object** button to insert the object into the publication.

5. Align the object vertically with the top of the page, relative to the page margins.

6. Replace the sample text *Newsletter Title* with the text **What's Brewing?**

STEP-BY-STEP 5.10 Continued

7. Replace the sample text *Business Name* (or *Your organization*) with the text **Beans & Beyond**.

8. Replace the sample text *Newsletter Date* with the text **Spring/Summer**.

9. Change the color scheme to Sienna. The top portion of the newsletter should look similar to Figure 5-14.

FIGURE 5-14
Masthead object in publication

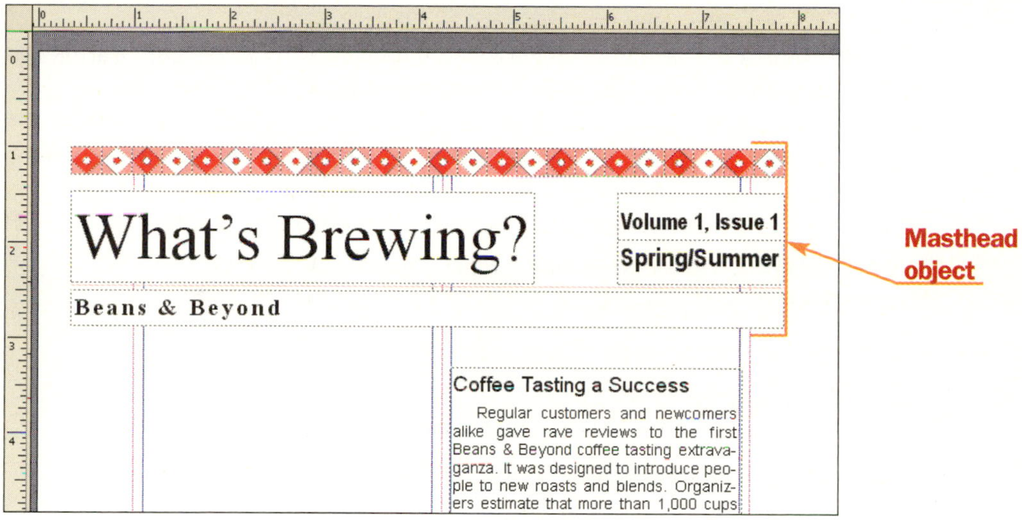

10. Save changes and leave the **Brew** file open to use in the next exercise.

Tables of Contents

Use a *table of contents* to direct the reader to specific articles, stories, or chapters in a publication. Although traditionally associated with long publications, a table of contents can be useful in short publications such as newsletters, as well. A table of contents usually includes a list of the headlines or titles on the left and the page numbers where the items begin on the right. It may or may not have *dot leaders* along the line between the two columns.

Extra for Experts

A few programs, including Page-Maker, have features for generating a table of contents that automatically updates the page numbers if you add, delete, or rearrange content. First, you apply styles to mark the paragraphs you want to include in the table, and then you select the command to generate the table and insert it in a text box.

If your program can automatically set up a table of contents, you simply select the design you want to use, replace the sample text with the correct headlines, titles, and page numbers, and then size and position the object in the publication. If you are using a program such as PageMaker that does not include design objects, either manually create a table of contents as shown in Figure 5-15, or skip the following exercise.

S TEP-BY-STEP 5.11

1. In the **Brew** file, open the gallery or dialog box that lists available design objects.

2. Select the **Tables of Contents** category, and then select the **Accessory Bar** design. Click the **Insert Object** button to insert the object into the publication.

3. Size and position the object to fit in the left column between the masthead and the existing article.

4. Replace the list of titles (*Inside Story*) with the following list so it looks similar to Figure 5-15:

   Perc or Drip? Which Brewing Method's Right for You

   Costa Rica: A Central American Paradise

   Meet the Owner: An Interview with Vera McGill

   Letters to the Editor

   Just for Laughs

   Check This Out! Links to Interesting Web Sites

   Taste Test

FIGURE 5-15
Table of contents in publication

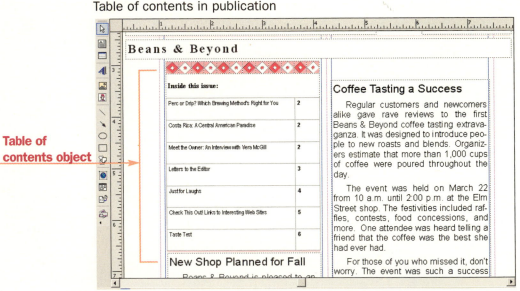

Table of
contents object

5. Save changes and leave the **Brew** file open to use in the next exercise.

Logos

A *logo* is a symbol representing a company or organization, which may include text, graphics, or both. Usually, logos are designed using a different program, such as a graphics program, or by hand, but they are often printed in publications as part of stationery *letterheads*, in the masthead of a newsletter, or even as a watermark. A letterhead is the area on a sheet of stationery where the name, address, and other information about a company or individual are printed. If a logo has been saved as a graphics file, you can simply insert it in a publication as you would any graphics file. If it has been drawn or printed, you can scan it in. If you don't have an existing logo, you may be able to use your desktop publishing program to create one by inserting, sizing, and positioning text and graphics.

If you are using a program such a Publisher that can automatically create a logo, you simply select the logo design you want to use, replace the sample text with the name of your organization, and then replace the sample picture with the picture of your choice. You can size and position the logo anywhere in the publication. The result is a professional-looking logo in minutes.

S TEP-BY-STEP 5.12

1. In the **Brew** file, open the dialog box or gallery that lists available design objects. Alternatively, insert the graphics file **DP Step 5-12a** into the white space in the lower-right corner of the page, and then skip to step 6.

2. Select the **Logos** category, and then select the **Open Oval Logo** design. Click the **Insert Object** button to insert the object into the publication.

3. Drag the object over into the white space in the lower-right corner of the page.

4. Replace the picture (the pyramid shape above the text) with the picture file **DP Step 5-12b** from the data files.

5. Replace the sample text with the text **Beans & Beyond**.

STEP-BY-STEP 5.12 Continued

6. Resize the object to fill the white space—about 3 inches wide by 1.5 inches high. When you are finished, the whole page should look similar to Figure 5-16.

FIGURE 5-16
Completed page

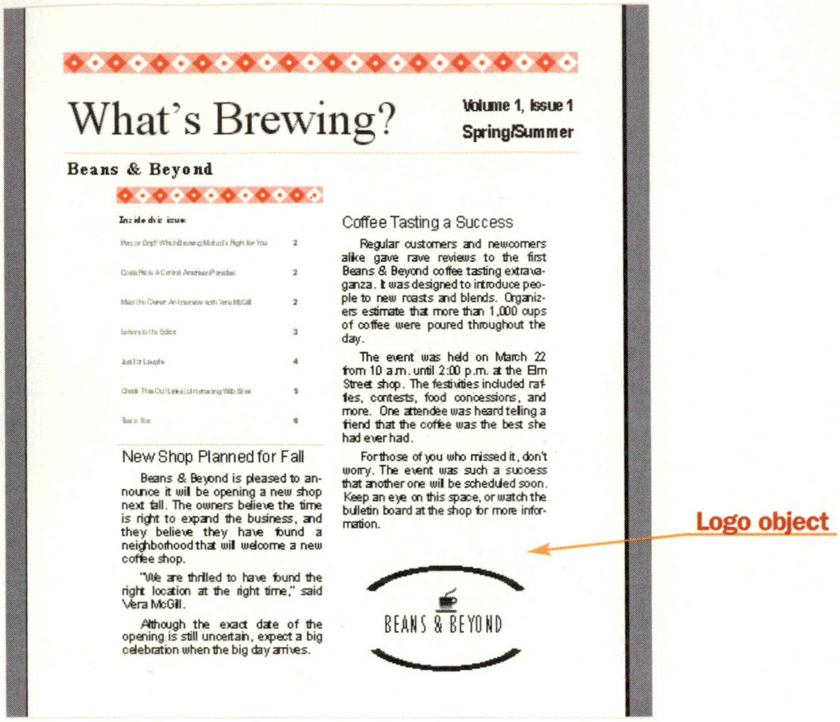

What's Brewing?

Volume 1, Issue 1
Spring/Summer

Beans & Beyond

New Shop Planned for Fall

Beans & Beyond is pleased to announce it will be opening a new shop next fall. The owners believe the time is right to expand the business, and they believe they have found a neighborhood that will welcome a new coffee shop.

"We are thrilled to have found the right location at the right time," said Vera McGill.

Although the exact date of the opening is still uncertain, expect a big celebration when the big day arrives.

Coffee Tasting a Success

Regular customers and newcomers alike gave rave reviews to the first Beans & Beyond coffee tasting extravaganza. It was designed to introduce people to new roasts and blends. Organizers estimate that more than 1,000 cups of coffee were poured throughout the day.

The event was held on March 22 from 10 a.m. until 2:00 p.m. at the Elm Street shop. The festivities included raffles, contests, food concessions, and more. One attendee was heard telling a friend that the coffee was the best she had ever had.

For those of you who missed it, don't worry. The event was such a success that another one will be scheduled soon. Keep an eye on this space, or watch the bulletin board at the shop for more information.

7. Print one copy of the **Brew** file.

8. Save changes and close the file. Close your desktop-publishing program.

SUMMARY

In this lesson, you learned:

- The RGB color system is used to define color on monitors, and the CMYK color system is used to define color in print.
- You can define custom colors by using a color bar or by keying a color system value.
- You can add a gradient, pattern, or texture to a fill, and a pattern to a stroke.
- Shadows and 3-D effects create the illusion of depth on the page.

- A dropped capital is a decorative effect that makes the first letter in a paragraph stand out from the rest of the text.

- Some programs have utilities that let you turn text into graphics objects, and some programs let you add text to shapes.

- You can insert horizontal rules before and/or after a paragraph.

- Some programs let you apply pictures as borders around rectangular objects.

- You can insert a watermark in the background of any page in a publication.

- Some programs come with objects already designed for use as logos, mastheads, and tables of contents.

VOCABULARY *Review*

Define the following terms:

CMYK	Letterhead	Spot color
Color system	Logo	Table of contents
Dot leader	Masthead	Texture
Dropped capital	Pattern	Tint
Gradient	Process color	Transparency
Horizontal rule	RGB	Watermark
Hue	Shadow	

REVIEW *Questions*

TRUE / FALSE

Circle T if the statement is true or F if the statement is false.

T (F) **1.** The color system used for displaying colors on a monitor is called CMYK.

(T) F **2.** CMYK values are usually entered as percentages.

T (F) **3.** Transparency measures the amount of white added to a color.

(T) F **4.** Patterns may be applied to both fills and strokes.

(T) F **5.** A radial gradient blends colors out from a central point.

T (F) **6.** All desktop publishing programs have features for transforming text into graphics objects.

T *F* 7. You can place rules only on the left and right of a paragraph of text.

T F 8. Watermarks are sometimes used as proof of authenticity.

T F 9. Logos may be included as part of a letterhead.

T *F* 10. A shadow is the only special effect that creates the illusion of depth.

3 - P effects

WRITTEN QUESTIONS

Write a brief answer to the following questions.

1. Name at least two reasons for using spot color when printing a publication.

2. What is the difference between a texture fill and a pattern fill?

3. What is a common use for a dropped capital?

4. List at least two benefits of converting text to a graphics object.

5. Name at least two ways to apply borderlines to text boxes.

FILL IN THE BLANK

Complete the following sentences by writing the correct word or words in the blanks provided.

1. A(n) _logo_ is a symbol representing a company or organization.

2. Use a(n) _table of contents_ to direct a reader to specific articles, stories, or chapters in a publication.

3. A(n) _watermark_ is a semitransparent image usually inserted in the background of printed publications.

4. A(n) _drop cap_ is a decorative effect in which the first character in a paragraph is larger than the other characters.

5. Use a(n) _linear_ gradient to blend colors horizontally across a shape.

6. _brightness_ is the range of a color from black to white.

7. To make a color completely see-through, set the _transparency_ to 100%.

8. The colors of ink used in four-color printing are often called _process_ color.

9. The Pantone Matching System is an example of a(n) _spot_ color system.

10. The *K* in CMYK stands for _black_.

PROJECTS

PROJECT 5-1

1. Launch your desktop publishing program and create a new blank full-page document with 1-inch margins.

2. Save the file as **GHA.** You are going to design letterhead stationery for a medical office.

3. Change to Master Page view. Because you want the letterhead information displayed on all pages, you will insert the data on the master page.

4. Insert a horizontal ruler guide at 2 inches on the vertical ruler, and another one at 9 inches on the vertical ruler.

5. Insert a text box 7 inches wide by 1.5 inches high. Align the bottom of the text box on the top ruler guide, and center it horizontally between the margins.

6. Insert and format text as follows:
   A. On the first line in the text box, use a 36-point serif font such as Sylfaen and key **Good Health Associates, Inc.**
   B. Center the text horizontally and vertically in the text box.
   C. Insert a 1-point horizontal rule below the paragraph, sized to extend from the left margin to the right margin.

7. Insert another text box 7 inches wide by 1.5 inches high. Align the top of the text box on the bottom ruler guide, and center it horizontally between the margins.

8. Insert and format text as follows:
    A. On the first line in the text box, use the same serif font you used in step 6 in 14 points to key **320 Matheson Street ~ Healdsburg, California ~ 95448**, and then press **Enter**.
    B. Key **Telephone (707) 555-5555 ~ Fax (707) 555-6666 ~ Email mail@gha.com**.
    C. If the tilde characters (~) appear too high in relation to the other text on the line, format them using the Subscript font effect.
    D. Center all lines horizontally, and align them vertically with the bottom of the text box.
    E. Position the insertion point in the first line of text, and insert a 1-point horizontal rule above the paragraph, sized to extend from the left margin to the right margin.

9. Insert a heart shape near the top of the page, sized at 0.5 inches by 0.5 inches. (If you cannot draw a heart using your program's drawing tools, draw a different shape such as a star.) Format the shape as follows:
    A. Position the shape horizontally 1 inch from the upper-left corner and vertically 0.5 inches from the upper-left corner. Set the text wrap to None.
    B. Open the custom color dialog box and select the CMYK system.
    C. Enter the following values: Cyan: **0**; Magenta: **55**; Yellow: **15**; Black: **0**. Name the color if necessary.
    D. Click the **OK** button until all dialog boxes are closed and the color is applied.
    E. If possible, apply a 3-D effect to the shape, such as style 10, which tilts the face down and to the right and extends the top and left sides.

10. Use the **Copy** and **Paste** commands to duplicate the shape. Flip or reflect the shape horizontally, and then position the duplicate horizontally 1 inch from the upper-right corner and vertically 0.5 inches from the upper-right corner.

11. Create a watermark as follows:
    A. Insert a clip art picture of a medical staff. If you cannot locate a suitable picture, use **DP Project 5-1** from the data files.
    B. Set the image control color to washout, or adjust the lightness and contrast as necessary. (Try 85% lightness and somewhere between 15% and 55% contrast.)
    C. Size the picture to about 5.5 inches square, and center it horizontally and vertically relative to the margins.

12. Change back to regular view.

13. Print one copy of the publication.

14. Save changes and close the **GHA** file. Leave your desktop publishing program open to use in Project 5-2.

PROJECT 5-2

1. In your desktop publishing program, open **DP Project 5-2** from the data files. This is a version of the CNO Newsletter you worked on previously. You are going to enhance the document with borders, lines, dropped capitals, and other effects.

2. Save the file as **CNONews3**.

3. On page 1, insert a masthead design object in a simple style, such as Checkers. Format the object as follows. (If your program does not have masthead design objects, use text boxes to insert the masthead information.)
   A. Center the object horizontally between the left and right margins, and position it 0.5 inches from the upper-left corner of the page.
   B. Replace the sample text *Newsletter Title* with the text **CNO News**.
   C. Replace the sample text *Business Name* (or *Your organization*) with the text **Community Network Organization**.
   D. Replace the sample text *Newsletter Date* with the text **Fall/Winter**.
   E. Change the color scheme to Harbor, or any scheme that uses dark green. If no color schemes are available, create a custom dark green. (For example, CMYK: C: **67**; M: **31**; Y: **37**; K: **36**.) If the green appears too dark, select or create a brighter green.

4. On page 1, insert a table of contents design object in the same style you used for the masthead. Format the object as follows. (If your program does not have table of contents design objects, use text boxes to insert the information.)
   A. Replace the first three story names (*Inside Story*) with the following: **Officer Nominations, Holiday Helpers Needed, Letters to the Editor**. Each story is on page 2.
   B. Delete the remaining items in the table. (Select all of the information, click **Table** on the menu bar, click **Delete**, and then click **Rows**.)
   C. Size and position the object to fit in the white space in the lower-right corner of the page.

5. Position the insertion point in the first paragraph under the headline *Annual Fundraiser*, and apply a dropped capital letter sized to drop 3 lines. Adjust the text box depth, if necessary, to display all text again.

6. Position the insertion point in the headline text *Volunteer News*, and apply a 2-point dark green horizontal rule before the paragraph.

7. Switch to page 2 and select the text box containing the headline *Letters to the Editor*. Apply a simple art border, such as solid block checks, around the object. If your program does not have art borders, apply a heavy, dashed line border. If necessary, adjust the line spacing in the text box to 1 line, and the paragraph spacing to 6 points after each paragraph to fit all text in the text box.

8. Insert dark green 2-point horizontal rules before the first paragraph in each text box in the left column.

9. Position the insertion point in the first paragraph under the headline *Holiday Helpers Needed* and create a dropped capital letter that drops 2 lines. Adjust text boxes as necessary to show all text.

10. Print one copy of each page—either using double-sided printing or on two sheets.

11. Save changes and close the **CNONews3** file. Close your desktop publishing program.

SCANS ⊕ WEB PROJECT

For a history or social studies project, use the Internet to research a major holiday celebrated in a country other than the United States. For example, you might research the Indian holiday of Diwali, Chinese New Year, or Cinco de Mayo. Look for information about the history of the holiday and ways in which the holiday is observed or celebrated. When you have finished the research, use your desktop publishing program to create a greeting card for the holiday, including pictures and text.

SCANS ✋ TEAMWORK PROJECT

As a group, plan and design an advertisement for a travel destination you would like to visit. Think of four or five possible spots, and then vote to select one. Look up information about the location, either in books and magazines or on the Web. If you have time, you might contact a travel agent for information. Make a list of the highlights appealing to visitors, and try to think up a slogan or catch phrase that would catch a reader's attention. Locate pictures to illustrate the ad. Consider using a watermark, logo, or other design element.

When you have the information you need, plan the advertisement publication. Decide on the page setup, including the page size, sheet size, and orientation. For example, you may want to make a poster, a postcard mailer, or a banner. Mock-up the ad so you can see where to place text and graphics. When you are ready, use your desktop publishing program to create the publication document. Insert all text and objects, and position them on the pages so the document is appealing and easy to read. When you are finished, check the spelling and then print the publication.

CRITICAL*Thinking*

ACTIVITY 5-1

Use your desktop publishing program to design and create a book jacket for a book you have read, or for a report you are preparing. Plan the publication carefully, considering the page size and sheet size and all the components that must be included. For example, the document will be printed only on one side, but it will probably have five pages: a back page, a front page, and a spine (the strip along the binding between the back and front), as well as folds for the front and back covers. Use a ruler to measure the actual book so you know how large a sheet to use and how large the pages must be. Write the text and either create or locate the graphics, and then insert the data into the publication. Adjust the size and position of all objects, and enhance the publication using color, horizontal rules, and other effects. When you are satisfied with the publication, check the spelling, print it, and share it with your class.

PUBLISHING A DOCUMENT

OBJECTIVES

Upon completion of this lesson, you should be able to:

- Plan for publication.
- Perform prepress checks.
- Set properties for desktop printing.
- Enable trapping.
- Print a composite and color separations.
- Save a file for commercial printing.
- Deliver files to a commercial printer.

Estimated Time: 1.5 hours

VOCABULARY

Bleed

Camera-ready

Composite

Compress

Crop

Crop marks

PostScript

PostScript Printer
  Description file

Print properties

Printer's spreads

Proof

Publish

Reader's spreads

Separations

Trapping

A document created with a desktop publishing program is not really complete until it is *published*. Publishing is the method you use to output the document so you can distribute it to readers. The two main methods of publishing are printing the document on your desktop printer or having it printed by a commercial printer. A third option is to print a copy on your desktop printer, and then have it reproduced at a copy shop. In this lesson, you learn how to decide the type of publication best suited for a particular project and how to prepare a document for publishing.

Plan for Publication

You make some decisions regarding publication before you even start a project. As you learned in Lesson 1, you should always start by determining the physical aspects of the publication, such as page size, paper stock, method of binding, number of colors, and the number of copies you will need. And, of course, you must consider your budget. All these factors affect the decision of how to publish the completed document. For example, if your desktop printer cannot accommodate the paper size you want to use, you must consider a commercial printer. If you

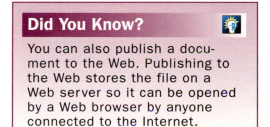

Did You Know?

You can also publish a document to the Web. Publishing to the Web stores the file on a Web server so it can be opened by a Web browser by anyone connected to the Internet.

plan to fold a booklet or staple a newsletter in the upper-left corner, you might not need a commercial printer. But if you want a more sophisticated binding you may have no other choice. Other things to consider include how fast you need the document published; the quality you expect in the finished product; and extra options, such as embossing or foil stamping.

Select a Publication Method

As mentioned, the basic choices for publishing a document are to use your desktop printer, a commercial printer, or a copy shop. Use the following guidelines for deciding which method is best for a particular job.

- In general, if you need only a few copies of a publication and are working within a tight budget, your desktop printer may be the best choice. Keep in mind, however, that the quality of the publication depends a great deal on the specific printer you are using. A laser printer provides the best quality output, followed by an inkjet printer. Other considerations include the time you must spend manning the printer, the cost of ink or toner, the necessity of folding or binding by hand, and whether your printer can handle the project specifications such as page size, color, or double-sided printing.

- Use a copy shop if you need to produce many copies, if you have a tight budget, or if you need the publication in a hurry. A copy shop may also be able to handle folding or basic binding techniques such as stapling. When you use a copy shop, the quality of the finished product depends on the quality of the original being reproduced, as well as on the available equipment. Before you commit to a copy shop, consider generating a test copy so you can determine if it meets your standards.

- Finally, you should use a commercial printer if you want the highest quality product and if you can afford it. Other benefits of using a commercial printer include access to more binding options, the ability to handle special orders, and the knowledge and advice an experienced printer can provide.

Select a Commercial Printer

If you decide to use a commercial printer, then the next step is choosing one. The cost of the job should not be the only factor to influence your decision. You will have to work closely with the printer from the very outset of the project, so you should find someone you are comfortable with and who you trust. Following are some of the questions you should ask a commercial printer before you even begin designing the publication:

- What type of color will be used—spot, process, or a combination—and must you use a specific color matching system?

- Does the commercial printer want the document file in a particular format, such as PostScript, or is your program's file format suitable?

- How does the commercial printer want the file delivered? Can it be on a disk or CD or sent electronically on the Internet?

- Does the printer have in stock the type and quantity of paper you've selected?

- Does the printer have the necessary facilities for folding or binding the publication as required?

- What type of proof do you need to submit? Can you print a composite and color separations on your desktop printer, or does the printer require *camera-ready* film? Camera-ready film is film made of the finished pages that can be used to publish the document.

■ For bound or folded publications, should you submit pages formatted as *printer's spreads* or *reader's spreads*? Reader's spreads are basically facing pages—such as page 2 on the left and page 3 on the right. In printer's spreads, the pages are arranged in the order that they must be printed for the page order to be correct when the publication is bound. For example, in a 4-page folded booklet, page 4 is on the left of the sheet and page 1 is on the right of the sheet.

Did You Know?

Most desktop publishing programs automatically format multipage documents as printer's spreads. If you want to print reader's spreads for proofing, you probably have to select an option in the Print dialog box.

Perform Prepress Checks

No matter which method of publication you select, before you publish the document, you should be sure to use a spelling checker and to proofread the file for errors. (Checking spelling is covered in Lesson 1.) You should also look over the design and layout to determine if there are any improvements to make. For example, you may need to nudge the location of a headline in a newsletter, or expand the size of a text box so all the text is displayed.

Hot Tip

Often we read what we expect to read instead of what is really there. To catch spelling errors you might otherwise miss, try looking at the words in reverse order from the end of a story to the beginning. It's also a good idea to have someone else proofread as well.

Check Page Design

Some desktop-publishing programs, such as Publisher, include tools for checking the design of a publication. A design checker works similar to a spelling checker. It locates and highlights design problems, such as too much text to fit in a text box, and may find grammar and punctuation problems as well. To start the checker, click Tools on the menu bar, and then click Design Checker. The design checker may display a dialog box asking which pages to check. Click OK to check them all, or key the specific page numbers. Click OK to start the check. When the checker finds a problem, it displays a dialog box similar to the one in Figure 6-1. You can choose to ignore the problem, ignore all occurrences of the problem, or close the dialog box. You cannot continue the check until you select an option or fix the problem. You do not have to close the dialog box to fix the problem. Simply drag the box out of the way and work in the publication. Click the Explain button to start the Help program and display information about how to fix the problem. When the problem is corrected, click the Continue button to restart the check.

FIGURE 6-1
Design Checker dialog box

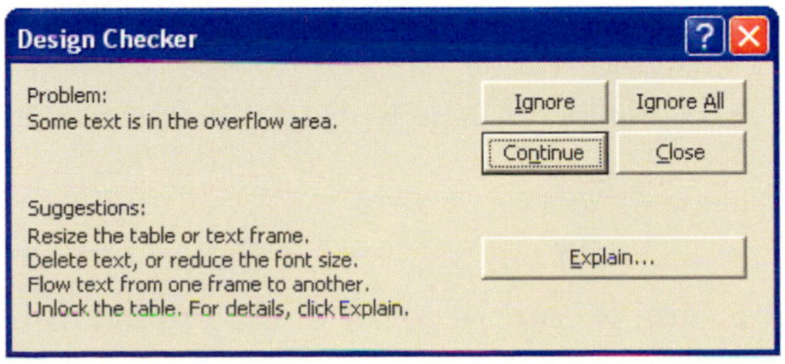

Design Checker	? ✕
Problem: Some text is in the overflow area.	Ignore Ignore All Continue Close
Suggestions: Resize the table or text frame. Delete text, or reduce the font size. Flow text from one frame to another. Unlock the table. For details, click Explain.	Explain...

If your program has a design checker, use it to complete the following exercise. If you are using a program such as PageMaker that does not have a design checker, you can complete the exercise simply by examining the publication on your computer screen to find problems and correct them.

STEP-BY-STEP 6.1

1. Launch your desktop publishing program, and open **DP Step 6-1** from the data files.

2. Save the file as **Mailer**. This publication is a version of the postcard mailer you used in previous lessons.

3. Run a spelling checker to identify spelling errors. If the checker finds any errors, correct them.

> **Note** ☑️
>
> If you do not have the fonts required for this file, check the data files for this lesson, or use another serif font, such as Times New Roman.

4. Start the design checker if one is available in your program. For example, click **Tools** on the menu bar, and then click **Design Checker**. Click the **OK** button to check the publication with the default settings. The program stops when it comes to the first problem—a text box that is too small to display all of the text it contains. If your program does not have a design checker feature, try to locate the text box on page 1 that is too small to display all text.

5. Select the problem text box, and resize it so it is about 1.3 inches high. You can do this by dragging the top sizing handle up or by keying the value in the appropriate dialog box. Once the box has been resized, all of the text appears. If necessary, move the text box up so it doesn't overlap other content on the page.

6. Click the **Continue** button to resume the check. A text box on page 2 is also too small to display all the text it contains. This time, correct the problem by changing the font size.

7. If your program has an AutoFit or Copy fitting feature, select it to automatically resize all the text in the text box to fit. If not, resize the text to 12 or 13 points.

8. Click the **Continue** button to resume the check. The checker should locate two spaces following a period in a text box on page 1. Typing two spaces after a punctuation mark is an incorrect keyboarding technique.

9. Delete one of the spaces. (If necessary, display nonprinting characters so you can see the spaces.)

10. Click the **Continue** button to resume the check. Correct or ignore any other problems that the Design Checker identifies, and then click the **OK** button to complete the check.

11. Save changes and leave the **Mailer** file open to use in the next exercise.

Print Page Proofs

You should always print a sample copy or *proof* of the publication to review before you print all copies or send the publication to a commercial printer. You should proofread the printout for spelling errors that your spelling checker does not catch, and for design problems such as inconsistent line weight, misaligned objects, or mismatched colors that show up more clearly in print. Also, you can see the entire publication at once, and even give it to someone else to check as well. For desktop printing, you can also use a proof to determine if the colors you have selected reproduce the way you expect.

Some desktop publishing programs and some desktop printers have options to control the quality of the output when you print proofs. For example, you may be able to set your desktop printer for a lower quality printing in order to use less ink, or, if you want to check the text but are not concerned with the graphics, you may be able to set your program so it does not print graphics objects. Likewise, if you want to simply scan the proof to see if objects are aligned, you may be able to print thumbnails of each page, which saves paper. These options are usually selected in the Print dialog box, or in one of the print or printer properties dialog boxes. You learn more about print properties in the next exercise.

Before printing, make sure the desktop printer is correctly set up for use with your computer. This means it is physically attached to your computer or network and the printer driver software has been correctly installed. You should also make sure that the proper size paper is correctly loaded in the printer and the printer is turned on. You may want to install fresh ink cartridges or toner to ensure the best color quality.

As you have already learned, to print a copy of a publication on your desktop or network printer, click File on the menu bar and then click Print. A Print dialog box similar to the one in Figure 6-2 opens. Set properties as necessary, and then click the OK or Print button in the Print dialog box to generate the file. Alternatively, to print a single copy of the document using the default settings, click the Print button on the toolbar.

FIGURE 6-2
Print dialog box

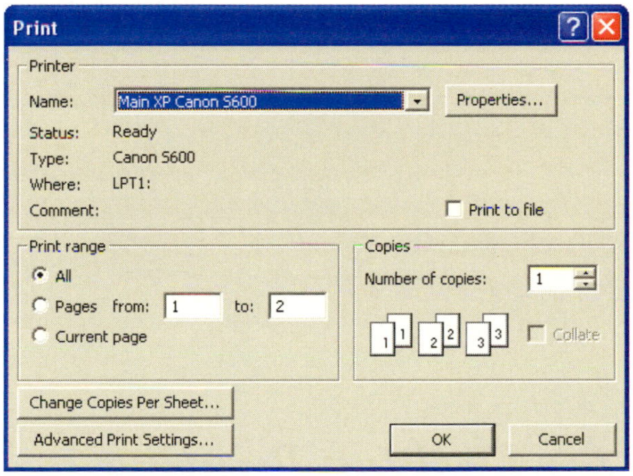

STEP-BY-STEP 6.2

1. With the **Mailer** file open in your desktop publishing program, click **File** on the menu bar and then click **Print**.

STEP-BY-STEP 6.2 Continued

2. If your printer is capable of different quality output, select the option for draft printing. This option is probably available in your printer's Properties dialog box, which should look similar to Figure 6-3. To open the dialog box, click a button such as **Properties** or **Setup** in the Print dialog box. Select an option such as Draft or Fast, and then click the **OK** button.

FIGURE 6-3
Properties dialog box for a Canon inkjet printer

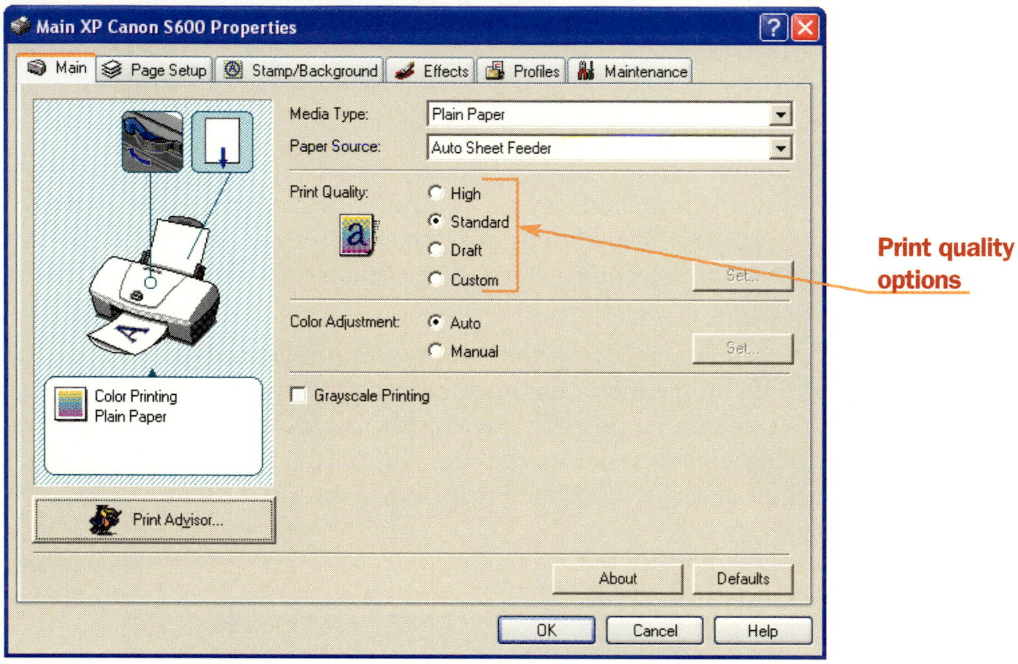

3. Click the **OK** or **Print** button to print one copy of each page on a separate sheet of paper.

4. Proofread the printout for spelling and design errors. There is one spelling error and one grammatical error that the spelling checker probably did not find. When you locate the errors, circle them on the printout in red, and then correct them in the file.

5. Save changes and leave the **Mailer** file open to use in the next exercise.

Set Properties for Desktop Printing

Print properties are the settings that control the way a publication prints on your desktop printer. They fall into two basic categories: *printer options*, which are specific to the printer model you are using; and *print options*, which are specific to the program and the publication document. For example, printer options may include the draft quality, while print options might include whether to print graphics or how many copies of a page to print on one sheet of paper.

You access the print properties through your program's Print dialog box. The available options and the way they are organized depend on your desktop publishing program, your printer, and the publication you are working with. Usually, however, you click a button such as

Properties or Setup to open your printer's Properties dialog box. You click a different button such as Advanced Print Settings or Options to open a Print Settings or Print Options dialog box, similar to the one in Figure 6-4. There may be other buttons for accessing other dialog boxes as well. In each dialog box, select the appropriate options, and then click OK to return to the Print dialog box. When you have set all the necessary properties, click the OK or Print button in the Print dialog box to print the publication.

FIGURE 6-4
Print Settings dialog box

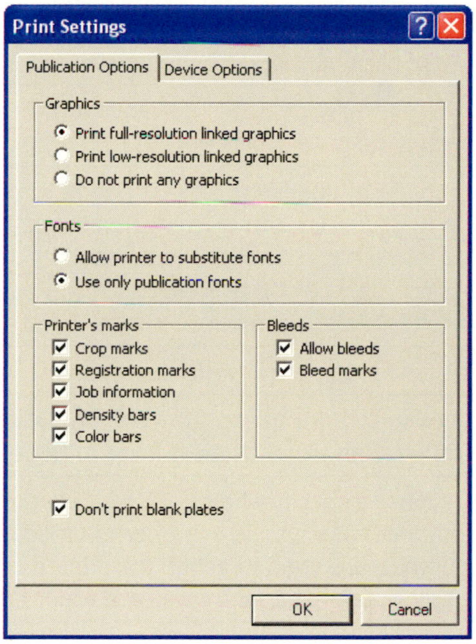

In addition to properties, keep in mind that certain types of publications require special setup or handling to print correctly. For example, duplex (double-sided) printing may require you to print one page, then reinsert the paper correctly in the printer to print the next page. Banners and posters may print on multiple sheets of paper, which must then be arranged to create the complete publication. Conversely, you may be able to print more than one postcard on the same sheet, and then trim them to size.

Some effects also require special handling. For instance, you print a *bleed*, which is an effect created by an object running off the edge of the page, by using options in the Page Setup dialog box to set the publication to print on a sheet size larger than the page size. Position the object in the document so it extends beyond the edge of the page. After printing, you *crop*, or trim, the paper to the appropriate page size.

Table 6-1 lists some common print properties. Keep in mind, however, that because the specific properties available on your computer depend on the printer and the program you are using, you may not have all the properties listed, or you may have more.

TABLE 6-1
Common print properties

PROPERTY	DESCRIPTION
Printer	Select the printer to print the document. Other options may change depending on the printer selected.
Number of copies	Key the number of copies of each page that you want to print.
Collate	Select this option to print pages consecutively. Deselect this option to print all copies of each page before proceeding to the next page.
Print range	Use these options to specify the exact pages to print. Select All to print all pages, key a range separated by a hyphen to print all pages within the range, and/or key specific page numbers separated by commas to print only those pages. Other options may be available, such as printing the current page only, printing only odd- or even-numbered pages, or printing blank pages.
Orientation	Select either landscape or portrait orientation.
Reverse	Select this option to print pages from the end of the document to the beginning, rather than from the beginning to the end.
Printer's marks	Use these options to specify whether to print elements such as **crop marks,** which indicate where the paper should be cut or trimmed down to the correct page size, or color bars, which are used to gauge the printed colors. Marks are displayed only if the paper size is at least 1 inch taller and wider than the page size.
Fonts	Use these options to specify whether to allow font substitution.
Page setup	Depending on your printer, you may be able to scale the output by a percentage of the original size or select an option to control the way the document fits on the printed page. For example, you may be able to select Poster printing or Banner printing, to print thumbnails of each page, and to choose how many copies of each page to print per sheet. Other options may include printing reader's spreads or printer's spreads and tiling the pages.
Graphics or Proof	Use these options to specify whether to include graphics in the printout.
Print quality	Select the quality level you want to use. The higher the quality, the better the output. This option usually determines the resolution, the amount of ink, or number of colors used to print a document.
Color	Use these options to specify grayscale, black and white, or four-color printing. In some programs, or for some publications, you may be able to set options for printing color separations, screens, and/or bleeds.

S TEP-BY-STEP 6.3

1. With the **Mailer** file open in your desktop publishing program, click **File** on the menu bar and then click **Print**.

2. If available, select the option for double-sided printing. You may find this option in your printer's properties dialog box. If the option is not available, select to print only page 1. This option is in the Print dialog box.

3. Select the option to print crop marks. You may find this option in the Print Settings or the Print Options dialog box.

4. Click in the Copies or Number of copies box and key **2**.

> ### Did You Know?
>
> Some desktop printers have a nonprintable region, which is the area on the top, bottom, left, and right of a page on which data cannot be printed. If your printer has a nonprintable region, it is listed in the printer-specific Properties dialog box. You should take your printer's nonprintable region into consideration when designing a document.

5. Click the **OK** or **Print** button to print two copies. If you have duplex printing, both sides of the postcard should print. If not, only page 1 should print. If both pages printed, skip to step 9. Otherwise, continue with the following steps to complete the publication.

6. Reinsert the printed sheets into your printer, positioned correctly to print page 2 on the reverse side.

7. In the **Mailer** file, make page 2 active, click **File** on the menu bar, and then click **Print**.

8. Select to print only page 2, and then repeat steps 3 through 5. You should now have two copies of the **Mailer** publication.

9. Using the crop marks as guides, trim the paper to the publication page size. You can use scissors, but to get a straighter edge, use a paper cutter.

10. Save changes and leave the **Mailer** file open to use in the next exercise.

Enable Trapping

Sometimes adjoining colors are printed slightly out of register, which means they are not aligned properly. When that happens, there may be gaps or overlaps between the colors. *Trapping* is a technique used to adjust the position of adjoining colors to avoid such gaps or overlaps. Most desktop publishing programs have automatic trapping that you can turn off or on. By default, your program uses typical trapping settings appropriate for most publications. You can adjust the trapping settings in most desktop publishing programs to fine-tune the way trapping is applied. For example, you may be able to specify the trap width or set custom trapping for objects.

To enable trapping for a publication, open the trapping preferences dialog box, which should look similar to Figure 6-5. For example, click Tools on the menu bar, click Commercial Printing Tools, click Trapping, and then click Preferences. In some programs, you simply click File on the menu bar, click Preferences, and then click Trapping. Select the option to enable trapping, and then click OK.

FIGURE 6-5
Trapping Preferences dialog box

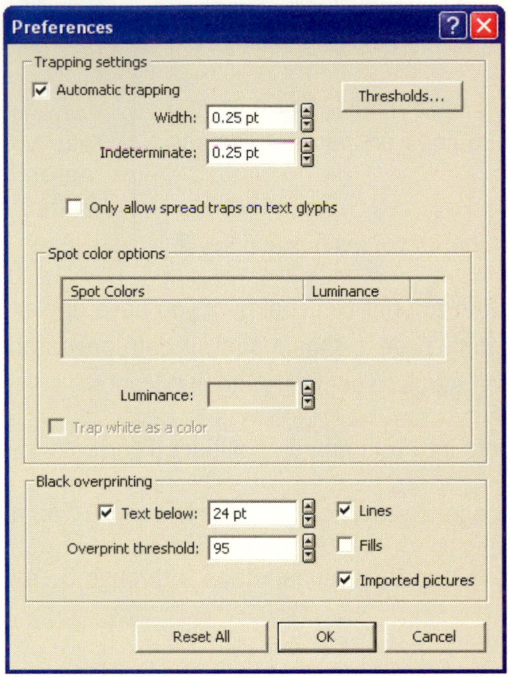

STEP-BY-STEP 6.4

1. In the **Mailer** file, open the trapping preferences dialog box.

2. Select the option to enable trapping, and then click the **OK** button.

3. Save changes and leave the **Mailer** file open to use in the next exercise.

Prepare a Composite and Color Separations

A commercial printer will probably want you to submit a final *composite* proof, which is an accurate copy of the publication, as well as *separations*, which are printouts showing the layout of each color—black, cyan, magenta, and yellow for process color printing, and each spot for spot color printing—on separate sheets of paper. A composite is the default method of printing. All components and all colors are printed on each page. You printed a composite of the Mailer file earlier in this lesson. If you want to print separations, you must select that option in the Print dialog box. You may also select whether to print a separation page for each color in the publication, or for only a selected color. Note that separations generally print in black and white because they are used to note the position of each color, not to match colors.

In some programs, such as PageMaker, the options for printing separations are always available in one of the print properties dialog boxes. In other programs, however, the color printing options are not available until you set up the file for commercial color printing.

Set Up a File for Commercial Color Printing

If you are using a program such as Publisher that requires you to set up the file for commercial color printing, click Tools on the menu bar, click Commercial Printing Tools, and then click Color Printing. A Color Printing dialog box similar to the one in Figure 6-6 is displayed. Select the type of printing process you want to use, and then click OK. You can select spot color, process color, or a combination of the two. Your program may also offer RGB or single-color options.

FIGURE 6-6
Color Printing dialog box

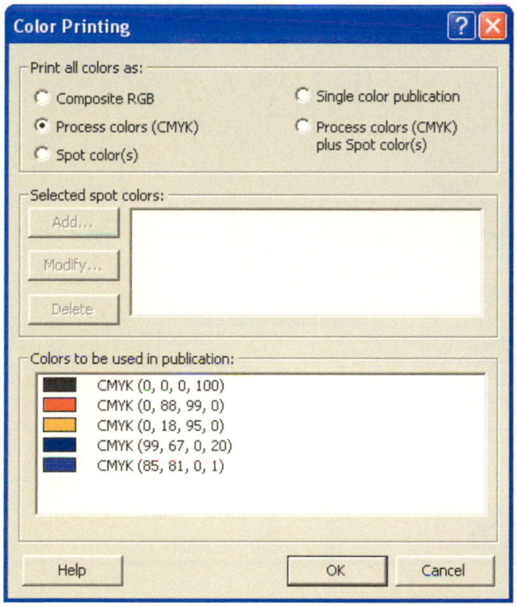

If you are using a program that requires you to set up the publication for commercial printing, complete the following exercise. If not, you can skip to the next exercise.

S TEP-BY-STEP 6.5

1. In the **Mailer** file, click **Tools** on the menu bar, click **Commercial Printing Tools**, and then click **Color Printing**.

2. Click the **Process colors (CMYK)** option button, and then click the **OK** button.

3. Save changes and leave the **Mailer** file open to use in the next exercise.

Print Separations

If your publication is set up for commercial printing, or if your program lets you print separations for all publications, the option for printing separations is found in a print properties dialog box. For example, click File and then click Print. If the Composite and Separations options are not listed, click the Color button. When you select the option to print separations, the list of available colors becomes active, as shown in Figure 6-7. Select All to print all colors, or select the specific color you want to print.

FIGURE 6-7
Options for printing separations

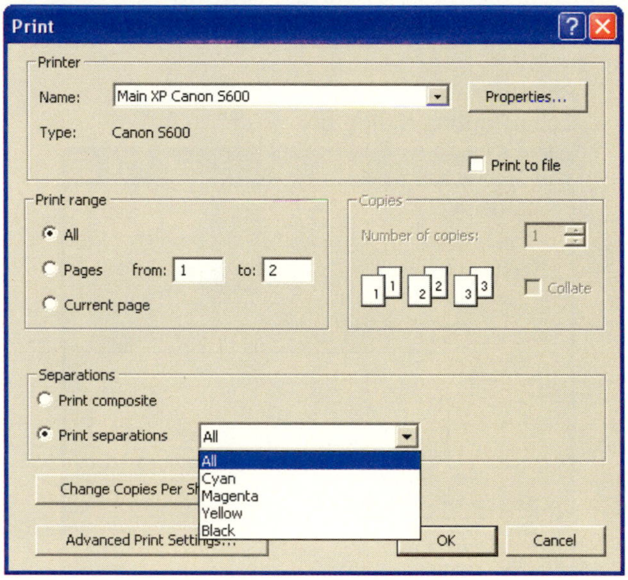

STEP-BY-STEP 6.6

1. In the **Mailer** file, click **File** on the menu bar, and then click **Print**. The Print dialog box opens. Select the option to print all separations. If the option is not listed in the Print dialog box, click the **Color** button and then select the option.

2. Click the **OK** or **Print** button to print the separations. One page prints for each color.

3. Save changes and leave the **Mailer** file open to use in the next exercise.

Save a File for Commercial Printing

Before you deliver a publication to a commercial printer, you must correctly prepare your publication files. Usually, that means saving the file in a format that the commercial printer can use and making sure that all graphics and fonts used in the publication are available. If your commercial printer uses the same program you use, or has the capability to convert your file, you may be able to submit the file in its native, or default, file format. You must, however, be sure that all graphics and fonts are embedded in the file, or you must submit the graphics and font files as well.

Luckily, most desktop publishing programs have a tool for preparing a file for commercial printing. This utility, which is usually called something like Pack and Go or Save For Service Provider, automatically sets up all the files needed to generate the publication, including the publication file, fonts, and graphics. In some cases, it actually packs all the files together in one new file. In other cases, it simply copies and organizes the necessary files.

If the commercial printer cannot use your file in its default file format, you may have to convert to a different format. Many commercial printers request files in *PostScript* format. PostScript is a page description language used to define page layout and design for printing specifically on PostScript printers, which are printers that use the PostScript language.

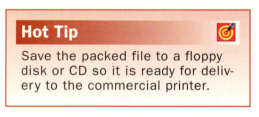

Hot Tip

Always consult your commercial printer before submitting files and proofs. Most printers have a list of requirements detailing exactly what you need to provide.

Pack the Publication Files

To reproduce the document correctly, the commercial printer must be able to open and use all components of the publication file including the fonts and graphics. If fonts and graphics are embedded in the publication, your commercial printer should be able to use them. You can manually make sure all the files are available, but it is easier to use a file preparation utility that comes with your desktop publishing program. In addition to compiling the necessary files and packing them into a single file, most programs also generate a list of the packed files, including information such as whether a font is embedded and a graphics file is linked. Usually, the utility also creates a Readme or Report file that contains information about the packed publication and possibly, how to extract the data.

The steps for using an automatic file preparation utility vary depending on the program you are using. Usually, you start the utility and then select options to control where the packed file is saved and exactly what is included in it. In any case, you start the utility by clicking File on the menu bar, clicking Pack and Go, and then clicking Take to a Commercial Printing

Hot Tip

Save the packed file to a floppy disk or CD so it is ready for delivery to the commercial printer.

Service. Select options, if necessary, and click the Next button to proceed through the steps necessary to complete the process. Alternatively, you may have to click Utilities on the menu bar, click Plug-ins, and then click Save For Service Provider. Select options and then click Package. Set options as desired, and then click Save.

The file preparation utility usually automatically names the files that it generates. It may use the name of the original publication file, or it may use a name such as packed01.

If your program does not have an automatic file preparation feature, you must make sure to deliver all font and graphics files to the commercial printer along with the publication file. Most printers will request a file list as well.

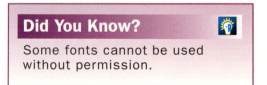

Did You Know?

Some fonts cannot be used without permission.

STEP-BY-STEP 6.7

1. Create a new folder named **DP Step 6-7** that you can use to store the packed files. Ask your instructor where to place the folder.

STEP-BY-STEP 6.7 Continued

2. In the **Mailer** file, start the file preparation utility that comes with your program. For example, click **File** on the menu bar, click **Pack and Go**, and then click **Take to a Commercial Printing Service**.

3. Click the appropriate button to continue. For example, click **Next**, or click **Package**.

4. Select or key the location where you want to store the packed file—the DP Step 6-7 folder you created in step 1—and then select the options you want to use for the packed file. You may have to click **Next** to select the options.

5. Click the **Save** or **Finish** button to complete the procedure. If a dialog box prompts you to print separations or composites, clear the selections, then click the **OK** or **Close** button to close the utility. The packed file is stored in the specified location.

6. Leave the **Mailer** file open to use in the next exercise.

Extra for Experts

Even if you do not use an automatic file preparation utility, your program may have tools for managing graphics and fonts. Consult your program's Help files for more information.

Save a PostScript File

Most desktop publishing programs have tools for converting a file to PostScript format. In some programs, you start off using the Save As command just as you do to save the file in any other format. However, if you select PostScript from the Save as type list and then click the Save button, the Save as PostScript File dialog box opens. You *must select a PostScript printer from the Printer list*, as well as other print properties for printing the PostScript file. Click the Save button to save the file. If you do not have a PostScript printer available, you will not be able to save the file in PostScript format.

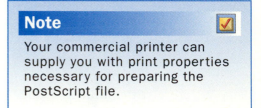

Note

Your commercial printer can supply you with print properties necessary for preparing the PostScript file.

In other programs, you create the PostScript file using the Print Options dialog box. Click File on the menu bar, and then click Print. From the Printer list, select a PostScript printer, and then select the appropriate *PostScript Printer Description file* (PPD), which is a file that provides information about the printing device, from the PPD list. (You should ask your commercial printer which printer and PPD to use.) Click the Options button, select the Write PostScript to File check box in the Print Options dialog box, and then key a name and specify a location for the PostScript file. Select additional printer options as necessary, and then click the Save button to save the file.

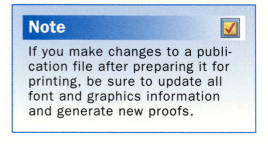

Note

If you make changes to a publication file after preparing it for printing, be sure to update all font and graphics information and generate new proofs.

STEP-BY-STEP 6.8

1. In the **Mailer** file, select the command for saving the file in PostScript format. In some programs, this is the **Save As** command on the **File** menu, and in other programs it is the **Print** command on the **File** menu.

STEP-BY-STEP 6.8 Continued

2. Select **PostScript** as the file type, or select a PostScript printer and PPD, and the option to write to a file.

3. If necessary, select the location where you want to store the file.

4. Click the **File name** box, and then key the filename **PSMailer**.

5. Select properties, or click the **Save** button to open the Save As PostScript File dialog box so you can select properties, including a PostScript printer if it is not already selected. You must select a PostScript printer in order to save the file in PostScript format.

6. Click the **Save** button to save the file. (If a message box appears, click **OK** to continue.)

7. Save and close the **Mailer** file and your desktop publishing program.

Extra for Experts

To save a copy of a publication file in a format other than PostScript, click File on the menu bar, click Save As, select the file format from the Save as type list, and then click the Save button. The formats in the Save as type list vary depending on the program you are using.

Deliver Files to a Commercial Printer

When the files are 100% ready to go, you must deliver them to the commercial printer. You usually have two choices for delivery: on removable media, such as a CD-R or CD-RW, or electronically via the Internet. Ask your printer which method you should use.

Remember, you may have to deliver the font and graphics files in addition to the publication file. Font files are stored in the Fonts folder, which is in the Windows folder on your hard drive (or network). A Fonts folder window is shown in Figure 6-8. Be sure to deliver font files for all styles of the font used in the publication. For example, include the bold and italic versions of the font.

FIGURE 6-8
Fonts folder window

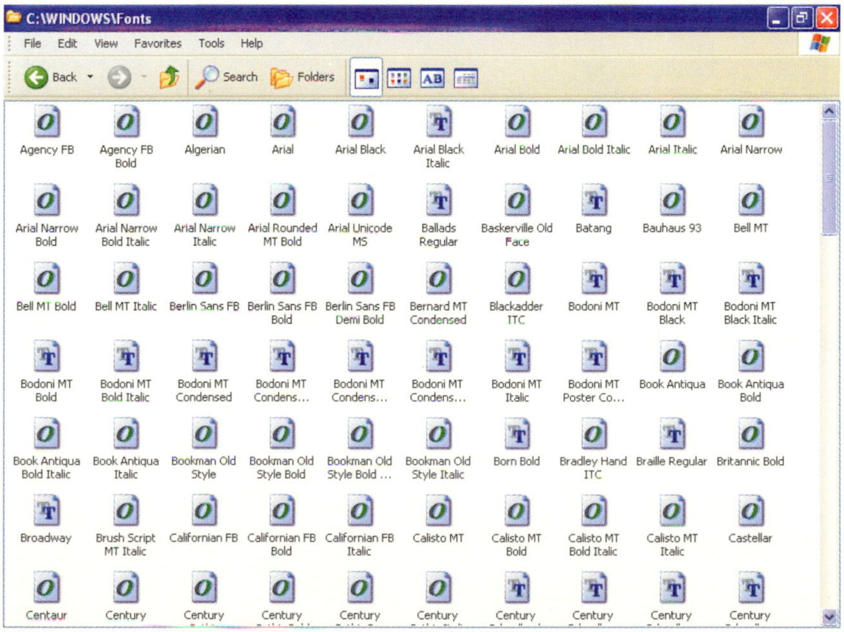

If you are submitting more than one file, your commercial printer may want you to *compress* or zip them into one file. A compressed file is smaller than a lot of individual files and is usually easier to manage. The printer can unzip or extract the files as necessary.

Compress Files

Although you do not have to compress the files before delivery, it is easier to send one compressed file over the Internet instead of many other files. Also, the printer may request a compressed file. Some versions of Windows come with a compression utility you can use to zip or compress the files, or you can use any compression utility. Select all the files you want to compress, then right-click the selection and click the appropriate command for zipping or compressing the files. For example, with the Windows compression tool, click Send to. On the submenu, click Compressed (zipped) Folder. Windows compresses the files into one folder. You can identify the zipped folder because its icon has a zipper on it, as shown in Figure 6-9. By default, the zipped folder has the same name as the first compressed file. To rename the folder, right-click it and click Rename. Key the new name and then press Enter. To extract the files, right-click the zipped file or folder and click Extract All.

FIGURE 6-9
Compressed folder icon

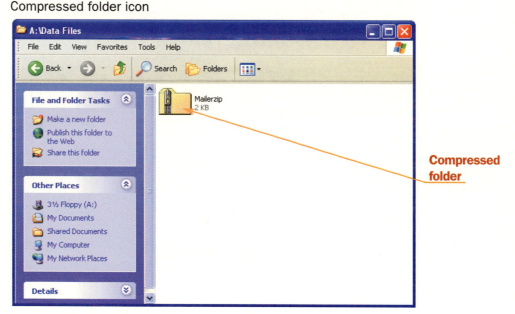

Compressed folder

In the following exercise, you use data files and font files supplied with this book. Your instructor may want you to use the actual PostScript file or the packed files you created in previous exercises, as well as the font files stored in the Fonts folder in the Windows folder on your computer.

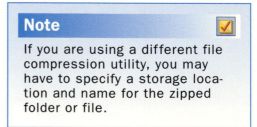

Note

If you are using a different file compression utility, you may have to specify a storage location and name for the zipped folder or file.

STEP-BY-STEP 6.9

1. From the Windows desktop, use My Computer or Windows Explorer to navigate to the folder where the data files are stored.

2. Press and hold **Ctrl** and click the following files to select them: **DP Step 6-9a** (the PostScript file), **DP Step 6-9b** (a TIFF graphics file), **GOUDOS** (Goudy Old Style font), **GOUDOSI** (Goudy Old Style Italic font), **GOUDOSB** (Goudy Old Style Bold font), **COPRGTB** (Copperplate Gothic Bold font), and **TCCM____** (Tw Cen MT Condensed font).

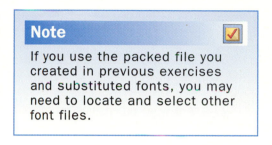

Note

If you use the packed file you created in previous exercises and substituted fonts, you may need to locate and select other font files.

3. Use your compression utility to compress the files. For example, if you are using the Windows compression utility, right-click the selection and click **Send to** on the submenu, then click **Compressed (zipped) Folder**. (You may have to supply a name and click the Add button before your program compresses the files. See the next step to supply the filename.)

4. Right-click the compressed folder and click **Rename**. Key the filename **Mailerzip**, and then press **Enter**.

5. If you did not store the **Mailerzip** folder in the folder where you have stored others files for this lesson, right-click the **Mailerzip** folder, click **Cut**, navigate to the folder where you have stored other files for this lesson, right-click a blank area in the folder window, and click **Paste**.

Deliver Files on Removable Media

If your commercial printer requests the file(s) on a disk or CD, simply copy the necessary files to the disk. If you are copying a lot of files, you may want to compress or zip them first. You copy files to a disk using your operating system. First, insert the destination disk in the appropriate storage device. For example, insert the CD-R in the CD-R drive. Then, navigate to the window where your publication files are stored. Select the file or files to copy, click Edit on the menu bar, and then click Copy. Navigate to the My Computer window and select the storage device that contains the destination disk. Click Edit on the menu bar, and then click Paste. You should attach a label to the disk and write the filename, your name, and the date on it, as well as any other information to help the commercial printer identify the contents. You can then hand deliver or ship the disk along with the composite and separations and a file list.

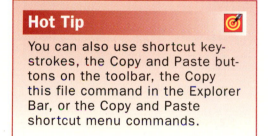

Hot Tip

You can also use shortcut keystrokes, the Copy and Paste buttons on the toolbar, the Copy this file command in the Explorer Bar, or the Copy and Paste shortcut menu commands.

STEP-BY-STEP 6.10

1. Insert the destination disk into the appropriate storage device. For example, insert a CD-R or CD-RW into a CD-R drive, or insert a floppy disk into a floppy disk drive.

2. From the Windows desktop, navigate to the folder where the data files are stored.

STEP-BY-STEP 6.10 Continued

3. Click the **DP Step 6-10** compressed folder to select it. Click **Edit** on the menu bar, and then click **Copy**.

4. Navigate to the My Computer window and select the device that contains the destination disk.

5. Click **Edit** on the menu bar, and then click **Paste**. Windows copies the folder to the disk.

6. Remove the disk and label it with the filename, your name, and the date. It is now ready to deliver to the commercial printer.

7. Use a word processing program, a text editor, a database program, a spreadsheet program, or a piece of paper and a pen to create a list of all the files you have copied to the disk.

Deliver Files Electronically

If your commercial printer requests the file(s) electronically, send them via e-mail using your e-mail account. Log on to the Internet using your ISP account, and then start your e-mail program. Create a new message and key the recipient's e-mail address in the Send to box. Key descriptive information in the Subject box, such as the job number or the publication name. Attach the file or compressed file to the message, and then send the message. Ask the printer to confirm receipt. You may need to ship the file on a disk as well, along with all proofs and file lists.

> **Extra for Experts**
>
> Your printer may have an FTP site to which you can upload files. To use an FTP site, you need FTP client software, an account number, and a password.

STEP-BY-STEP 6.11

1. Log on to your Internet Service Provider, and start your e-mail program.

2. In the To box, key the address of the commercial printer.

3. In the Subject box, key **Files for postcard mailer**.

4. In the message text area, key **Please reply to confirm receipt**, and then key your name and e-mail address.

5. Click the button for attaching a file, then locate and select the **DP Step 6-11** compressed folder.

6. Click the **Send** button in your e-mail program to send the message and its attachment.

7. Close your e-mail program and log off. If necessary, disconnect from the Internet.

SUMMARY

In this lesson, you learned:

- You can use a desktop printer to publish a document if you need only a few copies or are concerned about the cost.

- You can have a copy shop reproduce a publication if you need many copies, are in a hurry, and are concerned about the cost.

- You should have a commercial printer publish a document if you want the best quality, need many copies, have special printing requests, and have enough money in the budget.

- Before printing, you should check the spelling and design in a publication.

- Some programs have a design checker utility that can locate problems such as too much text in a text box, or double spaces after punctuation.

- You set print properties to control the way a document prints, but the properties vary depending on your printer, your desktop publishing program, and the publication.

- Commercial printers usually require a composite proof and separations.

- Trapping helps eliminate gaps and overlaps between adjoining colors.

- Many programs have a utility that automatically prepares a file for commercial printing.

- You may have to save a file in PostScript format for your commercial printer.

- You can deliver a publication file to a commercial printer on disk or electronically.

- In some cases, you must deliver font and graphics files as well.

VOCABULARY *Review*

Define the following terms:

Bleed	PostScript	Proof
Camera-ready	PostScript Printer	Publish
Composite	Description file	Reader's spreads
Compress	Print properties	Separations
Crop	Printer's spreads	Trapping
Crop marks		

REVIEW *Questions*

TRUE / FALSE

Circle T if the statement is true or F if the statement is false.

T F **1.** You can print a PostScript file only on a PostScript printer.

T F **2.** All printers have the same printer properties.

T F **3.** Once you run a spelling checker, you don't have to worry about spelling errors in your publication.

T F **4.** Use a copy shop to reproduce a publication if you need it in a hurry.

T F **5.** To avoid overlapping between adjoining colors, you should adjust the separation.

T F **6.** Commercial printers always have all the font files needed for printing a publication.

T F **7.** One way to deliver files is to copy them onto a CD-R and then ship the CD-R to the printer.

T F **8.** Compressed files usually take up less disk space than files that have not been compressed.

T F **9.** Font files are usually stored in the Type folder.

T F **10.** Use the collate print option to print pages consecutively.

WRITTEN QUESTIONS

Write a brief answer to the following questions.

1. List at least two pros and two cons of publishing a document on your desktop printer.

2. List at least three questions you should ask a commercial printer.

3. What is the difference between a printer's spread and a reader's spread?

4. List at least two situations in which you need a special setup or handling to print a publication on a desktop printer.

5. Why do color separations print in black and white?

FILL IN THE BLANK

Complete the following sentences by writing the correct word or words in the blanks provided.

1. A(n) _____ is a file that provides information about a PostScript printing device.

2. If a font is not _____ in the publication file, you must send the font file to the commercial printer.

3. Print _____ to show the layout of colors in a publication.

4. _____ is a technique used to adjust the position of adjoining colors during printing.

5. Printed _____ indicate where paper should be trimmed or cut to the correct page size.

6. A(n) _____ is an effect created by an object running off the edge of the page.

7. You should always review a(n) _____ of the publication before you have it published.

8. Use a(n) _____ to publish your document if you want the highest quality.

9. Print _____ are the settings you use to control the way a publication prints on your desktop printer.

10. A(n) _____ is an accurate copy of your publication, including all graphics and colors.

PROJECTS

PROJECT 6-1

1. Launch your desktop-publishing program, and open **DP Project 6-1** from the data files. This is a version of the CNO Newsletter you have worked with in previous lessons.

2. Save the file as **CNONews4**.

3. Run the spelling checker. Ignore all proper names, and correct any other spelling errors as necessary.

4. Run the design checker to locate and fix the following problems, and any other problems you or the checker find. If your program does not have a design checker, manually look for and fix design problems.

   A. The text box containing the headline *Annual Fundraiser* is not large enough to fit all the text. Fix the problem by decreasing the spacing after paragraphs to 8 points.

   B. The text box containing the headline *Officer Nominations* is also not large enough to fit all the text. This time, increase the height of the text box as necessary.

   C. There is a double space following a period in the text box in the right column on page 1. Delete the extra space.

5. Set printer properties to print one draft-quality proof of each page on separate sheets of paper.

6. Print the proofs.

7. Proofread the proofs for spelling and grammatical errors that the spelling checker did not catch, and for design problems that the design checker did not catch. Mark the problems on the printed proofs, and fix them in the publication file.

   A. There are two spelling/grammatical errors in the story headlined *Volunteer News*.

   B. There are two spelling/grammatical errors in the story headlined *Officer Nominations*.

   C. There are design problems with two horizontal rules on page 2. One rule is thicker than the other rules on the page and is not aligned with the left margin. Another rule is not aligned with the right column margin.

   D. There is a design problem with the alignment of the text box at the top of the right column on page 1. It would look better if the text were aligned vertically with the text in the left column.

8. Set printer properties to print two high-quality, double-sided color copies of the **CNONews4** file. If necessary, print page 1, then reinsert the sheet in the printer and print page 2 on the reverse side.

9. Save changes and close the **CNONews4** file. Leave your desktop-publishing program open to use in Project 6-2.

PROJECT 6-2

1. In your desktop-publishing program, open the file **DP Project 6-2a**. This is a version of the invitation you worked with previously.

2. Save the file as **CNOInvite3**.

3. Run the spelling checker and design checker to identify and correct errors.

4. Set print properties to print a draft-quality proof of the document.

5. Print the draft, and then proofread for spelling, grammatical, and design problems. Correct any problems that you find.

6. Enable trapping.

7. If necessary, set up the publication for commercial color printing using both spot and process colors.

8. Print a composite of the publication.

9. Print separations of the publication.

10. If your program has an automatic file preparation utility, use it to prepare the publication files for the commercial printer. Save the files on a floppy disk, a CD-R, or a new folder set up for this purpose, named **DP Project 6-2**. (If your program asks you to locate the clip art files inserted on pages 2 and 3, you will need access to the CD from which they were inserted, or you can navigate to the data files for this lesson and select and open DP Project 6-2c and DP Project 6-2d.)

11. Save a copy of the publication in PostScript format, with the name **PSCNOInvite3**. You must have a PostScript printer available in order to save the file in PostScript format.

12. Compress the PostScript file and all necessary graphics and font files together and rename the compressed folder **CNOzip**. Locate the files on your computer, or use the data files provided. (If you use an automatic file packing utility, don't worry if there are fewer graphics files than are listed below. Some programs may have fewer graphics files in the publication. Also, if your program substituted fonts, you may need different font files.)
    Graphics files: DP Project 6-2b, DP Project 6-2c, DP Project 6-2d, DP Project 6-2e, DP Project 6-2f, DP Project 6-2g.
    Font files: GARA, GARDBD, GARAIT, COPRGTB, COPRGTL

13. Copy the **CNOzip** folder to a floppy disk or CD.

14. Save changes and close the **CNOInvite3** file. Close your desktop-publishing program.

WEB PROJECT

In addition to the options of printing a publication on the desktop, using a copy shop, or using a commercial printer, a fourth option is to publish to the Web. Use the Internet to research some of the differences between designing a page for printing and designing a page for publishing on the World Wide Web. Start by looking for information about the basic principles of design as used for printed documents and for Web pages. Look for the different ways to use color; for example, most printed documents use dark text on a light background, while many Web pages use light text on a dark background. Are there different concepts concerning alignment or white space? See if you can find information about fonts that look better onscreen than in print, or why you should select certain types of graphics for use on the Web and others for use in print. Use the information you find to write a report using a word processing program or create a chart using a spreadsheet program comparing print publishing design with Web publishing design.

TEAMWORK PROJECT

As a group, use a telephone book or other business directory to compile a list of commercial printers and copy shops in your community. If you have a database program or a spreadsheet program, use it to enter information about each business, including the name, address, telephone number, fax number, and e-mail address. You may want to include additional information such as specialties, a contact's name, or even the hours of operation. If you do not have a database or spreadsheet program, you can record the information in a notebook.

Think of a publication you would like to create for your class, school, or community. You can pick any type of publication, such as a newsletter, a poster, a banner, a flyer, a brochure, an advertisement, or a booklet. If you like, you can even use one of the publications you planned and created in an earlier lesson. Plan the publication from scratch, including paper stock, sheet size, color, page setup, and number of copies. Contact at least two commercial printers on your list and ask them for assistance planning the publication. Tell them up front that this is a class project, and that it is unlikely you will actually be contracting with them to print the publication. If they are uncooperative, thank them and then try a different business in your list. For example, ask them the type of color process they use, what type of files they prefer working with, and how they like the files delivered. Ask them if they have any advice about paper stock, what the time frame for completing the job would be, and, of course, how much it would cost. Record the answers along with the other information about the printer.

Contact at least two copy shops and ask them for information about reproducing copies of the publication. Ask them if they have color copying, if they have self-service options, and if they have any advice based on the type of publication and the number of copies you need. Also, remember to ask them the cost, and how long it would take.

Based on the information you have gathered, decide whether you would want to use a commercial printer, a copy shop, or simply print the publication yourselves on your desktop printer. Use a word processing program to write a proposal for producing the publication. Include specifications about the publication and a recommendation for how and where to publish the document. Include the reasons for your recommendation. If you do not have a word processing program, handwrite the proposal. Present the proposal to your class.

CRITICAL *Thinking*

ACTIVITY 6-1

Design and create a booklet providing tips and hints about desktop publishing that could be used as a handout in a desktop publishing class. Start by planning the booklet from scratch. Think about the audience and how you want to present the information. Consider how the booklet will be published, its size and its length, and whether you will use color in it or just black and white text and graphics. Also consider how long it will take to create the booklet and develop a realistic schedule to guide you through the process. Build in time to have your classmates review your work at each stage so you can improve it as you go along. Record specifications in a word processing or spreadsheet document so you can refer to them as you create the booklet.

Next, organize the information to include in the booklet. Do you want to include technical information about printers and software programs, or just information about design and organization? If necessary, research the information to include using books or the Internet, or by talking to an instructor or commercial printer. Use a word processing program or text editor to store the information electronically.

Plan how to format the text in the booklet. Will you simply key paragraphs of information, or do you want to use different elements to break up the text and make the booklet more appealing visually? Look at other publications to see how they do it. (Look at this book for ideas, such as the list of objectives at the beginning of each lesson, the way the headings are formatted, and how tips and notes are presented in boxes.) Select or create a font scheme, and select the appropriate font sizes to use for each element. Record the specifications in a word processing or spreadsheet document so you can refer to them when you create the booklet. Having specifications ensures consistency throughout the booklet.

Decide what type of graphics to include. Do you want to use lines or borders? Are there pictures to include? If so, are they already in a graphic file format, or do you need to convert them or create them? Do you have permission to use them? Prepare the graphics files so you have them ready to insert. Think of a title for the booklet and how you want the cover page to look.

Use your desktop publishing program to create the booklet. Set up the pages to match the specifications that you planned. Copy and paste the text from the word processing or text editor document, or key the text directly into the publication. Apply the text formatting specifications you selected. Insert, size, and position graphics objects to complement the text. Print a draft copy of the booklet and ask your classmates to review it and make comments. If necessary, make changes or adjustments to improve the booklet.

Prepare the booklet for publication. Check the spelling and the design. Print another proof and review it carefully for errors. Make improvements, if necessary, and then review it again. When you are satisfied that the booklet is complete, print it and share it with your class.

DESKTOP PUBLISHING

REVIEW *Questions*

TRUE / FALSE

Circle T if the statement is true or F if the statement is false.

T F   1. Using a commercial printer is usually the fastest way to publish a document.

T F   2. Prepare separations for a publication to avoid gaps or overlaps between adjoining colors during printing.

T F   3. Horizontal alignment adjusts the position of paragraphs in relation to the left and right margins of a text box.

T F   4. Tabs are used to adjust the horizontal position of text across a single line.

T F   5. Layout guides do not print.

T F   6. A headline is repeated at the top of every page in a publication.

T F   7. Some clip art Web sites require you to register and pay for downloading pictures.

T F   8. A spot color is ink that is mixed during printing.

T F   9. Horizontal rules do not print.

T F 10. By default, text wraps from the end of one line in a text box or frame to the beginning of the next line.

MATCHING

Match the correct term in Column 1 to its description in Column 2.

Column 1   **Column 2**

___ **1.** Reader's spread   **A.** A prototype or sample of a publication

___ **2.** Gutter   **B.** Pages that must be printed on the same sheet of paper so the page order is correct when the publication is bound

___ **3.** Footer

___ **4.** Printer's spread   **C.** Pages that are printed in consecutive order

___ **5.** Color scheme   **D.** The file format used for digital photographs

___ **6.** GIF   **E.** A decorative text effect used to highlight the first character in a paragraph

___ **7.** Mock-up   **F.** The area between the bottom margin and the bottom of the page

___ **8.** JPEG
   G. The inside page edges

___ **9.** Dropped capital
   H. The area on a page that has no text or graphics

___ **10.** White space
   I. The file format used most often for cartoons and logos

   J. A set of coordinated colors

   K. The area between the top margin and the top of the page

FILL IN THE BLANK

Complete the following sentences by writing the correct word or words in the blanks provided.

1. Set the _____ to adjust the space between two specific characters.

2. The method used to attach the pages of a publication to one another is called the _____.

3. _____ formatted files are often used for graphics in desktop publishing documents because they reproduce well when printed and support transparency.

4. Use a(n) _____ to quickly apply a set of formatting settings to text in a publication.

5. In many programs, you insert graphic objects into a(n) _____ frame.

6. When you _____ an object in a publication, the object is not connected to the source file in any way.

7. A(n) _____ is a hardware device that uses light to capture a digital version of printed or handwritten data.

8. When you _____ an object, it pivots around its reference point.

9. To print across the wide side of a page, select _____ orientation.

10. Use the _____ around the edges of a page displayed on screen to temporarily store objects.

PROJECTS

PROJECT 1

1. Launch your desktop publishing program and create a new blank document using the default settings.

2. Save the document as **Poster**.

3. Set up the page layout for the **Poster** publication as follows:
   A. Publication type: Poster
   B. Page size: 18 inches wide by 24 inches high
   C. Paper size: Letter
   D. Orientation: Portrait
   E. Page overlap: 0.5 inches. (In some programs you specify overlap—or tiling—when you print, not when you set up the page layout.)
   F. Margins: 1.5 inches on all sides
   G. No double-sided printing

4. Insert a horizontal ruler guide at 13 inches on the vertical ruler.

5. Search your program's clip art collection to locate pictures of a band or orchestra, and then insert the picture into the **Poster** publication. Resize and position the picture to fill the space above the horizontal ruler guide—approximately 14.5 inches wide by 11 inches high.

6. Insert another horizontal ruler guide at 16.75 inches on the vertical ruler, and then insert a text box or text frame sized to fit in the space between the two horizontal ruler guides—approximately 14.75 inches wide by 3.5 inches high.

7. In a 42-point sans serif font, such as Arial Rounded MT Bold, key the following five lines of text.

   Calling All Musicians!

   Perfect Pitch Community Band

   Needs You!

   All Band Instruments

   All Levels of Ability

8. Format the text as follows:
   A. Apply the Small Cap text effect to the second line of text.
   B. Adjust the paragraph spacing before and after the second line of text to 12 points.
   C. Change the leading or line spacing between the last three lines of text to 0.9 lines. All the text should fit within the text box, but if not, increase the text box height slightly.
   D. Center all text horizontally.

9. Insert two new horizontal ruler guides, one at 17.5 inches and one at 19.5 inches on the vertical ruler, and then insert a text box sized to fit between them. The text box should be approximately 14.75 inches wide by 2 inches high.

10. Using a 26-point serif font, such as Georgia, justified alignment, and leaving 3 points of space before and after each paragraph, key the following two paragraphs of text:

    Rehearsals are Wednesdays from 7 p.m. to 9 p.m. in the HHS Band Room. Concerts are scheduled for October, December, February, and April. Registration fee is $25.00.

    For more information or to sign up, call Nelson Beauchamp, Director, at 555-1234, or email him at nbeauchamp@ppcb.org.

11. Insert four clip art pictures of different musical instruments in the space between the bottom margin and the lower text box. For example, insert a picture of a saxophone, a guitar, a trumpet, and a keyboard. Select pictures that are similar in color and style.
    A. Size each clip art picture to approximately 2.5 inches wide by 2 inches high.
    B. Distribute the pictures horizontally to space them evenly across the page.

12. Prepare the publication for printing on your desktop printer.
    A. Check the spelling in the publication.
    B. Check the design of the publication.
    C. Print a draft quality proof to proofread and check. If necessary, set the Tiling option to 0.5 in a print options dialog box to control the overlap.

13. Print at least one copy of the completed publication. It will require nine sheets of paper. Crop and assemble the individual sheets to complete the publication.

14. Save changes and close the **Poster** file. Leave your desktop publishing program open to use in Project 2.

PROJECT 2

1. Create a mock-up of a four-page booklet to use as a program for the Perfect Pitch Community Band's Fall concert.
   A. The booklet is to print on two sides of a single sheet of 8.5-inch by 11-inch paper, which will be folded in the middle.
   B. You need to include a title and the date on the front (page 1), a list of band members on page 2, the list of music on page 3, and information about the band on the back (page 4).

2. In your desktop publishing program, open **DP Project 2a** from the data files. This file contains all the text you need to complete the publication.

3. Save the file as **Program**.

4. If your program has font schemes and color schemes, apply the Breve font scheme and the Citrus color scheme. If your program does not have font and color schemes, don't worry. You can manually apply colors and fonts in the following steps.

5. On page 1, size the text box to 3 inches wide by 0.5 inches high. Center it horizontally between the left and right margins, and position it vertically 3.5 inches from the top of the page.

6. Draw a new text box, sized to 3 inches wide by 1 inch high. Align it with the right margin horizontally and with the bottom margin vertically. Connect the first text box to the new text box, and then format the text as follows:
   A. Apply the **Title 3** style to the text in the first text box. Alternatively, apply 28-point Bodoni MT Black, or a similar sans serif font. Center the text horizontally.
   B. Apply the **Heading 3** style to both paragraphs in the second text box. Alternatively, apply 14-point Bodoni MT bold, or a similar font, and leave 4 points of space before and after each paragraph. Right-align both paragraphs horizontally, and align them vertically with the bottom of the text box.

7. Use WordArt or another text art program to create two graphics text objects as follows. If you do not have a text art program, create text boxes, use a decorative font to key the text, and then modify and format the text as desired.
   A. Create an object using a wave style and a two-color horizontal gradient fill. If possible, change the colors for the gradient to orange (C= 0; M= 56; Y= 97; K= 0) and rust (C= 5; M= 96; Y= 98; K= 5).
   B. Key the text **Perfect Pitch** in a 36-point serif font such as Times New Roman.
   C. Center the object horizontally and position it 1.75 inches from the top of the page vertically.
   D. Create a second object using the same style and colors.
   E. Key the text **Community Band** in a 32-point serif font such as Times New Roman.
   F. Center the object horizontally, and position it 2.5 inches from the top of the page vertically.

8. On page 2, resize the text box containing the text *Perfect Pitch Community Band* to 3 inches wide by 0.75 inches high and align it with the top margin vertically and between the left and right margins horizontally. Format the text as follows:
   A. Apply the **Heading 2** style to the first line, and then center the text horizontally. Alternatively, apply 16-point Bodoni MT or a similar sans serif font in bold.
   B. Apply the **Heading 4** style to the second line, and then center the text horizontally. Alternatively, apply 12-point Bodoni MT or a similar sans serif font in bold and italic.
   C. Insert a dark green, 2-point thick horizontal rule after the second line. (Try the custom color C= 76; M= 24; Y= 86; K= 23. If the color appears too dark, try increasing the brightness or developing your own custom color.)

9. Divide the page into two vertical columns, or insert a vertical ruler guide at 2.5 inches on the horizontal ruler, and then resize the second text box on page 2 to 1.5 inches wide by 4.25 inches high. Position it in the left column horizontally, and 2 inches from the top of the page vertically.

10. Draw a new text box in the right column, also sized to 1.5 inches wide by 4.25 inches. Align it vertically 2 inches from the top of the page. Link the text box on the left to the new text box. Format the text in both text boxes in the Body Text 2 style (12-point Franklin Gothic Book), and then modify the formatting as follows:
    A. Apply the **Heading 3** style to all instrument names (14-point Bodoni MT, bold).
    B. Set the line spacing to 1 space and leave 3 points of space before and after each paragraph. (If necessary, adjust the height of the text boxes so all text is displayed.)
    C. Insert a horizontal ruler guide at 2.25 inches on the vertical ruler.
    D. If necessary, nudge the text box in the left column until the text *Flute* is sitting on the ruler guide. Nudge the text box in the right column until the text *Alto Saxophone* is sitting on the ruler guide.

11. On page 3, resize the text box to 3 inches wide by 6 inches high. Center it vertically on the page, and position it between the left and right margins. Format the text as follows:
    A. Apply the **Heading 6** style to the name of each piece of music (12-point Franklin Gothic Demi, bold, with 3 points of space before and after each paragraph).
    B. Apply the **Body Text 2** style to the paragraphs listing the composers' and arrangers' names (12-point Franklin Gothic Book, with 10 points of space after each paragraph).
    C. Apply a 0.25-inch hanging indent to the paragraphs listing the composers' and arrangers' names.

12. On page 4, resize the text box to 3 inches wide by 3 inches high and align it vertically with the bottom margin. Format the text as follows:
    A. Apply the **Body Text 2** style (12-point Franklin Gothic Book, with 10 points of space after each paragraph) to all of the text.
    B. Justify the first paragraph of text.
    C. Convert the remaining lines into a bulleted list, using a simple round black bullet.

13. Insert a music-related clip art picture such as a band conductor or a musician. Size it to approximately 3 inches wide by 2.75 inches high, and position it in the white space between the text box and the top margin.

14. Change to Master Page view and insert the picture **DP Project 2b** from the data files. Format the picture as follows:
    A. Change the color to Washout, or adjust the contrast and lightness settings to wash out the image so it can be used as a watermark.
    B. Resize the picture to 10 inches wide by 8 inches high.
    C. Center the picture horizontally and vertically on the sheet.

15. Change back to regular view and prepare the document for desktop publication.
    A. Check the spelling and design. Ignore or correct errors.
    B. Print a draft quality proof to check.

16. Print at least one copy of the booklet using duplex or two-sided printing.

17. Save changes to the **Program** file, and close your desktop publishing program.

SIMULATION

Before starting to work in your desktop-publishing program, take the time to plan each project completely. Working alone or with a partner, review the steps and then create a schedule for completing the job. Set up a timeline with appropriate milestones. Establish criteria that you believe should be met for each stage of the project, and create a rubric that you can use to gauge your accomplishments. Periodically, have your classmates review your work and offer comments. Incorporate their suggestions as you continue your work.

You are a marketing assistant for Swift River Travel, a travel agency. The company is promoting new winter getaway tours. You are responsible for designing publications to advertise the information.

JOB 1

The travel agents have asked you to design a brochure providing information about tour packages to four ski and snowboarding resorts in New England and Quebec, Canada. To complete this job, you research the destinations using the Internet and locate appropriate graphics as well as facts and highlights about the destinations. Then, you design the brochure and insert the data. When the publication is complete, print it.

Part 1

1. Use the Internet to locate information about the following ski resorts. If you cannot use the Internet, you may be able to obtain the information from a ski or snowboarding shop or from a travel agent. You may also be able to contact the resort directly.

   - Bretton Woods Mountain Resort in Bretton Woods, New Hampshire (www.brettonwoods.com)

   - Okemo Mountain Resort in Ludlow, Vermont (www.okemo.com)

   - Sunday River Ski Resort in Bethel, Maine (www.sundayriver.com)

   - Mont Tremblant Resort in Tremblant, Quebec, Canada (www.tremblant.com)

2. Find facts about each resort, such as the following:

   - number of ski trails

   - number of acres of skiing and boarding terrain

   - number of lifts

   - capacity for artificial snowmaking

   - average annual snowfall

   - distance from the nearest major city or cities

   - additional unique or interesting facts

3. Write the information down in a notebook, or copy it from the Web page into a word processing or text editing document. Save the document as **Skiinfo**.

4. Download at least one picture of each location. Save the picture of Bretton Woods as **Bwpic**; the picture of Okemo as **Okpic**; the picture of Sunday River as **SRpic**; and the picture of Tremblant as **MTpic**. If you save more than one picture of any of the resorts, save them as separate files and add consecutive numbers to the filenames.

Part 2

1. Create a mock-up of a trifold brochure, using a standard 8.5-inch by 11-inch sheet of paper in landscape orientation. Fold the page into thirds, and mark the front panel with an F and the back panel with a B. Unfold the sheet of paper and number the panels on the inside 1, 2, and 3, and the panels on the outside 4, 5, and 6. The inside panels are all on page 1 of your document, and the outside panels, which include the front and back, appear all on page 2 of your document.

2. Launch your desktop publishing program and open **DP Job 1a** from the data files.

3. Save the document as **Brochure**.

4. Change the page layout for the **Brochure** publication as follows:
   A. Publication type: Custom
   B. Orientation: Landscape
   C. Page size: 11 inches wide by 8.5 inches high
   D. Paper size: Letter
   E. Margins: 0 inches on all sides
   F. No double-sided printing

5. Switch to Master Page view and divide the page into 3 columns, leaving no space between columns, then switch back to regular page view. Remember, on page 1 is the content for the inside panels of the brochure, and on page 2 is the content for the outside panels of the brochure. The middle panel on page 2 is the back panel, and the right panel on page 2 is the front panel.

6. If available, select the Binary font scheme. On both pages 1 and 2, insert two horizontal ruler guides—one at 2 inches on the vertical ruler and one at 6 inches on the vertical ruler.

7. Position the text boxes as follows:
   A. On page 1:
   Place the Bretton Woods text box in the left column between the top margin and the first horizontal ruler.
   Place the Sunday River text box in the middle column between the top margin and the first horizontal ruler.
   Place the Mont Tremblant text box in the right column between the top margin and the first horizontal ruler.
   B. On page 2:
   Place the Okemo Mountain text box in the left column between the top margin and the first horizontal ruler guide.
   Place the two-line Swift River Travel text box in the right column between the top margin and the first horizontal ruler guide.
   Position the seven-line Swift River Travel text box centered horizontally and vertically in the middle column.

8. Format all except the text box in the middle column of page 2 as follows:
   A. Change the text box margins (or inset) to 0.5 inches on the top, left, and right and 0.04 inches on the bottom. (**Hint:** Select and modify all text boxes on page 1 at the same time, and then all text boxes on page 2 at the same time.)
   B. Apply the **Heading 2** style to all resort names (16-point Verdana, bold, with a 0.14-inch space after each resort name) and the **Body Text 2** style to the locations (12-point Georgia).
   C. In the third column on page 2, apply the **Title 3** style to the text *Swift River Travel* (28-point Verdana, bold, with a 0.14-inch space after the paragraph) and the **Tagline** style to the text *"Your Key to Adventure"* (9-point Georgia, bold, italic).
   D. Center all text horizontally.
   E. Apply a blue, 2-point horizontal ruler after the second paragraph in each text box, except for the middle box on page 2, which is formatted in the next step.

9. Format the text in the text box in the middle column of page 2 as follows:
   A. Apply the **Heading 2** style to the first line (16-point Verdana, bold).
   B. Apply the **Tagline** style to the second line (9-point Georgia, bold, italic).
   C. Apply the **Address** style to the remaining lines (8-point Georgia).
   D. Center all text.
   E. Apply a 2-point blue line before the first line and after the last line. If necessary, increase the spacing between the rule and the baseline of the text.

10. In all three columns on page 1, and in the left and right panels on page 2, insert a text box between the two horizontal guides. Size it to fill the space (approximately 3.5 inches wide by 4 inches high). Set the text box margins (or inset) to 0.5 inches on the left and right and 0.04 inches on the top and bottom. Using the information you gathered in Part 1, key or copy information into the text boxes in the panels under a resort name. Alternatively, use the information in **DP Job 1b**, a data file in Microsoft Word format.
    A. Enter one or two sentences describing the resort, or something unique about the resort. Press **Enter** and key **Fast Facts:** and then press **Enter** again. Key a list of five or six facts about the resort.
    B. Apply the **Body Text 2** style (12-point Georgia, with 9 points of space after each paragraph) to the list items and the description sentence(s), and apply the **Heading 5** style (12-point Georgia, bold, with 9 points of space after each paragraph) to the text *Fast Facts*.
    C. Apply a basic small round bullet to the list items.
    D. Justify the description sentence(s).
    E. If necessary, improve the design by adjusting the line or paragraph spacing. For example, change the line spacing in the middle panel of page 1 to leave 36 points of space before the text *Fast Facts*.

11. In the right column on page 2, key the following

    Check It Out!

    Super Winter Escapes

    Packaged tours to four thrilling resorts:

    Bretton Woods, New Hampshire

    Sunday River, Maine

    Mont Tremblant, Quebec, Canada

    Okemo Mountain, Vermont

12. Format the text as follows:
    A. Line 1: **Title 4** style (18-point Verdana, bold), centered horizontally. If you did not apply a style, increase the leading to add some space between lines.
    B. Line 2: **Heading 6** style (12-point Verdana, bold), centered horizontally. If you did not apply a style, increase the leading slightly to improve appearance.
    C. Line 3: **Body Text 5** style (10-point Verdana, bold, italic, with 9 points of space after the paragraph), aligned left.
    D. Lines 4, 5, 6, and 7: **Body Text 2** style (12-point Georgia, with 9 points of space after each line), aligned left.
    E. Center the text vertically in the text box.

13. In all three columns on page 1, and in the left column on page 2, insert pictures of each resort into the space between the lower horizontal ruler guide and the bottom margin. Size each picture to approximately 3 inches wide by 2 inches high and align the tops of the pictures with the horizontal ruler guide. If you do not have picture files, insert **DP Job 1c** for Bretton Woods; **DP Job 1d** for Sunday River; **DP Job 1e** for Mont Tremblant; and **DP Job 1f** for Okemo.

14. Create a text box along the bottom edge of each picture and key the source information for the text and graphics in 8-point Georgia, centered. For example, for Bretton Woods, key **Source for data and picture: www.brettonwoods.com.** Include other source data as necessary, such as the date.

15. In the right column on page 2, insert a clip art picture of a skier into the space between the bottom margin and the lower horizontal ruler guide.

16. Prepare the document for publication on your desktop printer.
    A. Check the spelling and design.
    B. Print a draft-quality proof.

17. Print the **Brochure** file, using double-sided or duplex printing. Save it and close the file, but leave your desktop publishing program open to use in Job 2.

JOB 2

Your supervisor has asked you to initiate a monthly internal newsletter to help keep the staff up to date on company news. First, you need to design a template for the newsletter that you can save and use as a starting point each month. Then, you insert graphics and text to complete the publication.

Part 1

1. In your desktop publishing program, create a new blank publication using the default settings.

2. Save the file as **SRTNews**.

3. Adjust the page setup as follows:
    A. Publication type: Full page
    B. Orientation: Portrait
    C. Page size: 8.5 inches wide by 11 inches high
    D. Paper size: Letter
    E. Margins: 1 inch on all sides
    F. No double-sided printing
    G. No facing pages

4. Insert a new page so there are a total of two pages in the publication, and then create two columns on each page.

5. If available, insert the Crossed Lines Masthead design object, and align it with the top of the page vertically, centered horizontally. Replace the sample text *Organization Name* (or *Your Organization*) with the text **Swift River Travel**. Replace the sample text

Newsletter Name with the text **SRT Update**. Replace the sample text *Newsletter Date* with the text **Winter**. If the design object is not available, create the masthead as follows:

A. Insert a text box sized about 0.5 inches high and 5 inches wide, aligned with the top and left of the page. In the text box, key the text **Swift River Travel**, using a 13-point serif font (such as Times New Roman) in bold all-capital letters. Fill the text box with a bright blue color, and change the font color to white. Apply a 1-point white (or paper) horizontal rule after the paragraph.

B. Insert another text box sized about 1.25 inches high and 5 inches wide. Position it vertically so its top is aligned with the bottom of the other text box, and horizontally with the left of the page. Using the same serif font in about 56 points, key the text **SRT Update**. Fill the box with the same bright blue, and change the font color to white.

C. Insert two more text boxes, each sized about 0.5 inches high by 1.5 inches wide. Position them to the right of the other text boxes, one above the other, so the top of one is aligned with the bottom of the other. The top box should be aligned with the top margin of the page. Using a sans serif font, such as Arial Narrow, key **Volume 1, Issue 1** in the top text box, and **Winter** in the bottom text box. Adjust font size and style as desired.

D. If necessary, adjust the size and position of the text boxes to improve the appearance of the masthead. Select all four text boxes and group them.

6. Change to Master Page view and insert page numbers in the lower-right corner of the page. Precede the number with the word **Page**. You can do this by creating a footer or by inserting a text box or text block.

7. Change back to regular page view.

8. On page 1, insert a horizontal ruler guide at 3 inches on the vertical ruler on page 1.

9. On page 2, insert a text box sized to approximately 3 inches wide by 4.75 inches high.

10. Key the following lines of text
SRT Update is published by employees of Swift River Travel for internal use only. Information contained in this newsletter is not meant as any type of advertising or promotion. It is not meant for distribution to outside clients or other agencies.
For more information, call (941) 555-5555.

11. Format the text with an 18-point serif font, such as Times New Roman. Justify the text. Apply a light gray fill or shade to the text box and a 4-point bright blue border line on all sides. Set paragraph spacing to leave 6 points before and after each paragraph. Align the text box in the lower-left corner of the page.

12. Save the changes, and then save the **SRTNews** file as a template file named **Newstemp**.

13. Close all open files.

Part 2

1. In your desktop publishing program, create a new document based on the **Newstemp** template.

2. Save the file as **SRTNews2**.

3. Insert two text boxes on page 1, each one sized to 3 inches wide by 6.5 inches high. Position one in the left column, with its top aligned with the horizontal ruler guide; and position the other in the right column, also with its top aligned with the horizontal ruler guide.

4. Switch to page 2, and insert three text boxes as follows
   A. Size one text box to approximately 3 inches wide by 3.25 inches high and position it in the upper-left part of the page.
   B. Size one text box to approximately 3 inches wide by 1.5 inches high, and position it in the upper-right part of the page.
   C. Size the third text box to approximately 3 inches wide by 4.75 inches high and position it in the lower-right part of the page.

5. Open the file **DP Job 2** from the data files. You may open this text file in your desktop publishing program, or in a text editor such as Notepad. Copy and paste the text from the text file into the text boxes in the **SRTNews2** publication as follows. (Note that if you open the text document in Notepad, each paragraph may appear as a single line.)
   A. Copy and paste the first four paragraphs of text into the text box in the left column of page 1.
   B. Copy and paste the next four paragraphs of text into the text box in the right column of page 1.
   C. Copy and paste the next eight paragraphs of text into the text box in the upper-left part of page 2.
   D. Copy and paste the next two paragraphs of text into the text box in the upper-right part of page 2.
   E. Copy and paste the last three paragraphs of text into the text box in the lower-right part of page 2.

6. Close the **DP Job 2** text file without saving any changes.

7. Format the text as follows:
   A. Format all headlines (the first line in each text box) with a sans serif font, such as Arial, in 16 points.
   B. Format the remaining text with a serif font, such as Times New Roman, in 12 points.
   C. Set the line spacing of all text to 1 space between lines and 6 points before and after each paragraph.
   D. Apply a 4-point blue horizontal rule before the first paragraph (the headline) in the three text boxes you inserted on page 2. (You may need to adjust the spacing options for the rules if they crowd the text.)

8. Insert clip art pictures as follows:
   A. Insert a picture of a snowboarder or skier on page 1. Size the picture to about 2 inches wide by 1.5 inches high. Position it about 2.5 inches from the left edge of the page and about 7.25 inches from the top of the page. Set the text wrap to square.
   B. Insert a picture of a beach on page 1. Size the picture to about 2 inches wide by about 1.8 inches high. Position it to align with the right margin horizontally, and about 4 inches from the top of the page. Set the text wrap to square.
   C. Insert a picture of a computer class on page 2. Size it to about 3.25 inches wide by about 2 inches high. Position it about 4 inches from the left edge of the page and about 2.75 inches from the top of the page. Set the text wrap to square. Apply a 0.75-point border line around all sides of the picture.
   D. Insert a picture of a family on page 2. Size it to about 2 inches wide by about 1.5 inches high, and then center it horizontally in the text box at the bottom right of the page. Set the text wrap to Top and Bottom.

9. Adjust the size and position of text boxes as necessary to make sure they are neatly aligned and large enough to display all text. For example, try to align the horizontal rule at the top of the text box in the lower-right part of page 2 with the top border of the text box in the lower-left part of the page. You may also try nudging the pictures to adjust the way text wraps around them.

10. Prepare the document for publishing by a commercial printer.
    A. Check the spelling and the design.
    B. If necessary, enable color printing for commercial printers, using the CMYK process color system.
    C. Enable trapping.

11. Print a composite proof and separations for all colors.

12. Use your program's automatic file preparation utility to pack all necessary files onto a removable disk, such as a floppy disk or a CD.

13. Save the **SRTNews2** file and close it. Close your desktop-publishing program.

THE WINDOWS OPERATING SYSTEM

Microsoft Windows is the *operating system* that controls the way your computer works. An operating system is a software program that provides the instructions that allow you to communicate with your computer and all of its attached devices. Among other things, you use Windows to launch and exit programs, to find and open files, and to install new programs and hardware devices. This appendix covers some useful Windows features.

About Windows

There are different versions of Windows, but they all function in basically the same way. Information is displayed in *windows*, or rectangular areas, on your desktop. Some windows, called *folders*, are used to store files just like paper folders hold paper files in your desk drawer. When you open a folder window, it displays a list of all the files stored in that folder. Other windows, called program windows, are used to display a running program. There are also windows called *dialog boxes* that convey information between you and your computer.

Windows has a *graphical user interface* (GUI), which means you use easy-to-understand visual elements to communicate with your computer. Pictures called *icons* represent programs. Plain English commands are listed on easy-to-find *menus*. You can use a mouse or a keyboard or a combination of the two to make selections. One of the most convenient features of Windows is that it provides a common platform for all Windows programs. This means there are similarities in the way different programs look and function, so they are easier to learn and use.

The Windows Desktop

Depending on your version of Windows and the way your computer or network is set up, when you turn on your computer, you see either the Windows *desktop* or a *sign-in* screen. The Windows desktop is the main screen or workspace from which you can access all the tools you need to use your computer. The sign-in screen lists the names of all the people authorized to use the computer. From the sign-in screen, you click your name and then enter your password, if necessary, to display the desktop.

The default Windows XP desktop is shown in Figure A-1. Your desktop may look quite different because different versions of Windows have different default desktops, and your computer may be customized with different programs, different colors, and a different background. In any case, you should be able to locate the components described in Table A-1. You can also use *ScreenTips* to identify elements on your screen. ScreenTips are descriptions that appear when the mouse pointer rests on an item such as an icon or a *button*.

FIGURE A-1
Default Windows XP desktop

TABLE A-1
Desktop Components

COMPONENT NAME	DESCRIPTION
Start button	A button on the taskbar used to open the Start menu, from which you can access everything stored on your computer, including programs and files.
Taskbar	A row that usually appears at the bottom of the screen, used to display buttons and icons that provide quick access to common tasks. The taskbar displays the Start button, the Notification area, and buttons representing open programs and files. You can also opt to display toolbars such as Quick Launch on the taskbar.
Quick Launch toolbar	A list of icons representing commonly used programs. Click an icon to launch the program.
Recycle Bin icon	An icon representing the Recycle Bin folder, where deleted files and folders are stored until you remove them permanently.

TABLE A-1 (continued)

COMPONENT NAME	DESCRIPTION
Notification area	An area at the end of the taskbar used to display information about system components. Usually, the clock/calendar is displayed in the Notification area, as well as information about hardware devices such as printers and networks that are currently in use.
Mouse pointer	The mouse pointer indicates the current location of the mouse on your screen. It usually looks like an arrow, but the mouse pointer can change in shape depending on the current action. For example, it looks like an hourglass when the computer is busy processing a command.

Use the Mouse

You use your mouse and keyboard to make selections and issue commands in Windows. The mouse pointer represents the current location of the mouse on your screen. You move the mouse pointer by sliding the mouse on your desk or on a mouse pad. The four basic mouse actions are click, double-click, right-click, and click-and-drag.

■ *Click* means to press and release the left mouse button. This action is usually done to select an item, but sometimes is used to launch a program or open a window.

■ *Double-click* means to press and release the mouse button twice in rapid succession. Use this action to launch a program or open a window.

■ *Right-click* means to press and release the right mouse button. Right-click is used to open a shortcut menu of common commands.

■ *Click-and-drag* means to press and hold the left mouse button, and then slide the mouse to a different location. Click-and-drag is used for moving selected items.

Your mouse may also have a scroll wheel. Spin the wheel to shift the screen display up and down through the contents of a window.

Note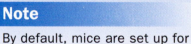

If the taskbar is not displayed, your computer probably has been customized to hide it when it is not in use. This leaves more room to display data on the screen. Move the mouse pointer to the side of the screen where the taskbar is usually displayed (try the bottom first), and it should appear.

Note

By default, mice are set up for right-handed users. If you are left handed, ask your instructor for information about seting up the mouse for your use.

Use the Keyboard

In addition to the standard text characters and numbers, most computer keyboards have special keys for quickly accessing computer features and commands. Table A-2 describes some common Windows keys.

TABLE A-2
Common Windows keys

KEY	DESCRIPTION
Modifier keys (Ctrl, Alt, Shift)	These keys are used in combination with other keys or mouse actions to select commands or perform actions. For example, pressing the Ctrl key and the *S* key at the same time usually saves the current file.
Directional keys	The directional keys include the up, down, left, and right arrows, as well as the Home, End, Page Up, and Page Down keys. These keys move the insertion point or selection box around the screen, or shift the display to show a different part of a window.
Enter key	The Enter key is used to execute a command or to start a new paragraph when you are keying text.
Escape key (Esc)	The Escape key is used to cancel a command.
Editing keys	The editing keys include Insert, Delete, and Backspace. They are used when you are keying data to control the way information is entered.
Function keys (F1–F12)	Usually found in a row above the standard keyboard keys, these keys are often assigned as shortcut keys for commands in programs. For example, F9 is often used to update information, and F2 is often used to repeat the most recent action.
Windows logo key	Usually located on either side of the spacebar, this key is used to open or close the Start menu, and in combination with other keys for other purposes.
Application key	Usually found to the right of the spacebar, this key is used in place of a right-click to open a shortcut menu of commands.

Launch a Program

Depending on how your computer is set up, there may be program icons displayed on the desktop or the taskbar. If so, click or double-click an icon to launch the program. If the program is not represented by a desktop icon, use the Start menu. The Start menu displays links to commonly used programs. Click the program name to launch the program. Figure A-2 shows both the Windows XP Start menu (on the left) and the Classic Windows Start menu (on the right).

FIGURE A-2
Windows XP Start menu and Classic Windows Start menu

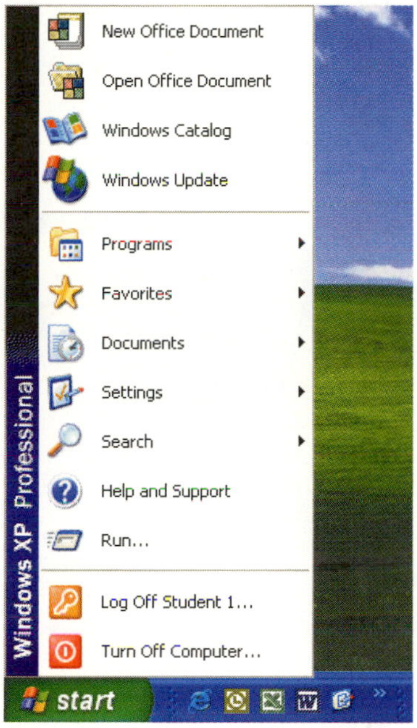

To access any program installed on your computer, use the All Programs menu. Click the Start button to open the Start menu, and then click Programs or All Programs. A list of all programs installed on your computer is displayed, as shown in Figure A-3. Click the name of the program you want to launch. The program opens in a program window on the desktop.

Note ✅

If there is a right-pointing arrowhead next to a menu item, that means the item has a *submenu*. Click the item to open the submenu, and then click the program you want to launch. If there is an ellipse (…), it means the command opens a dialog box. If there is a shortcut key combination, press that combination to quickly select the command without using a menu.

FIGURE A-3
All Programs menu

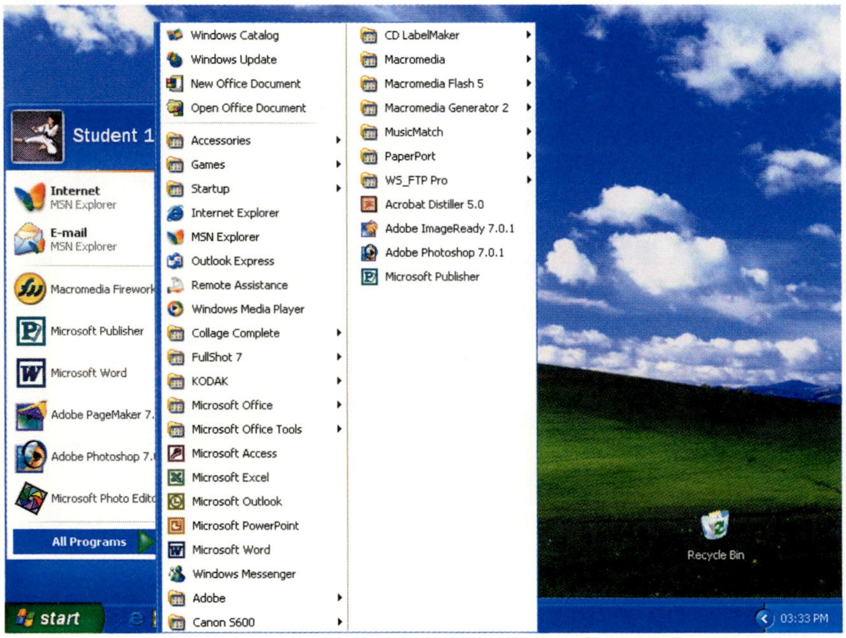

Most program windows have common elements, such as a title bar, a menu bar, and a toolbar. To exit a program, you can click the Program Close button, which is an X in the upper-right corner of the window, or you can click File on the menu bar, and then click Exit. A typical program window is shown in Figure A-4.

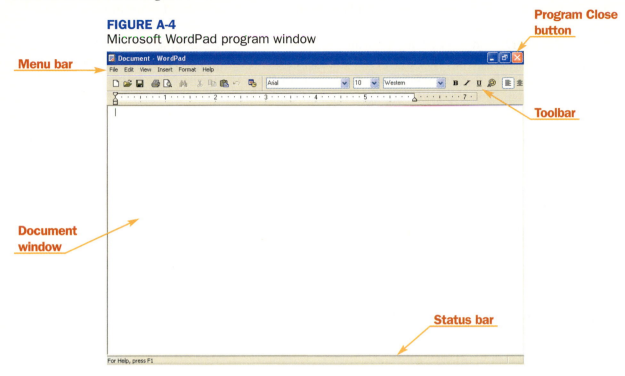

FIGURE A-4
Microsoft WordPad program window

Menu bar

Program Close button

Toolbar

Document window

Status bar

The Windows Filing System

One of the main functions of Windows is to help you keep the contents of your computer organized. Windows uses a multilevel filing system called Windows Explorer to keep track of *files* and *folders*. Files are the documents that store data, and folders are storage areas where you place files and other folders so you can find them easily.

Storage Devices

At the base of the filing system are the *disk drives* or other storage devices, which are the hardware devices on which the file and folder data is written electronically. Local storage devices are attached directly to your computer. Network storage devices may be attached anywhere on the network. You may have one or more of the following attached directly to your computer or to your network:

■   Hard disk drive, which is fixed inside the computer case

■   Floppy disk drive, which has a slot so you can insert and remove a disk

■   CD or DVD drive, which has a drawer in which you can insert and remove a CD or DVD disk

Disk drives are named using letters. A floppy disk drive is always named drive A. If there is a second floppy disk drive, it is called drive B. The hard disk drive stored in your computer is usually called drive C. Additional drives are named using consecutive letters, so a CD drive may be drive D, a DVD drive may be drive E, and so on. You can usually add descriptive names or labels to the drive letter to help identify the storage device. To see a list of your *local* storage devices, click the Start button and then click My Computer on the Start menu. The My Computer window opens as shown in Figure A-5. Alternatively, double-click the My Computer icon on the Windows desktop. Remember, the contents of the My Computer window vary depending on the contents of your computer system.

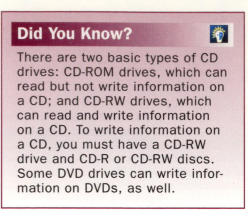

Did You Know?

There are two basic types of CD drives: CD-ROM drives, which can read but not write information on a CD; and CD-RW drives, which can read and write information on a CD. To write information on a CD, you must have a CD-RW drive and CD-R or CD-RW discs. Some DVD drives can write information on DVDs, as well.

FIGURE A-5
My Computer window in Windows XP

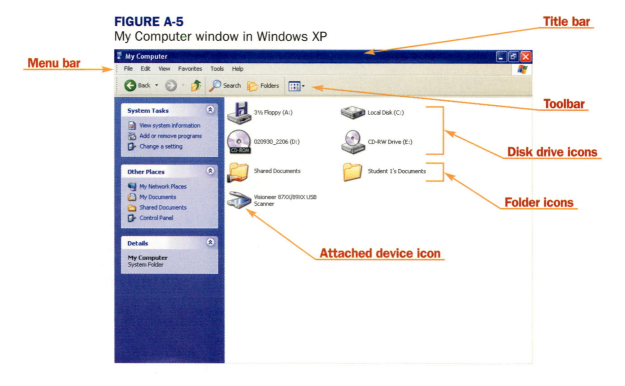

Folders

Files can be stored directly on a disk, but to keep things organized, you usually store them in folders, which are then stored in other folders, or on a disk. Windows comes with some default folders used for storing system information and data files. You can create new folders at any time. The default folders are usually listed on the Start menu or are represented by icons on the desktop. The following list describes some of the Windows default folders:

> **Note** ☑
>
> To see the network storage devices, click the Start button, and then click My Network Places on the Start menu to open the My Network Places window. Alternatively, double-click the Network Neighborhood icon on the Windows desktop.

- My Documents is the default storage location for data files.

- Shared Documents is used to store documents that can be opened by anyone on the network.

- My Computer displays the components of your computer system, such as disk drives and other attached devices.

- Control Panel provides access to your computer components so you can customize and control settings and options.

- Recycle Bin is used to store deleted files and folders until you choose to remove them permanently.

Navigate Through the Contents of Your Computer

To view the contents of a disk or folder, you open the window that displays the item, and then open the item itself. For example, to see the contents of a floppy disk in drive A, you click the Start button to open the Start menu and then click My Computer to open the My Computer window. In the My Computer window, you double-click the drive A icon to open the drive A window.

Most folder windows have similar characteristics, including a title bar, a menu bar, and possibly toolbars. The contents list is displayed in the main folder window. Some versions of Windows display additional information in the Explorer Bar pane along the left side of the window. You can change the contents of the Explorer Bar depending on what you are doing. By default, it displays the links bar, which lists links to common folders such as My Computer or My Documents. Click a link to open the folder.

You can change the Explorer Bar to display Folders if you want to navigate using a hier-archical tree diagram as shown in Figure A-6 (in versions of Windows prior to Windows XP, this feature is called Windows Explorer). Click the Folders button to display the hierarchical tree. Click an item in the tree to display its contents in the main folder window. Click a plus sign next to an item to expand the tree, or click a minus sign to collapse the tree.

FIGURE A-6
Folders Explorer Bar in Windows XP

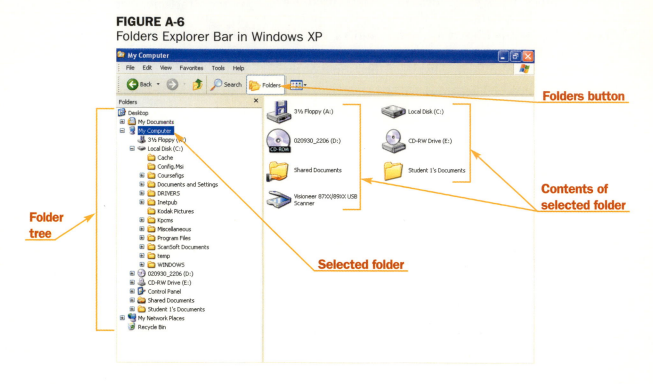

There may also be Back, Forward, and Up commands on the toolbar at the top of the window. Click Back or Forward to scroll through all of the windows you have opened recently, and click Up to open the folder in which the current folder is stored.

Change the Window Display

You can change the way items are displayed in a folder window. Click the Views button on the toolbar or the View command on the menu bar, and then click one of the following:

■ Thumbnails to display an icon or picture with the item name.

■ Tiles to display a smaller icon or picture with the item name, type, and size.

■ Icons to display a smaller icon or picture with the item name.

■ List to list the items by name.

■ Details to list the items including specific information such as name, type, size, and modification date, as shown in Figure A-7.

FIGURE A-7
Folder in Details view

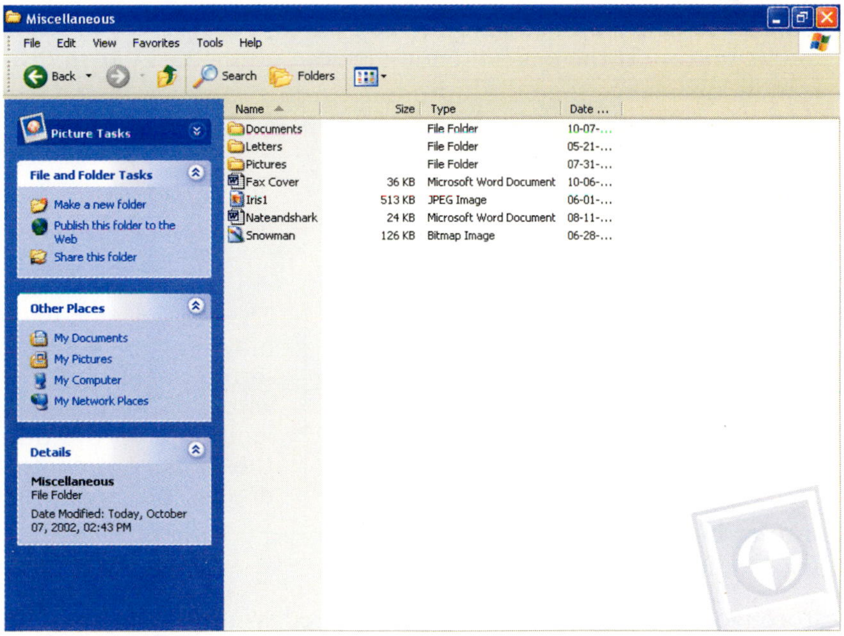

You can also change the sort order and grouping of the items in a folder window. Click View on the menu bar and then click Arrange Icons by. Click the sort order or grouping option you want to use.

Note

In some versions of Windows, folders containing picture files have a Filmstrip view option you can use to preview the images.

Work with Windows

As mentioned, information is displayed in windows on the Windows desktop. The two basic types of windows are program windows, used to display an open program, and folder windows, used to display lists of the contents of folders and storage devices. You can have more than one window open at a time, but only one can be active. The active window is the one in which you are currently working. All open windows have a button on the taskbar. To make a different window active, click its taskbar button. If there is not enough room on the taskbar to display buttons for each open window, Windows may group the buttons according to program and display one button for each group. When you click a group button, a menu of windows appears so you can click the specific window you want to make active.

Size and Position Windows

Windows open in the size and position they were in when you last used them. All windows have control buttons in the upper-right corner that you can use to change the window's size and position.

> **Note** ✅
>
> The current document or file may also have control buttons in the upper-right corner of the window. The program control icons are on the title bar, while the document control buttons are on the menu bar.

- Click the Maximize button to increase the size of a window to fill the entire desktop.

- Click the Minimize button to reduce a window so it is just a button on the taskbar.

- Click the Restore Down button to restore a maximized window to its previous size and position. The Restore Down button is available only in a maximized window.

- Click the Close button to close the window.

You can also drag a window by its title bar to move it to a different location on the desktop, and you can drag the borders of a window that is not maximized to change its size.

To arrange all open windows on the desktop, right-click a blank area of the taskbar and select one of the following commands:

■ Cascade Windows to overlap the windows, showing only the title bars. The active window is on top, as shown in Figure A-8.

■ Tile Windows Horizontally to arrange the windows across the width of the screen. You can see a portion of all windows. The title bar of the active window is brighter than the others.

■ Tile Windows Vertically to stack the windows from the top to the bottom of the screen. You can see a portion of all windows, and the title bar of the active window is brighter than the others.

FIGURE A-8
Cascading windows

Install a Program

If you purchase a new program, you must install it on your computer so you can use it. Usually, you install a program from a CD-ROM. When you insert the CD-ROM in the CD-ROM drive, the installation usually begins automatically. You simply follow the instructions on the screen to install and set up the program. During the installation, you may have to enter information about your computer or about the program you are installing. For example, you may have to enter a key or code number and select the folder in which you want to store the program files. If the program does not start automatically, you can use the Add New Programs command in the Control Panel. If you use the Add New Programs command, you need to know the name of the installation or set-up file. Usually, it is setup.exe or install.exe.

Before you purchase a new program, read the package to make sure it is compatible with your computer system. The system requirements are usually listed on the back or side of the package. Most stores do not let you return opened software. To determine if a program is compatible, ask yourself the following questions:

- Does the program run on the version of Windows you have installed?

- Does your computer have enough memory to run the program?

- Does your computer have enough disk space to install the program?

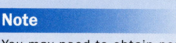

Note ☑

You may need to obtain permission from a system administrator or network administrator before installing a new program.

- Does the program require a particular hardware device or component, such as a video adapter card or monitor resolution?

You can locate information about your computer system in the System Properties dialog. To open the System Properties dialog box, right-click the My Computer icon and then click Properties, or open the Control Panel and either double-click the System icon, or click *See basic information about your computer*. In the System Properties dialog box, you can locate such information as the version of Windows running on your computer, the amount of memory you have installed, and the processor speed.

To find out how much disk space you have available, open My Computer, right-click on the icon for your hard drive, and click Properties.

Install a Hardware Device

*H*ardware devices are components that are connected to your computer system and controlled by your computer's microprocessor. Hardware devices can include your printer, modem, scanner, digital camera, video camera, microphone, speakers, keyboard, monitor, mouse, and disk drives.

> **Note** ☑️
>
> You may need permission from a system administrator or network administrator to install a hardware device.

Before you can use a hardware device, you must install it on your computer. The first step in hardware installation is to connect the device to the computer. Some devices, such as internal modems, are attached to slots inside the computer, and other devices, such as printers, are attached by cables to ports on the outside of the computer. Still others, such as a wireless mouse, communicate via wireless connections such as infrared or satellite. Local devices are attached directly to your computer, and network devices are attached to the network. If a device installs inside the computer, you may want to consult a professional. If the device connects to a port outside the computer, you can install it yourself.

Next, you must install the correct device driver, which is a software program that provides the instructions that let the device communicate with Windows. Usually, the device driver comes on a floppy disk or CD-ROM with the device. Alternatively, you may be able to download it from the manufacturer's Web site. Windows comes with drivers for common hardware devices.

In most cases, when you plug the device into your computer, Windows detects it automatically and begins the installation procedure. Simply follow the instructions displayed on your screen to complete the installation and set-up. If the installation does not start automatically, you can use the Add New Hardware command in the Control Panel.

Use a Help Program

*W*indows and most Windows programs come with built-in help programs you can use to get information while you work. The Help program depends on the version of Windows you are using.

To start the Windows XP Help program, click the Start button to open the Start menu and then click Help and Support. The Help and Support Center screen is displayed, as shown in Figure A-9. You can click a link to go to a general topic page, from which you can click links to locate the specific information you need, or you can key a topic in the Search box and click the Go button. Windows displays a list of links to information about the topic.

FIGURE A-9
Windows XP Help and Support Center

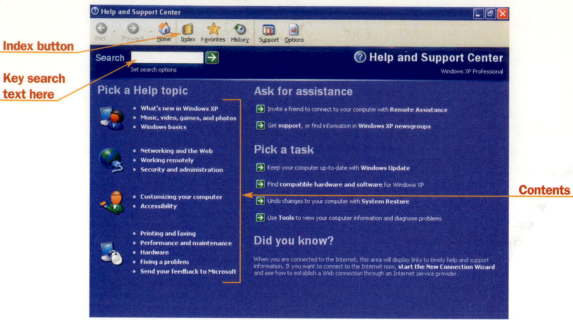

To start the Help program in a version of Windows prior to XP, click the Start button to open the Start menu and then click Help.

The program window has two panes. On the left you can select to use the Contents, Index, or Search tools. The specific help information is displayed on the right.

- Contents lists the major topics for which help is available. Click a book icon to display a list of subtopics, and then click a subtopic to display the information.

- Index provides an alphabetical list of help topics. You can scroll through the list to find the topic you need, or you can key a topic in the keyword search box to jump to that topic. Click a topic in the list to display the information.

- Search lets you search through all of the available help pages for a keyword. Key the word in the keyword search box, and then click the List Topics button to display a list of topics that contain that word. Click a topic in the list to display the information.

Note

The Help programs that come with Windows programs all use a similar method for locating topics. You'll find that most offer a Contents page, an Index page, and a Search page in the left pane, and display the help information in the right pane.

GLOSSARY

A

Active Current, or in use.

Additive colors Colors that, when combined in full value, add up to white. Red, green, and blue are additive colors.

Align Position an object horizontally or vertically relative to the top, bottom, left, or right of the publication area.

All-over balance A type of balance in which objects are positioned using a grid-like design with focal points scattered throughout in order to direct the eye through the design.

Analogous colors Colors that are next to each other on the color wheel.

Ascenders The parts of characters that extend up above the main line of text.

B

Balance A basic principle of design that describes the visual weight of objects and the way they are arranged.

Banner headline A headline that extends across the entire width of the page.

Baseline The bottom of a line of text.

Bindery A business that folds, binds, and trims publications.

Binding Securing pages or sections of a book or booklet using stitching, staples, wire, plastic, tape, or glue.

Bitmap A type of graphic in which the image is created using a series of dots.

Bleed Printing that extends to the edges of the paper.

Boundaries Nonprinting lines that mark the outer edges of objects, such as text boxes and frames.

Brightness A measurement of the amount of white or black added to a hue. Sometimes called *tint*. Also, a description of paper indicating how much light the paper reflects.

C

Callout Text used to call attention to something else on the page. Usually connected by a line to the particular item.

Camera-ready Pages or artwork ready to be captured on film for reproduction.

Cast-coated paper Paper that has a finish similar to a glossy photograph.

Clip art Pictures and other types of files that can be inserted into a document.

Clipboard A temporary storage area in your computer's memory where data that has been cut or copied is stored until it is pasted into a new location.

CMY A color system or model used for printing that creates colors by blending different levels of cyan, magenta, and yellow.

CMYK A color system or model used for printing, that creates colors by blending different levels of cyan, magenta, yellow, and black.

Color bar A linear palette that displays gradations in color ranging from red to violet.

Color depth The number of colors used in an image or on a screen.

Color scheme A set of coordinated colors.

Color system A system used to define standard colors, such as RGB (red, green, blue), which is used for computer monitors, or CMYK (cyan, magenta, yellow, black), which is used for printing. Sometimes called a *color model*.

Color wheel A circular palette that displays gradations in color ranging from red to violet.

Compatible   Able to work together.

Complementary colors   Colors that are opposite each other on the color wheel.

Composite   A proof that includes all text, colors, graphics, and other objects on the same page.

Compress   Shrink in size.

Consistency   The use of repetition to create a uniform and predictable design.

Contrast   The degree of separation between the color values of different parts of the same publication. Also, a basic principle of design in which elements with opposite or complementary features are juxtaposed in order to create visual interest.

Cool colors   The colors ranging from green to violet on the color wheel.

Coordinates   Points on a page used to position an object. The X coordinate positions the object horizontally and the Y coordinate positions the object vertically.

Crop   To cut or remove portions of an object.

Crop marks   Lines that are printed on a proof to indicate where the page should be cut down to size.

D

Default   A standard setting or mode of operation.

Descenders The parts of characters that extend below the baseline of text.

Destination   The location to which you copy a file or paste a selection.

Device driver   A software program that enables a computer to communicate with a hardware device.

Digital camera   A camera that takes pictures in digital format.

Discretionary hyphens   In some desktop publishing programs, hyphens that you insert manually.

Distort   To change the height or width of an object without retaining the original proportions.

Distribute   Adjust the space between objects in an image or publication.

Dot leader   Dots repeated along the line preceding a tab stop.

Download   Copy files from one computer to another, usually from a network to a computer on the network.

Drawing objects   Objects such as shapes that you draw in a document using the drawing tools. Usually, drawing objects are vectors.

Dropped capital   A decorative effect in which the first character in a paragraph is increased in size and inset or offset from the other lines in the paragraph.

Duplex printing   Printed on both sides of a sheet of paper.

E

Em dash   A special character that is roughly the width of a letter *M*. Usually used in place of two hyphens.

Embed   To paste an object into a publication without maintaining a connection to the source file.

Emboss   An effect used to make text appear to be inset into the page.

Emphasis   The use of color, lines, or shapes in order to highlight or focus attention on a particular aspect of an image.

En dash   A special character that is roughly half the width of an em dash. Usually used in place of the words *to* or *through*.

F

Facing pages   A left-hand page and a right-hand page set to open opposite each other. Also called *mirrored pages* or *two-page spread*.

Field   A code representing a value that may change, such as a page number.

File format   The way data in a file is saved. Usually, a file format is associated with a particular program so that the program can read the data in the file.

Fill   The area inside a shape.

Finish   The characteristics of the surface of paper.

Flip   To reverse an image horizontally or vertically.

Floating object   An object that can be sized and positioned anywhere on the page.

Font   A set of characters in a particular typeface.

Font effects   Attributes applied to a character in a font set.

Font scheme   A collection of coordinated fonts.

Font size   The height of an uppercase letter in a font set, measured in points.

Font style   The slant and weight of a character in a font set.

Footer   The area between the bottom margin and the bottom of the paper.

Frame   A placeholder object used to contain text or graphics.

Frame inset   The margin between the edge of the frame and the text or graphics in the frame.

G

Galleys   Printed proofs of publication pages.

GIF   Graphics Interchange Format. GIF files are popular for use on the World Wide Web. They can contain up to 256 colors. They are used for cartoons, logos, graphics with transparent areas, and animations.

Grade   A rating used to categorize paper. There are seven basic grades: bond, uncoated book, coated book, text, cover, board, and specialty.

Gradient   Color that shades gradually from a dark hue to a light hue.

Graphics   Images that you use to enhance the work you do on your computer, including drawing, photographs, cartoons, charts, and maps.

Graphics tablet   A hardware device on which you write or draw with a stylus in order to input data into your computer.

Grayscale   A color scheme that uses a range of blacks, whites, and grays.

Grid guides   Nonprinting lines used to define columns and rows on pages in a publication, to assist in positioning and sizing objects.

Group   Combine multiple objects together into one unit.

Guides   Nonprinting gridlines used to help align and position objects in a document.

Gutter   The space between a margin and the binding or between columns.

H

Halftone   A reproduction of a photograph on paper.

Hardware device   A piece of hardware equipment, such as a printer or a modem, that is connected to a computer.

Header   The area between the top margin and the top of the paper.

Horizontal alignment   The position of an object in relation to the left and right margins.

Horizontal rule   A horizontal line inserted before or after a paragraph of text.

Hue   Color.

Hyphen   A character used to indicate the break in a word from the end of one line to the beginning of the next line.

Hyphenation zone   The area along the right margin in which words will be hyphenated.

I

I-beam   The shape of the mouse pointer when you are working in a text-entering or text-editing mode.

Import   Open a file created with one program in a different program.

Imposition   The placement and position of multiple pages printing on a single sheet of paper.

Indents   Temporary margins set in a text box.

In-line object   An object inserted like a character on a line of text.

Insertion point   A flashing vertical line that indicates where characters will be inserted in a text block.

J

JPEG   Joint Photographic Experts Group. This format is used for photographs and other high-color images. It supports millions of colors and can be compressed. It does not support transparency.

Justified   An alignment option in which words are spaced so that the ends of lines are even with both the left and right margin.

K

Kerning   The spacing between certain pairs of characters.

Key word   A word or phrase that is used in a file or on a Web site, or that describes that file or Web site.

L

Landscape orientation (wide)   See *Orientation*.

Layout guides   Nonprinting gridlines used on every page of a publication to ensure consistency throughout a document.

Leading   The spacing between lines of text.

Letterhead   The text and graphics printed at the top or bottom of stationery, usually to identify a company name, address, and other contact information.

Linear gradient   A gradient pattern in which the colors blend horizontally across an object.

Link   To paste an object in a publication maintaining a connection to the source file. When changes are made to the source file, the object can be updated.

Logo   A combination of text and graphics used as a symbol to represent a company or other organization.

M

Manual hyphens   Hyphens that are inserted manually rather than automatically to control where a word breaks at the end of a line of text. In some programs, they are called *discretionary hyphens*.

Margins   The area between the edges of the page and the objects in the document.

Master page   A model or template used to contain text and/or objects that will appear on every page in the publication. In some programs, a publication can have more than one master page.

Masthead   The banner headline displayed across the top of a newsletter. Also, a list of people involved in creating the publication.

Mirrored pages   Facing pages or a two-page spread.

Mock-up   A prototype, model, or sample of a publication.

Monochromatic   A color scheme that uses black and one other color.

O

Objects   Elements, such as text boxes and graphics, that are inserted or embedded in a publication file.

Opacity   A measurement of the level of transparency of color.

Orientation   The way a document is printed across a sheet of paper. Portrait orientation—or tall—

prints the document across the short side of a page, while landscape orientation—or wide—prints the document across the long side of the page.

Overlap   A setting used when printing a large-sized publication on smaller, multiple sheets of paper. Overlap specifies how much of each sheet will overlap with adjacent sheets in order to ensure that the content aligns correctly when the printed sheets are arranged. Sometimes called *tiling*.

P

Page layout   The organization used to design a page in a publication.

Page size   The dimensions of the page on which a document is printed.

Pantone Matching System   A color system or model used to define spot color.

Paper size   The dimensions of the paper on which a document is printed. Sometimes called *sheet size*.

Pattern   A bitmap graphic used as a fill in some graphics programs. Also, a repetitive graphic design used in an image.

Picture frame   A frame used as a placeholder for a graphics object.

Pixel   A single tiny dot used as a unit of measure and to define images on a computer screen. Short for *picture element*.

Points   A unit of measure used for type. There are 72 points in an inch.

Portrait orientation (tall)   See *Orientation*.

PostScript   A page description language used to define the way text and graphics will be printed.

PostScript Printer Description file   The file that stores the instructions for a PostScript printer.

Print properties   Settings that control the way a file will print.

Printer's spreads   Multiple pages laid out for printing on the same sheet so that, when the publication is bound, the pages are in the correct order.

Process color   Cyan, magenta, yellow, and black, which are the colors of ink used in four-color printing.

Proof A printed copy of a publication used for checking the design, spelling, and layout.

Proofreader's marks Symbols written on a proof to inform a printer or editor of changes that should be made.

Proportion A basic principle of design that describes the size and location of an object in relation to other objects in an image.

Publication type An option in some desktop publishing programs that specifies the kind of document you are creating, such as a poster or booklet. Usually, when you select a publication type, the program automatically applies page layout settings designed specifically for that type.

Publish Make a publication available for reading, either in print or on the World Wide Web.

R

Radial balance A type of balance in which objects are distributed evenly around a focal point.

Radial gradient A gradient pattern in which the colors blend out from a center point.

Raster image Bitmap images.

Reader's spreads Multiple pages laid out for printing in consecutive order.

Reference point A point in an object used to identify an axis for rotation, reflection, and other transformations.

Reflect In some programs, the term used to describe the action of flipping or reversing an object.

Relative spaces Spaces that adjust in width only due to the font size, not due to the alignment or justification of the text.

Resolution The quality or sharpness of an image, usually measured in pixels per inch or pixels per centimeter. Sometimes resolution is written as an equation, like this: vertical dots per inch $\times$ horizontal dots per inch.

RGB An acronym for Red Green Blue, a color system used for blending colors on computer monitors.

Rotate To pivot an object around its center point.

Ruler guides Nonprinting gridlines used on a single page of a publication.

Rules Horizontal and vertical lines that print.

S

Sans serif font A type of font in which the characters have straight edges without serifs.

Saturation A measurement of the intensity of color.

Scale To change the size of an object. Also, the size of an object.

Scanner A hardware device used to transfer printed images or text into a computer file.

Scratch area An area outside the edges of a publication where text and graphics may be stored temporarily.

Screen An effect used to change the tint of a color.

Search site A Web site that provides tools for locating other Web sites even if you don't know a specific address.

Secondary colors The colors created by mixing the primary colors. Especially, orange, green, and violet.

Separations Printed pages of the layout of each color in a publication.

Separator character The character that follows a number or bullet in a list.

Sepia A brown tint.

Serif font A type of font that has lines and curlicues on the edges of characters.

Shadow An effect that creates the illusion of depth and dimension.

Shapes Drawing objects that can be inserted in a document.

Sheet size Paper size.

Signature A group of pages printed on the same sheet of paper.

Sizing handles Small rectangles that are displayed around the edges of the current or selected object. They can usually be used to resize the object.

Skew To slant an object along its horizontal or vertical axis.

Source The location from which you copy a file or object.

Spot color A process used primarily in printing in which a color is premixed to a color standard, such as the Pantone Matching System, and is not mixed during the printing process.

Stack   Arrange objects in overlapping layers.

Standoff   The distance between an object and the text wrapped around it.

Stock   Paper.

Story   The text in a text box or article.

Stroke   The line used to draw an object.

Style   A collection of saved formatting settings.

Subtractive colors   Colors that absorb light. Cyan, magenta, yellow, and black are subtractive colors.

Swatches   Blocks of color displayed on a color palette.

Symmetrical balance   A type of balance in which a design is the same on both sides of a center axis, either horizontally or vertically.

T

Tab leaders   Characters repeated along a line preceding a tab stop.

Table of contents   A list of all headings in a publication. Usually, the table of contents also includes the page numbers on which the headings are printed.

Tabs   Nonprinting characters used to align text at a single point.

Template   A file used to create other files. Templates store formatting and page layout settings as well as standard or sample text and graphics.

Text box   An object used to contain text.

Texture   A pattern applied to a fill or stroke to make it look as if color is applied over a textured surface.

TIFF   Tagged Image File Format. TIFF files are used for storing bitmap images. This format is commonly used in desktop publishing and other multimedia applications.

Tiling   Overlap.

Tint   The brightness of a color.

Toggle   A feature or command that can be turned on or off. Also, the action of turning a feature or command on or off.

Toolbox   An onscreen element used to display a collection of tools or buttons.

Tracking   The spacing between text characters.

Transform   Modify an object by either scaling, distorting, skewing, rotating, or flipping.

Transparency   A medium used for slides and overhead projectors. Also, the level of opacity of a color.

Trapping   A process used to avoid overlap and gaps between adjacent colors during the printing process.

TrueType fonts   Fonts that reproduce when printed the same as they appear on screen.

TWAIN   The software language used by devices such as scanners and some digital cameras. It interprets data so that it can be read by a computer.

Two-page spread   A left-hand page and a right-hand page that open opposite each other. Also called *facing pages*.

V

Value   The range from black to white in a hue.

Variety   A term used to describe the use of various elements of design in order to create visual interest in an image.

Vector   A type of graphics in which the image is created using lines and curves defined by mathematical formulas.

Vector paths   The lines and curves that define a vector graphic.

Vertical alignment   The position of an object in relation to the top and bottom margin.

View   The way a file is displayed on-screen.

W

Warm color   The colors ranging from red to yellow on the color wheel.

Watermark   An object that is printed in the background. Usually, the brightness and contrast are adjusted so that the object appears very faint.

Weight   Thickness. Used to measure strokes and lines as well as paper.

White space   The blank area around objects.

Wizard   An automated series of dialog boxes that prompts you through the steps necessary to complete a procedure.

Wrap   To flow text automatically from the end of one line to the beginning of the next. Also, to flow text around objects.

Z

Zoom   The action of adjusting the magnification of a file by a percentage of its actual size. Also, the feature used for this purpose.

INDEX